Linux Essential Reference

The New Riders Professional Library

Cisco Router Configuration &
Troubleshooting
Mark Tripod, 0-7357-0024-9

Debian GNU/Linux:
Installation and Configuration
*John Goerzen and Ossama Othman,
0-7357-0914-9*

Developing Linux Applications
Eric Harlow, 0-7357-0021-4

GIMP Essential Reference
Alex Harford, 0-7357-0911-4

GTK+/Gnome Application
Development
Havoc Pennington, 0-7357-0078-8

KDE Application Development
Uwe Thiem, 1-57870-201-1

Linux Firewalls
Robert Ziegler, 0-7357-0900-9

Linux System Administration
*M Carling, Stephen Degler,
James Dennis, 1-56205-934-3*

Lotus Notes & Domino
Essential Reference
*Tim Bankes and Dave Hatter,
0-7357-0007-9*

MySQL
Paul DuBois, 0-7357-0921-1

Network Intrusion Detection:
An Analyst's Handbook
Stephen Northcutt, 0-7357-0868-1

Python Essential Reference
David M. Beazley, 0-7357-0901-7

Solaris Essential Reference
John Mulligan, 0-7357-0023-0

Understanding Data Communications,
Sixth Edition
Gilbert Held, 0-7357-0036-2

Linux Essential Reference

Ed Petron

New Riders

201 West 103rd Street, Indianapolis, IN 46290

Linux Essential Reference

Copyright © 2000 by New Riders Publishing

International Standard Book Number: 0-7357-0852-5

Library of Congress Catalog Card Number: 99-067430

Printed in the United States of America

First Printing: December, 1999

03   02   01   00   99   7   6   5   4   3   2   1

Interpretation of the printing code: The rightmost double-digit number is the year of the book's printing; the rightmost single-digit number is the number of the book's printing. For example, the printing code 99-1 shows that the first printing of the book occurred in 1999.

Trademarks

Warning and Disclaimer

Publisher
David Dwyer

Executive Editor
Laurie Petrycki

Acquisitions Editor
Katie Purdum

Managing Editor
Sarah Kearns

Editor
Robin Drake

Technical Reviewers
Debbie Daily
Herman Bolton

Product Marketing Manager
Stephanie Layton

Book Designer
Louisa Klucznik

Cover Production
Aren Howell

Indexer
Tim Wright

Proofreader
Erich Richter

Compositor
Wil Cruz

To the memory of my late brother Ken Petron, professional aviator and amateur musician, whose dedication and integrity inspired me and many others.

About the Author

Ed Petron is an independent computer consultant with more than a decade's experience as a programmer and system administrator working with mainframe and UNIX systems. He began using and studying Linux in 1995 with version 2.0.1 of the Slackware distribution. He now uses and contributes to the Debian distribution and has written several articles for *Linux Journal*. Ed holds a Bachelor of Music in keyboard performance (piano, harpsichord, and organ) from Indiana University and a Bachelor of Science in Computer Science from Chapman University. He is currently working on a Master of Science in Engineering with a concentration in computer science at California National University.

About the Technical Reviewers

Debbie Daily is currently a network system administrator for the Math department of Indiana University–Purdue University. She worked with mainframes for six years before returning to school to study computer science, with an emphasis on network security. Debbie began her UNIX career as a system administrator student intern while attending classes full time. She recently received her Bachelor of Science in Computer Science from Purdue University.

Herman Bolton holds a Bachelor of Science degree in computer science from the University of Pretoria, South Africa. He has been doing technical programming in C and C++ for the last 10 years on UNIX, VMS, and the last few years on Windows NT operating systems.

Contents

Acknowledgments

Many thanks to everyone at New Riders who helped support this project. When one realizes how much difference there is between raw manuscript text and finished book, one also develops a real appreciation for those people who handle production tasks such as proofreading, layout, indexing, and so on. Thanks also to development editor Robin Drake and technical editors Herman Bolton and Debbie Daily for providing many valuable suggestions concerning both content and structure. Of course, thanks to Laurie Petrycki and Katie Purdum not only for providing project management but also for providing me with the opportunity to work on this book in the first place.

Most of this book is based on information extracted from manual pages, texinfo pages, and various other sources. We should therefore recognize the many volunteers of the Free Software Foundation and the Linux Documentation Project, as well as any other individuals and organizations that have contributed free software and documentation.

On a more personal level, thanks to all the friends and acquaintances who provided moral support throughout the process. Many of them know little about computers, much less about Linux, but provided much-needed encouragement anyway.

Tell Us What You Think!

As the reader of this book, *you* are our most important critic and commentator. We value your opinion and want to know what we're doing right, what we could do better, what areas you'd like to see us publish in, and any other words of wisdom you're willing to pass our way.

As the Executive Editor for the Open Source team at New Riders Publishing, I welcome your comments. You can fax, email, or write me directly to let me know what you did or didn't like about this book—as well as what we can do to make our books stronger.

Please note that I cannot help you with technical problems related to the topic of this book, and that due to the high volume of mail I receive, I might not be able to reply to every message.

When you write, please be sure to include this book's title and author, as well as your name and phone or fax number. I will carefully review your comments and share them with the author and editors who worked on the book.

Fax: 317-581-4663

Email: newriders@mcp.com

Mail: Laurie Petrycki
            Executive Editor
            Open Source
            New Riders Publishing
            201 West 103rd Street
            Indianapolis, IN 46290

Introduction

This book is designed to be a reference for Linux users who know what they want to do but need to know how to do it. It assumes that the reader has already installed Linux and has a basic knowledge of UNIX concepts. Although not a tutorial, it may still be of value to the beginning Linux user if used in conjunction with one or more of the many tutorial books available.

Emphasis has been placed on the use of free software packages that are included with typical Linux distributions, with no specific distribution being favored over others. The book focuses on the use of the command-line interface and has purposely left out coverage of the X Window system. Unlike X applications, command-line commands often accept many different permutations and combinations of options that are not self-explanatory. Also, practically every Linux user uses commands, regardless of whether he or she uses X.

Notational Conventions

Most of the book contains formal descriptions of command syntax. The following rules apply when interpreting these descriptions:

- Command names and any other text that is to be typed literally is printed in a monospace font: `command option`.
- Variables that hold places for substitution are printed in an italic monospace font: `cat FILENAME`.
- Optional items are placed within brackets (`[ ]`).
- The ellipsis (`. . .`) is used to indicate zero or more occurrences of the preceding item.
- The vertical bar or pipe symbol (`|`) between parameters indicates that either parameter can be given.
- Required parts of a command may be placed within braces (`{ }`). This is most often used in conjunction with the vertical bar (`|`).

The following example illustrates the use of these conventions:

```
command { -a | -b } [ OPTION ... ] FILENAME ...
```

In this example, `command` is typed literally, along with either `-a` or `-b` as a required parameter. These are followed by zero or more `OPTION`s and one or more `FILENAME`s.

In the text, each command syntax description is accompanied by an explanation of the possible values for the parameters.

Many commands use flags prefixed with a hyphen (`-`) to distinguish the flag from other types of parameters such as filenames. For example:

```
command -ijk FILENAME ...
```

In these cases, it's usually possible to combine flags in one argument or give them separately. For example,

```
command -ij filea fileb
```

will usually be equivalent to

```
command -i -j filea fileb
```

The option descriptions generally point out these situations when they exist.

I

General Usage

1
Shell Utilities

The commands in this section are most useful as components of shell scripts. They perform such tasks as printing messages, performing simple arithmetic operations and conditional tests, input/output redirection, file and pathname manipulation, and other functions that are of interest to shell script writers.

Common Options

In addition to the options described in the following sections, each Linux shell utility command can be invoked with the following options:

Option	Description
--help	Prints a usage message listing all available options and exits successfully.
--version	Prints the version number and exits successfully.

Text Printing

These commands print text based on the values of variable and literal arguments passed to the commands.

echo

```
echo [ OPTION ... ] [ STRING ... ]
```

echo writes each *STRING* to standard output, with a space between each string and a newline after the last one.

Option	Description
-n	Don't print the trailing newline.
-e	Enables the interpretation of backslash-escaped characters in each *STRING*:
	\a Bell.
	\b Backspace.
	\c Suppress the trailing newline.

continues >>

>>continued

Option	Description
	\f Formfeed.
	\n Newline.
	\r Carriage return.
	\t Horizontal tab.
	\v Vertical tab.
	\\ Backslash.
	\NNN Character whose ASCII code is octal *NNN*. If *NNN* is not a valid octal number, it's printed literally.

printf

    printf FORMAT [ARGUMENT ...]

printf prints the specified *ARGUMENT*s according to the *FORMAT* string. The *FORMAT* argument is specified as it is with C printf.

The *FORMAT* argument is reused as necessary to convert all the given *ARGUMENT*s. The *FORMAT* argument for the printf command is functionally identical to that of the C printf library routine (see the printf(3) manual page for a complete description) except for the following:

- The printf shell command has one additional directive, %b, which prints its argument string with \ escapes interpreted in the same way as in the *FORMAT* string.

- The printf shell command interprets \0*000* in *FORMAT* as an octal number (if *000* is from zero to three octal digits) specifying a character to print, and x*HHH* as a hexadecimal number (if *HHH* is from one to three hex digits) specifying a character to print.

- An additional escape, \c, causes printf to produce no further output.

For example,

    printf '%f\n' 10

converts 10 to floating point, appends a newline character, and prints the following:

    10.000000

The same can be accomplished with this:

    printf '%f%b' 10 '\012'

The following command,

    printf '%.3f ' 3.1416 20.123 30.5

converts all three of the argument values to floating-point format and prints them with three digits of precision, like this:

    3.142 20.123 30.500

yes

```
yes [ STRING ... ]
```

yes prints the command-line arguments, separated by spaces and followed by a newline, running forever until it's killed. If no arguments are given, yes prints y followed by a newline forever until killed. The *STRING* arguments can consist of any arbitrary character string.

Conditions

The commands in this section perform simple arithmetic operations and execute conditional tests. They're used mainly to control the flow of execution in shell scripts.

expr

```
expr ARG ...
```

expr considers its arguments to be operators and operands. It evaluates the set of command-line arguments as an expression and writes the result to standard output. Expressions and subexpressions can be either integers or strings. Type conversions are made as necessary for compatibility with the operators to be applied. Type conversions that are necessary but impossible result in errors. expr will exit with a status of 0 for a nonzero or non-null result, 1 for a zero or null result, and 2 for an invalid expression.

The following table shows the operators (in order of increasing precedence):

Symbol	Description
¦	Relational OR.
&	Relational AND.
<, >, =, ==, <=, >=, !=	Comparison operations. = and == are equivalent.
+, -	Addition and subtraction.
*, /, %	Multiplication, division, modulus.
:	Pattern matching. The first argument is matched against the regular expression in the second argument.

The following functions can also be used:

Syntax	Description
match STRING REGEXP	expr match *STRING REGEXP* is equivalent to expr *STRING : REGEXP*, where *STRING* is matched against the pattern specified by the regular expression *REGEXP*. For more information on regular expressions, see Appendix A, "Regular Expressions."
substr STRING POSITION LENGTH	Returns the substring of *STRING* beginning at *POSITION* with length at most *LENGTH*.

continues >>

>>*continued*

Syntax	Description
`index STRING CHARACTER-CLASS`	Returns the first position of *STRING* where the first character in *CHARACTER-CLASS* is found. Returns **0** if not found.
`length STRING`	Returns the length of *STRING*.

For example, this command:

`expr 5 '*' 3 + 2`

prints the result **17** on standard output. Note that all components of the expression (including parentheses) must be separated. Quotes are needed for some shells (such as **bash**) to make sure that the multiplication operator * isn't expanded into a list of filenames.

Parentheses can be used to override the standard operator precedence, as in the following command:

`expr 5 '*' '(' 3 + 2 ')'`

In addition to the quotes around the * symbol, quotes may be necessary around the parentheses as well (**bash**, for example, will attempt to execute a subshell otherwise).

Boolean expressions yield either **0** for false or **1** for true. For example, both of the following print 1:

`expr 1 != 2`

`expr 1 '<=' 2`

<= needs to be in quotes for any shells that use < for input redirection (similarly for >=).

Pattern matching also outputs Boolean **0** or **1** results:

`expr a : [a-z]`

prints **1** and

`expr 1 : [a-z]`

prints **0**.

For more information on regular expressions, see Appendix A.

false

`false`

false does nothing except return an exit status of **1**, meaning failure.

test

`test [ EXPRESSION ]`

test returns an exit status of **0** (true) or **1** (false), depending on the evaluation of the expression formed from its arguments. Each part of the expression must be a separate argument.

The following options perform tests related to file access and permissions:

Option	Description
-b FILE	True if FILE exists and is a block special device.
-c FILE	True if FILE exists and is a character special device.
-d FILE	True if FILE exists and is a directory.
-e FILE	True if FILE exists.
FILE1 -ef FILE2	True if FILE1 and FILE2 have the same device and inode numbers; that is, if they're hard links to each other.
-f FILE	True if FILE exists and is a regular file.
-G FILE	True if FILE exists and is owned by the current effective group ID.
-g FILE	True if FILE exists and has its set-group-ID bit set.
-h FILE or -L FILE	True if FILE exists and is a symbolic link.
-k FILE	True if FILE has its "sticky" bit set.
FILE1 -nt FILE2	True if FILE1 is newer (according to its modification date) than FILE2.
-O FILE	True if FILE exists and is owned by the current effective user ID.
FILE1 -ot FILE2	True if FILE1 is older (according to its modification date) than FILE2.
-p FILE	True if FILE exists and is a named pipe.
-r FILE	True if FILE exists and is readable.
-S FILE	True if FILE exists and is a socket.
-s FILE	True if FILE exists and has a size greater than zero.
-t [FD]	True if FD is opened on a terminal. If FD is omitted, it defaults to 1 (standard output).
-u FILE	True if FILE exists and has its set-user-ID bit set.
-w FILE	True if FILE exists and is writable.
-x FILE	True if FILE exists and is executable.

The following options perform tests on strings:

Option	Description
STRING1 = STRING2	True if the strings are equal.
STRING1 != STRING2	True if the strings are not equal.
-n STRING or STRING	True if the length of STRING is nonzero.
-z STRING	True if the length of STRING is zero.

The following options perform numeric relational tests:

Option	Description
ARG1 -eq ARG2	ARG1 equals ARG2.
ARG1 -ne ARG2	ARG1 is not equal to ARG2.

continues >>

>>continued

Option	Description
ARG1 -lt ARG2	ARG1 is less than ARG2.
ARG1 -le ARG2	ARG1 is less than or equal to ARG2.
ARG1 -gt ARG2	ARG1 is greater than ARG2.
ARG1 -ge ARG2	ARG1 is greater than or equal to ARG2.

The following options can be used as connectives to form compound expressions:

Option	Description
! EXPR	True if EXPR is false.
EXPR1 -a EXPR2	True if both EXPR1 and EXPR2 are true.
EXPR1 -o EXPR2	True if either EXPR1 or EXPR2 is true.

The following **bash** script can be used to determine whether the file named as its first argument exists. If the file exists, the script will indicate whether it's a regular file.

```
#!/bin/bash

if test -e $1;
  then
  if test -f $1
    then echo $1 is a regular file;
    else echo $1 is not a regular file;
  fi;
else echo $1 not found;
fi;
```

true

```
true
```

true does nothing except return an exit status of **0**, meaning "success."

Redirection

Shells typically provide their own input/output redirection mechanisms. This section describes redirection performed by a separate command.

tee

```
tee [ OPTION ... ] [ FILE ... ]
```

tee copies standard input to standard output and also to any files given as arguments. If *file* doesn't exist, it's created.

Option	Description
-a or --append	Appends standard input to the given files rather than overwriting them.
-i or --ignore-interrupts	Ignores interrupt signals.

Filename Manipulation

The commands in this section operate on filenames and pathnames.

basename

```
basename NAME [ SUFFIX ]
```

basename removes any leading directory components from *NAME*. If *SUFFIX* is specified and is identical to the end of *NAME*, it's removed from *NAME* as well. basename prints the result on standard output. For example, the command

```
basename /usr/bin/script.pl
```

prints

```
script.pl
```

If the .pl extension is also given, the command

```
basename /usr/bin/script.pl .pl
```

prints

```
script
```

dirname

```
dirname NAME
```

dirname prints all but the final slash-delimited component of a string (presumably a filename). If *NAME* is a single component, dirname simply prints a period (.), meaning the current directory.

pathchk

```
pathchk [ OPTION ... ] NAME ...
```

pathchk checks the portability of filenames. For each *NAME*, pathchk prints a message if any of these conditions is true:

- One of the existing directories in *NAME* doesn't have search (execute) permission.
- The length of *NAME* is larger than its filesystem's maximum filename length.
- The length of one component of *NAME*, corresponding to an existing directory name, is larger than its filesystem's maximum length for a filename component.

pathchk has a single option, described in the following table:

Option	Description
-p or --portability	Instead of a length check, pathck checks the filename and its components against the POSIX.1 minimum length and character set specification.

Working Context

The commands in this section display or alter aspects of the current context such as terminal settings, current directory, and environment variables.

printenv

```
printenv [ VARIABLE ... ]
```

printenv prints environment variable values. If no VARIABLEs are specified, printenv prints the value of every environment variable. Otherwise, it prints the value of each VARIABLE that's set, and nothing for those that aren't set. It exits with a status of 0 if all variables specified were found, 1 if at least one specified variable was not found, and 2 if a write error occurred.

pwd

```
pwd
```

pwd prints the fully resolved name of the current directory. That is, all components of the printed name will be actual directory names—none will be symbolic links.

stty

```
stty [ SETTING ... ]
stty [ OPTION ]
```

stty prints or sets characteristics of the controlling terminal. Valid OPTIONs are as follows:

Option	Description
-a or --save or -all	Prints all current settings in human-readable form.
-g or --save	Prints all current settings in a form that can be passed to another stty command to restore them.

The possible SETTINGs are described in the following sections. Many of the values for SETTING can be negated (as described in the section tables) by preceding them with a hyphen (-).

Control Settings

Setting	Description
parenb	Generates the parity bit in output and expects the parity bit in input. Can be negated.
parodd	Sets odd parity (even if negated).
cs5, cs6, cs7, cs8	Sets character size to 5, 6, 7, or 8 bits.
hup or hupcl	Sends a hangup signal when the last process closes the TTY. Can be negated.
cstopb	Uses two stop bits per character (one if negated).
cread	Allows input to be received. Can be negated.
clocal	Disables modem control signals. Can be negated.
crtscts	Enables RTS/CTS flow control. Can be negated.

Input Settings

Setting	Description
ignbrk	Ignores break characters. Can be negated.
brkint	Makes breaks cause an interrupt signal. Can be negated.
ignpar	Ignores characters with parity errors. Can be negated.
parmrk	Marks parity errors (with a 255-0 character sequence). Can be negated.
inpck	Enables input parity checking. Can be negated.
istrip	Clears high (8th) bit of input characters. Can be negated.
inlcr	Translates newline to carriage return. Can be negated.
igncr	Ignores carriage return. Can be negated.
icrnl	Translates carriage return to newline. Can be negated.
ixon	Enables XON/XOFF flow control (Ctrl+S/Ctrl+Q). Can be negated.
ixoff or tandem	Enables sending of the stop character when the system input buffer is almost full, and the start character when it becomes almost empty again. Can be negated.
iuclc	Translates uppercase characters to lowercase. Can be negated.
ixany	Allows any character to restart output (only the start character if negated). Can be negated.
imaxbel	Enables beeping and not flushing the input buffer if a character arrives when the input buffer is full. Can be negated.

Output Settings

Setting	Description
opost	Post-process output. Can be negated.
olcuc	Translates lowercase characters to uppercase. Can be negated.
ocrnl	Translates carriage return to newline. Can be negated.
onlcr	Translates newline to carriage return-newline. Can be negated.
onocr	Don't print carriage returns in the first column. Can be negated.
onlret	Newline performs a carriage return. Can be negated.
ofill	Uses fill (padding) characters instead of timing for delays. Can be negated.
ofdel	Uses delete characters for fill instead of null characters. Can be negated.
nl1 or nl0	Newline delay style.

continues >>

>>continued

Setting	Description
cr3, cr2, cr1, or cr0	Carriage return delay style.
tab3, tab2, tab1, or tab0	Horizontal tab delay style.
bs1 or bs0	Backspace delay style.
vt1 or vt0	Vertical tab delay style.
ff1 or ff0	Formfeed delay style.

Local Settings

Setting	Description
isig	Enables interrupt, quit, and suspend special characters. Can be negated.
icanon	Enables erase, kill, werase, and rprnt special characters. Can be negated.
iexten	Enables non-POSIX special characters. Can be negated.
echo	Echoes input characters. Can be negated.
echoe or crterase	Echoes erase characters as backspace-space-backspace. Can be negated.
echok	Echoes a newline after a kill character. Can be negated.
echonl	Echoes newline even if not echoing other characters. Can be negated.
noflsh	Disables flushing after interrupt and quit special characters. Can be negated.
xcase	Enables input and output of uppercase characters by preceding their lowercase equivalents with \, when icanon is set. Can be negated.
tostop	Stops background jobs that try to write to the terminal. Can be negated.
echoprt or prterase	Echoes erased characters backward, between \ and /. Can be negated.
echoctl or ctlecho	Echoes control characters in hat notation (^C) instead of literally. Can be negated.
echoke or crtkill	Echoes the kill special character by erasing each character on the line as indicated by the echoprt and echoe settings, instead of by the echoctl and echok settings. Can be negated.

Combination Settings

Setting	Description
evenp or parity	Same as parenb -parodd cs7. Can be negated. If negated, same as -parenb cs8.
oddp	Same as parenb parodd cs7. Can be negated. If negated, same as -parenb cs8.
nl	Same as -icrnl -onlcr. Can be negated. If negated, same as crnl -inlcr -igncr onlcr -ocrnl -onlret.

Setting	Description
ek	Resets the erase and kill special characters to their default values.
sane	Same as cread -ignbrk brkint -inlcr -igncr icrnl -ixoff -iuclc -ixany imaxbel opost -olcuc -ocrnl onlcr -onocr -onlret -ofill -ofdel nl0 cr0 tab0 bs0 vt0 ff0 isig icanon iexten echo echoe echok -echonl -noflsh -xcase -tostop -echoprt echoctl echoke, and also sets all special characters to their default values.
cooked	Same as brkint ignpar istrip icrnl ixon opost isig icanon, plus sets the eof and eol characters to their default values if they're the same as the min and time characters. Can be negated. If negated, same as raw.
raw	Same as -ignbrk -brkint -ignpar -parmrk -inpck -istrip -inlcr -igncr -icrnl -ixon -ixoff -iuclc -ixany -imaxbel -opost -isig -icanon -xcase min 1 time 0. Can be negated. If negated, same as cooked.
cbreak	Same as -icanon. Can be negated. If negated, same as icanon.
pass8	Same as -parenb -istrip cs8. Can be negated. If negated, same as parenb istrip cs7.
litout	Same as -parenb -istrip -opost cs8. Can be negated. If negated, same as parenb istrip opost cs7.
decctlq	Same as -ixany. Can be negated.
tabs	Same as tab0. Can be negated. If negated, same as tab3.
lcase or LCASE	Same as xcase iuclc olcuc. Can be negated.
crt	Same as echoe echoctl echoke.
dec	Same as echoe echoctl echoke -ixany intr ^C erase ^? kill C-u.

Special-Character Settings

The following table describes the settings of special characters. Each setting must be followed by another command argument representing the actual value of the character. The value can be given literally, in hat notation (^C), or as an integer that may start with 0x to indicate hexadecimal, 0 to indicate octal, or any other digit to indicate decimal. A value of - or undef disables the character.

Setting	Description
intr	Sends an interrupt signal.
quit	Sends a quit signal.
erase	Erases the last character typed.
kill	Erases the current line.

continues >>

>>continued

Setting	Description
eof	Sends an end-of-file (terminates the input).
eol	Ends the line.
eol2	An alternate character to end the line.
swtch	Switches to a different shell layer.
start	Restarts the output after stopping it.
stop	Stops the output.
susp	Sends a terminal stop signal.
dsusp	Sends a terminal stop signal after flushing the input.
rprnt	Redraws the current line.
werase	Erases the last word typed.
lnext	Enters the next character typed literally, even if it's a special character.

Special Settings

Setting	Description
min *N*	Sets the minimum number of characters that will satisfy a read until the time value has expired, when -icanon is set.
time *N*	Sets the number of tenths of a second before reads time out if the minimum number of characters have not been read, when -icanon is set.
ispeed *N*	Sets the input speed to *N*.
ospeed *N*	Sets the output speed to *N*.
rows *N*	Tells the TTY kernel driver that the terminal has *N* rows.
cols *N* or columns *N*	Tells the kernel that the terminal has *N* columns.
size	Prints the number of rows and columns that the kernel thinks the terminal has.
line *N*	Uses line discipline *N*.
speed	Prints the terminal speed.
N	Sets the input and output speeds to *N*, with *N* being one of the following: 0, 50, 75, 110, 134, 134.5, 150, 200, 300, 600, 1200, 1800, 2400, 4800, 9600, 19200, 38400, exta, or extb. exta is the same as 19200. extb is the same as 38400. 0 hangs up the line if -clocal is set.

Many commands use the end of file (EOF) character to indicate end of input and terminate when it's detected. The standard EOF character is Ctrl+D (known to stty as ^D). The command stty eof ^E sets the EOF character to Ctrl+E if so desired.

tty

tty [*OPTION* ...]

`tty` prints the filename of the terminal connected to its standard input. It prints not a tty if the standard input is not a terminal. It returns an exit status of 0 if the standard input is a terminal, 1 if the standard input is not a terminal, 2 if given incorrect arguments, or 3 if a write error occurs.

`tty` has a single option available:

Option	Description
-s or --silent or --quiet	Prints nothing; only returns an exit status.

User Information

This section describes commands that print user-related data items such as groups and logins.

groups

groups [*USERNAME* ...]

`groups` prints the names of the primary and any supplementary groups for each given *USERNAME*, or the current process if no names are given. If names are given, the name of each user is printed before the list of that user's groups. The group lists are equivalent to the output of the command id -Gn.

id

id [*OPTION* ...] [*USERNAME*]

`id` prints information about the given *USERNAME* or the process running it if *USERNAME* isn't specified.

Option	Description
-g or --group	Prints only the group ID.
-G or --groups	Prints only the supplementary groups.
-n or --name	Prints the user or group name instead of the ID number. Requires -u, -g, or -G.
-r or --real	Prints the real (rather than effective) user or group ID. Requires -u, -g, or -G.
-u or --user	Prints only the user ID.

logname

logname

`logname` prints the calling user's name as found in the file /etc/utmp, and exits with a status of 0. If no /etc/utmp entry exists for the calling process, `logname` prints an error message and exits with a status of 1.

users

users [*FILE*]

users prints a single line containing a blank-separated list of usernames, one for each session. If a user is logged on more than once, the name appears more than once. By default, users reads from /etc/utmp, but will get its information from *FILE* if it's specified.

who

who [*OPTION*] [*FILE*] [am i]

who prints detailed information about each session. If invoked with no arguments, who prints the login name, terminal line, login time, and remote hostname or X display for each logged-on user.

If *FILE* is given, who uses that instead of /var/run/utmp as the name of the file containing the record of users who are logged on. /var/log/wtmp is commonly given as an argument to who to look at who has previously logged on.

Option	Description
-m	Same as whoami.
-q or --count	Prints only the login names and the number of users logged on. Overrides all other options.
-s	Ignored. Provided for compatibility with other versions of who.
-i or -u or --idle	Includes idle time for each session.
-H or --heading	Provides headings for columns.
-w, -T, --mesg, --message, or --writable	Includes information about each user's message status: + Allowing write messages. - Disallowing write messages. ? Cannot find terminal device.

whoami

whoami

whoami prints the username associated with the current effective user ID. It's equivalent to the command id -un.

System Context

These commands print or change system-wide information.

date

```
date [ OPTION ... ] [ +FORMAT ]
date [ -u ¦ --utc ¦ --universal ] [ MMDDHHMM [ [CC] YY] [ .SS ] ]
```

date can be used to print the current time and date according to *FORMAT* or to set the system clock. The following sections describe the available options and formats.

Options

Option	Description
-d *DATESTR* or --date=*DATESTR*	Displays the time and date in *DATESTR* instead of the current time and date.
-f *DATEFILE* or --file=*DATEFILE*	Formats each line in *DATEFILE* and displays it as with the -d option.
--rfc-822	Displays the time and date using the RFC 822-specified format, %a, %_d %b %Y %H:%M:%S %z. If --utc is also specified, uses GMT (Greenwich Mean Time) in place of %z.
-r *FILE* or --reference=*FILE*	Displays the last modification time and date of *FILE*.
-s *DATESTR* or --set=*DATESTR*	Sets the time and date to *DATESTR*.
-u or --utc or --universal	Prints or sets the time and date in Universal Coordinated Time.

Time Directives

The following directives related to time can be used in *FORMAT*:

Directive	Description
%H	Hour (00–23).
%I	Hour (01–12).
%k	Hour (0–23).
%l	Hour (1–12).
%M	Minute (00–59).
%p	Locale's AM or PM.
%r	12-hour time (*hh*:*mm*:*ss* AM or PM).
%s	Seconds since the epoch.
%S	Second (00–61).
%T	24-hour time (*hh*:*mm*:*ss*).
%X	Locale's time representation (%H:%M:%S).

continues >>

>>continued

Directive	Description
%z	RFC 822-style numeric time zone (for example, `-0600` or `+0100`), or nothing if no time zone is determinable.
%Z	Time zone (for example, `EDT`), or nothing if no time zone is determinable.

Date Directives

The following directives related to time can be used in *FORMAT*:

Directive	Description
%a	Locale's abbreviated weekday name (`Sun–Sat`).
%A	Locale's full weekday name, variable length (`Sunday–Saturday`).
%b	Locale's abbreviated month name (`Jan–Dec`).
%B	Locale's full month name, variable length (`January–December`).
%c	Locale's date and time—for example: `Sat Nov 06 12:02:33 EST 1999`
%d	Day of the month (`01–31`).
%D	Date (*mm/dd/yy*).
%h	Same as `%b`.
%j	Day of the year (`001–366`).
%m	Month (`01–12`).
%U	Week number of the year, with Sunday as the first day of the week (`00–53`). Days in a new year preceding the first Sunday are in week zero.
%V	Week number of the year, with Monday as the first day of the week, as a decimal (`01–53`). If the week containing January 1 has four or more days in the new year, it's considered week 1; otherwise, it's week 53 of the previous year, and the next week is week 1.
%w	Day of the week (`0–6`) with `0` corresponding to Sunday.
%W	Week number of the year, with Monday as the first day of the week (`00–53`). Days in a new year preceding the first Monday are in week zero.
%x	Locale's date representation (*mm/dd/yy*).
%y	Last two digits of the year (`00–99`).
%Y	Year (1970…).

Literal Directives

These directives produce literal strings:

Directive	Description
%%	Literal %.
%n	Newline.
%t	Horizontal tab.

Padding

By default, date pads numeric fields with leading zeroes. The following modifiers can be placed between % and the formatting directive to change the padding of numeric values:

Modifier	Description
-	Don't pad the field.
=	Pad the field with spaces.

Setting the Time and Date

When given an argument that doesn't start with +, date sets the system clock to the time and date specified. Only the superuser can set the clock. The general form for the argument is as follows:

MMDDHHMMCCYY.SS

where *MM* is the month, *DD* is the day of the month, *HH* is the hour, *MM* is the minute, *CC* is the century (optional), *YY* is the last two digits of the year (optional), and *SS* is the second.

hostname

hostname [*NAME*]

When invoked with no argument, hostname displays the name of the host system. When *NAME* is specified, the name is changed to *NAME*. Only the superuser can change the hostname.

uname

uname [*OPTION* ...]

uname prints information about the host machine and operating system. The following table describes the *OPTION*s available:

Option	Description
-a or --all	Prints all information provided by the other options.
-m or --machine	Prints the machine (hardware) type.
-n or --nodename	Prints the machine's network node hostname.
-p or --processor	Prints the machine's processor type.
-r or --release	Prints the operating system release.
-s or --sysname	Prints Linux, the operating system name (the default).
-v	Prints the operating system version.

Modified Command Invocation

This section describes commands that run other commands (generally specified as COMMAND [ARG ...]) in a context that differs from the current one (for example, in a modified environment or as a different user).

chroot

chroot NEWROOT [COMMAND [ARG ...]]

chroot runs COMMAND with the specified ARGs, with the root directory changed to NEWROOT. If COMMAND isn't specified, chroot uses the shell specified by the environment variable SHELL. If SHELL isn't set, /bin/sh -i is executed. Only the superuser can change the root directory.

env

env [OPTION ...] [NAME=VALUE ...] [COMMAND [ARG ...]]

env runs COMMAND with an environment modified by the NAME and VALUE pairs. If COMMAND isn't specified, the values of the new environment are printed as in printenv. The following OPTIONs apply:

Option	Description
-u NAME or --unset=NAME	Removes the variable NAME from the environment.
- or -i or --ignore-environment	Starts with an empty environment, ignoring the inherited environment.

nice

nice [OPTION ...] [[COMMAND [ARG ...]]]

nice executes COMMAND with the given ARGs at a modified scheduling priority. If no arguments are given, nice prints the current scheduling priority. If no adjustment is specified, 10 is added to the current priority.

nice takes a single OPTION, as described in the following table.

Option	Description
-n ADJUSTMENT or -ADJUSTMENT or --adjustment=ADJUSTMENT	Adds ADJUSTMENT to the scheduling priority.

nohup

nohup COMMAND [ARG ...]

nohup executes COMMAND and its ARGs with hangup signals ignored. The scheduling priority of COMMAND is increased by 5. If standard output is a terminal, it and standard error are redirected so that they're appended to the file nohup.out. If nohup.out can't be written to, they're appended to the file $HOME/nohup.out. If that file also can't be written to, the command is not run.

su

su [*OPTION* ...] [*USER* [*ARG* ...]]

su enables the invoking user to temporarily become *USER*. A shell is invoked with the specified *ARG*s. If no *USER* is given, *USER* defaults to root, the superuser. If *USER* has a password, su prompts for the password, unless the invoking user has an effective user ID of zero (the superuser). The shell to use is taken from *USER*'s `passwd` entry, or `/bin/sh` if none is specified there.

The following *OPTION*s apply:

Option	Description
-c *COMMAND* or --command=*COMMAND*	Passes *COMMAND* (a single command line to run) to the shell with a -c option, instead of starting an interactive shell.
-f or --fast	Passes the -f option to the shell.
- or -l or -login	Makes the shell a login shell.
-m or -p or --preserve-environment	Don't change the environment variables HOME, USER, LOGNAME, or SHELL.
-s *SHELL* or --shell=*SHELL*	Runs *SHELL* instead of the shell from *USER*'s passwd entry.

sudo

sudo [*OPTION* ...] *COMMAND*

sudo allows a permitted user to execute *COMMAND* as the superuser or as the user specified using the -u option. sudo determines who is an authorized user by consulting the file `/etc/sudoers`. A timestamp file with the same name as the user's name and contained in `/var/run/sudo` is used to determine whether password prompting is necessary. If the timestamp on this file is older than *N* minutes (where *N* was defined when sudo was compiled), the user will be prompted for the necessary password.

The following table describes the options accepted by sudo.

Option	Description
--	Stops processing command-line arguments.
-b	Runs the given command in the background. Shell job control cannot be used if the -b option is used.
-H	Sets the HOME environment variable to the home directory of the target user as specified in /etc/passwd.
-h	Prints the version and usage message and exits.
-k	Removes the user's timestamp file, thus requiring a password the next time sudo is run.
-l	Lists the allowed commands for the user on the current host.
-p *PROMPT*	Uses *PROMPT* instead of the default password prompt. If the password prompt contains the %u escape, %u will be replaced by the user's login name. Similarly, %h will be replaced by the local hostname.
-s	Runs the shell specified by the SHELL environment variable (if set) or the shell as specified in /etc/passwd.

continues >>

>>continued

Option	Description
-u USER	Runs COMMAND as USER instead of root. USER can be a username or #UID, where UID is the numeric user ID.
-V	Prints the version number and exits.
-v	Updates the user's timestamp file in /var/run/sudo and prompts for a password if necessary.

Suspending Execution

This section describes the means to delay or suspend the execution of shell scripts for a specified period of time.

sleep

```
sleep NUMBER[UNIT]
```

sleep pauses for an interval of time specified by NUMBER. UNIT is one of the following:

Option	Description
s	Seconds (default).
m	Minutes.
h	Hours.
d	Days.

Numeric Operations

These commands perform numerically related operations.

factor

```
factor [ NUMBER ... ]
```

factor prints prime factors for each NUMBER. If no NUMBERs are specified on the command line, factor reads them from standard input, delimited by newlines, tabs, or spaces.

seq

```
seq [ OPTION ... ] [ FIRST [ STEP ] ] LAST
```

seq prints a sequence of numbers from FIRST to LAST by STEP to standard output. By default, FIRST and STEP are both 1, and each number is printed on its own line. All numbers can be reals, not just integers.

Option	Description
-f FORMAT or --format=FORMAT	Prints all numbers using FORMAT. The default is %g. FORMAT must contain exactly one of the standard float output formats %e, %f, or %g.

Option	Description
-s *STRING* or --separator=*STRING*	Prints numbers separated by *STRING*. The default is the newline character.
-w or --equal-width	Prints all numbers with the same width by padding with leading zeroes.

2
Text Utilities

Most system and application data is stored in plain text format on Linux systems. The commands described in this chapter are used to perform commonly needed transformations of text data.

Common Options

In addition to the options described in the following sections, each command can be invoked with the following options:

Option	Description
--help	Prints a usage message listing all available options and exits successfully.
--version	Prints the version number and exits successfully.

Output Entire Files

The commands in this section output all data supplied to them. In some cases, the output data is an altered form.

cat

```
cat [ OPTION ... ] [ FILE ... ]
```

cat concatenates named files to standard output. This includes standard input if no files are specified or if FILE is -.

Option	Description
-A or --show-all	Same as -vET.
-b or --number-nonblank	Numbers all nonblank output lines starting with 1.
-e	Same as -vE.
-E or --show-ends	Displays $ at the end of each line.
-n or --number	Numbers all output lines starting with 1.

continues >>

>>continued

Option	Description
-s or --squeeze-blank	Replaces multiple consecutive blank lines with a single blank line.
-t	Same as -vT.
-T or --show-tabs	Displays tab characters as ^T.
-u	Ignored but provided for UNIX compatibility.
-v or --show-nonprinting	Displays control characters except for linefeed and tab with caret (^) notation. Characters with the high bit set are preceded by M-.

nl

nl [OPTION ...] [FILE ...]

nl concatenates named files to standard output and adds line numbers. This includes standard input if no files are given or FILE is -. Sections of logical pages are indicated by the following:

\:\:\:	Start of header.
\:\:	Start of body.
\:	Start of footer.

The characters \ and : can be overridden by the -d and --section-delimiter options described in the following table.

Option	Description
-b STYLE or --body-numbering=STYLE	Sets the numbering STYLE for each line of the body section of each logical page. Valid STYLE values are as follows: a numbers all lines. t numbers only nonempty lines (default for the body). n doesn't number lines (default for header and footer). pREGEXP numbers only lines that contain a match for the regular expression REGEXP.
-d CD or --section-delimiter=CD	Sets the section delimiter characters to CD (the default is \:). The second character D is optional and defaults to :.
-f STYLE or --footer-numbering=STYLE	Same as --body-numbering but applied to footers.
-h STYLE or --header-numbering=STYLE	Same as --body-numbering but applied to headers.
-i NUMBER or --page-increment=NUMBER	Increments line numbers by NUMBER (the default is 1).

Option	Description
-l *NUMBER* or --join-blank-lines=*NUMBER*	Treats *NUMBER* consecutive blank lines as one logical line for numbering and only numbers the last one. A blank line is one that consists of no characters, not even spaces or tabs.
-n *FORMAT* or --number-format=*FORMAT*	Sets the line number format. Valid values for **FORMAT** are as follows: ln left-aligns, no leading zeroes. rn right-aligns, no leading zeroes. rz right-aligns with leading zeroes.
-p or --no-renumber	Don't reset the line number at the start of a logical page.
-s *STRING* or --number-separator=*STRING*	Inserts *STRING* between the line number and the text line (the default is the tab character).
-v *NUMBER* or --starting-line-number=*NUMBER*	Sets the initial line number for each logical page to *NUMBER* (the default is 1).
-w *NUMBER* or --number-width=*NUMBER*	Line numbers are *NUMBER* characters wide (the default is 6).

od

```
od [ OPTION ... ] [ FILE ... ]
od -C [ FILE ] [[+]OFFSET[[+]LABEL]]
```

od rewrites input data as a sequence of ASCII representations of primitive data objects. This includes standard input if no files are named or if *FILE* is -. Each line of output begins with the byte offset of the first data object shown on that line. By default, od writes data in octal.

Option	Description
-A *RADIX* or --address-radix=*RADIX*	Selects the base in which the file offsets are printed. Valid values for *RADIX* are as follows: d Decimal. o Octal (default). x Hexadecimal. n None (no offsets printed).
-j *BYTES* or --skip-bytes=*BYTES*	Skips *BYTES* input bytes before formatting and writing. The number *BYTES* is interpreted as decimal unless it begins with one of the following: 0x or 0X Hexadecimal. 0 Octal.

continues >>

>>continued

Option	Description
	The number *BYTES* is interpreted as single bytes unless it ends with one of the following:
	b Blocks (*BYTES* is multiplied by 512).
	k Kilobytes (*BYTES* is multiplied by 1024).
	m Megabytes (*BYTES* is multiplied by 1048576).
-N *BYTES* or --read-bytes=*BYTES*	Outputs at most *BYTES* bytes of the input. Prefixes and suffixes are the same as for the -j option.
-s [*N*] or --strings[=*N*]	Outputs only string literals that are at least *N* characters in length. A *string literal* is defined as one or more ASCII characters followed by a null (zero) byte. If *N* is omitted, the minimum length defaults to 3.
-t *TYPE* or --format=*TYPE*	Specifies the format for the output. *TYPE* is a string of one or more of the following indicator characters. If more than one character is used, od writes one copy of the output line for each format specified, in the order specified.
	a Named character ('sp' for space, 'nl' for newline, and so on).
	c ASCII character or backslash escape (' ' for space, '\n' for newline, etc.).
	d Signed decimal.
	f Floating point.
	o Octal.
	u Unsigned decimal.
	x Hexadecimal.
	Except for types a and c, the type character can be followed by a decimal number indicating the number of bytes contained in the given data type. Alternatively, the size can be specified using one of the C compiler's built-in data types. For integers (d, o, u, and x):
	C Char.
	S Short.
	I Int.
	L Long.
	For floating point (f):
	F Float.
	D Double.
	L Long double.

Option	Description
-v or --output-duplicates	Outputs consecutive lines that are identical. By default, when two or more consecutive output lines would be identical, od outputs only the first line and puts an asterisk on the following line to indicate that there's duplication.
-w[N] or --width[=N]	Each output line represents N input bytes. This must be a multiple of the least common multiple of the sizes associated with the specified output types. If N is omitted, the default is 32. If the entire option is omitted, the default is 16.
-a	Outputs named characters. Equivalent to -ta.
-b	Outputs as octal bytes. Equivalent to -toC.
-c	Outputs as ASCII characters or backslash escapes. Equivalent to -tc.
-d	Outputs as unsigned decimal shorts. Equivalent to tu2.
-f	Outputs as floats. Equivalent to -tfF.
-h	Outputs as hexadecimal shorts. Equivalent to -tx2.
-i	Outputs as decimal shorts. Equivalent to -td2.
-l	Outputs as decimal longs. Equivalent to -td4.
-o	Outputs as octal shorts. Equivalent to -to2.
-x	Outputs as hexadecimal shorts. Equivalent to -tx2.

tac

tac [OPTION ...] [FILE ...]

tac concatenates named files to standard output with records (lines by default) reversed. These include standard input if no files are named or if FILE is -. Records are separated by instances of a string. By default, the separator is a newline at the end of each record.

Option	Description
b or --before	The separator is attached to the beginning of the record that it precedes in the file.
-r or --regex	Treats the separator string as a regular expression.
-s or separator=SEPARATOR	Uses SEPARATOR instead of newline as the record separator.

Output File Subsets

The commands in this section output selected parts of their inputs, such as the first few or last few lines.

csplit

csplit [*OPTION* ...] *INPUT PATTERN* ...

csplit splits *INPUT* (standard input if *INPUT* is -) into sections. Each section is output to a separate file. The section boundaries are determined by the *PATTERN* arguments described in the following table. An error occurs if a *PATTERN* argument refers to a nonexistent line of the input file. After all *PATTERN*s are matched, the remaining input is copied into one last output file. By default, csplit prints the number of bytes written to each output file after it has been created.

Pattern	Description
N	Creates an output file containing the input up to but not including line *N*. If followed by a repeat count, also creates an output file containing the next *N* lines of the input file once for each repeat.
/*REGEXP*/[*OFFSET*]	Creates an output file containing the current line up to (but not including) the next line of the input file that contains a match for *REGEXP*. The optional *OFFSET* is + or - followed by a positive integer. If it's given, the input up to the matching line plus or minus *OFFSET* is put into the output file, and the following line begins the next section.
%*REGEXP*%[*OFFSET*]	Same as the previous type except that no output file is created for the corresponding section. The type is to be used to suppress the generation of a section delimited by *REGEXP*.
{*REPEAT-COUNT*}	Repeats the previous pattern *REPEAT-COUNT* additional times. *REPEAT-COUNT* can be either a positive integer or an asterisk (*). The asterisk means that the repetition continues until the input is exhausted.

The output files' names consist of a prefix (xx by default) followed by a suffix. By default, the suffix is an ascending sequence of two-digit decimal numbers from 00 up to 99. In any case, concatenating the output files in sorted order by filename produces the original input file.

By default, if csplit encounters an error or receives a hangup, interrupt, quit, or terminate signal, it removes any output files that it has created so far before it exits.

The options are described in the following table.

Option	Description
-f *PREFIX* or --prefix=*PREFIX*	Uses *PREFIX* as the prefix for the output filename.
-b *SUFFIX* or --suffix=*SUFFIX*	Uses *SUFFIX* as the suffix for the output filename. When this option is specified, it's passed internally to the sprintf C library routine and must be suitable for conversion of a binary integer to string format. As such, only d, i, u, o, x, and X conversions are allowed. If this option is used, the --digits option is ignored.
-n *DIGITS* or --digits=*DIGITS*	Uses output filenames containing numbers that are *DIGITS* digits long instead of the default two digits.
-k or --keep-files	Don't remove output files when errors are encountered.
-z or --elide-empty-files	Suppresses the generation of zero-length output files. (In cases where the section delimiters of the input file are supposed to mark the first lines of each of the sections, the first output file will generally be a zero-length file unless you use this option.) The output file sequence numbers always run consecutively starting from 0, even when this option is specified.
-s or -q or --silent or --quiet	Don't print counts of output file sizes.

head

```
head [ OPTION ... ] [ FILE ... ]
head -NUMBER [ OPTION ... ] [ FILE ... ]
```

head prints the beginning (first 10 lines by default) of each file *FILE*. These include standard input if no files are named or if - is named. If more than one file is specified, head prints a one-line header consisting of ==> *FILE* <== before the output for each file. head accepts two option formats: the new one, in which numbers are arguments to the options (-q -n 1), and the old one, in which the number precedes any option letters (-1q).

Option	Description
-*COUNT*[*OPTIONS*]	This option is recognized only if it's specified first. *COUNT* is a decimal number optionally followed by a size letter (b, k, m) as in -c, or l to mean count by lines, or other option letters (cqv).
-c *BYTES* or --bytes=*BYTES*	Prints the first *BYTES* bytes instead of initial lines. Appending b (blocks) multiplies *BYTES* by 512, k (kilobytes) by 1024, and m (megabytes) by 1048576.
-n *N* or --lines=*N*	Outputs the first *N* lines.

continues >>

>>continued

Option	Description
-q or --quiet or --silent	Never print filename headers.
-v or --verbose	Always print filename headers.

split

split [OPTION] [INPUT [PREFIX]]

split creates output files containing consecutive sections of INPUT (standard input if none is given or INPUT is -).

Each output filename consists of PREFIX (x by default) followed by a group of letters a, b, and so on, such that concatenating the output files in sorted order by filename produces the original input file. (If more than 676 output files are required, split uses zaa, zab, etc.)

Option	Description
-LINES or -l LINES or --lines=LINES	Puts LINES lines of INPUT into each output file.
-b BYTES or --bytes=BYTES	Puts the first BYTES bytes of INPUT into each output file. Appending b multiplies BYTES by 512, k by 1024, and m by 1048576.
-C BYTES or --line-bytes=BYTES	Puts into each output file as many complete lines of INPUT as possible without exceeding BYTES bytes. For lines longer than BYTES bytes, put BYTES bytes into each output file until less than BYTES bytes of the line are left, then continues normally. BYTES has the same format as for the --bytes option.
--verbose	Writes a diagnostic to standard error just before each output file is opened.

tail

tail [OPTION ...] [FILE ...]
tail -NUMBER [OPTION ...] [FILE ...]
tail +NUMBER [OPTION ...] [FILE ...]

tail prints the last part (10 lines by default) of each FILE; it reads from standard input if no files are given or when given a FILE of -. If more than one FILE is specified, tail prints a one-line header consisting of ==> FILE <== before the output for each FILE.

tail accepts two option formats: the new one, in which numbers are arguments to the options (-n 1), and the old one, in which the number precedes any option letters (-1 or +1).

If any option-argument is a number N starting with +, tail begins printing with the Nth item from the start of each file, instead of from the end.

Option	Description
-COUNT or +COUNT	This option is recognized only if it's specified first. COUNT is a decimal number optionally followed by a size letter (b, k, m) as in -c, or l to mean count by lines, or other option letters (cfqv).
-c BYTES or --bytes=BYTES	Outputs the last BYTES bytes instead of final lines. Appending b (blocks) multiplies BYTES by 512, k (kilobytes) by 1024, and m (megabytes) by 1048576.
-f or --follow	Loops forever trying to read more characters at the end of the file, presumably because the file is growing. Ignored if reading from a pipe. If more than one file is given, tail prints a header whenever it gets output from a different file, to indicate the source of that output.
-n N or --lines=N	Outputs the last N lines.
-q or -quiet or --silent	Never print filename headers.
-v or --verbose	Always print filename headers.

Formatting

The commands in this section are used to rewrite the contents of files in a different format.

fmt

fmt [OPTION ...] [FILE ...]

fmt reads from the specified FILE arguments (or standard input if no FILEs are given) and writes to standard output.

By default, blank lines, spaces between words, and indentation are preserved in the output; successive input lines with different indentation are not joined; tabs are expanded on input and introduced on output.

fmt prefers breaking lines at the end of a sentence, and tries to avoid line breaks after the first word or before the last word of a sentence. A *sentence break* is defined as either the end of a paragraph or a word ending in any of . ? ! followed by two spaces or end of line, ignoring any intervening parentheses or quotes.

Option	Description
-c or --crown-margin	*Crown margin mode*: Preserve the indentation of the first two lines within a paragraph, and align the left margin of each subsequent line with that of the second line.

continues >>

>>continued

Option	Description
-t or --tagged-paragraph	*Tagged paragraph mode*: Like crown margin mode except that if indentation of the first line of a paragraph is the same as the indentation of the second, the first line is treated as a one-line paragraph.
-s or --split-only	Split lines only. Don't join short lines to form longer ones. This prevents sample lines of code and other such "formatted" text from being unduly combined.
-u or --uniform-spacing	Uniform spacing. Reduce spacing between words to one space and spacing between sentences to two spaces.
-*WIDTH* or -w *WIDTH* or --width=*WIDTH*	Fill output lines up to *WIDTH* characters (the default is 75). `fmt` initially tries to make lines about 7% shorter than this, to give it room to balance line lengths.
-p *PREFIX* or --prefix=*PREFIX*	Only lines beginning with *PREFIX* (possibly preceded by whitespace) are subject to formatting. The prefix and any preceding whitespace are stripped for the formatting and then reattached to each formatted output line. One use is to format certain kinds of program comments, while leaving the code unchanged.

fold

fold [*OPTION* ...] [*FILE* ...]

fold writes each *FILE* or standard input if none are given (- means standard input) to standard output, breaking long lines.

By default, fold breaks lines wider than 80 columns. The output is split into as many lines as necessary.

fold counts screen columns by default; thus, a tab may count more than one column, backspace decreases the column count, and carriage return sets the column to zero.

Option	Description
-b or --bytes	Count bytes rather than columns so that tabs, backspaces, and carriage returns are each counted as taking up one column, just like other characters.
-s or --spaces	Break at word boundaries; the line is broken after the last blank before the maximum line length. If the line contains no such blanks, the line is broken at the maximum line length as usual.
-w *WIDTH* or --width=*WIDTH*	Use a maximum line length of *WIDTH* columns instead of 80.

pr

pr [OPTION ...] [FILE ...]

pr writes each FILE or standard input if none are given (- means standard input) to standard output. Options are provided for pagination, multicolumn format, parallel printing of one file per column, and so on.

Option	Description
+FIRST_PAGE[:LAST_PAGE]	Begin printing with page FIRST_PAGE and stop with LAST_PAGE. Printing stops at end of file if :LAST_PAGE is omitted.
-COLUMN	With each single FILE, produce output in COLUMN columns and print columns down. Balance the number of lines in columns on each page. -COLUMN can't be used with -m.
-a -COLUMN	With each single FILE, print columns across rather than down. COLUMN must be greater than one.
-c	Print control characters using hat notation (for example, ^G); print other unprintable characters in octal backslash notation. By default, unprintable characters are not changed.
-d	Double space the output.
-e[IN-TABCHAR[IN-TABWIDTH]]	Expand tabs to spaces on input. The optional argument IN-TABCHAR is the input tab character (the default is <TAB>). The optional argument IN-TABWIDTH is the input tab character's width (the default is 8).
-f or -F	Use a formfeed instead of newlines to separate output pages. The default page length of 66 lines isn't altered, but the number of lines of text per page changes from 56 to 63 lines.
-h HEADER	Replace the filename in the header with the centered string HEADER.
-i[OUT-TABCHAR[OUT-TABWIDTH]]	Replace spaces with tabs on output. The optional argument OUT-TABCHAR is the output tab character (the default is <TAB>). The optional argument OUT-TABWIDTH is the output tab character's width (the default is 8).
-j	Merge lines of full length. Used together with the column options -COLUMN, -a -COLUMN, or -m. Turns off -w line truncation, no column alignment is used, and can be used with -s.
-l PAGE_LENGTH	Set page length to PAGE_LENGTH lines (the default is 66).
-m	Merge and print files in columns.
-n[NUMBER-SEPARATOR[DIGITS]]	Precede each column with a line number. With parallel files (m), precede only each line with a line number. NUMBER-SEPARATOR is printed after each number (the default is <TAB>). DIGITS is the number of digits per line number (the default is 5).

continues >>

>>continued

Option	Description
-N LINE_NUMBER	Start line counting at LINE_NUMBER.
-o N	Set indentation to N spaces (the default is zero).
-r	Don't print warning messages for files that can't be opened.
-s[SEPARATOR]	Use the string SEPARATOR to separate columns (the default is a space).
-t	Don't print the usual header (and footer) on each page, and don't fill out the bottoms of pages (with blank lines or a formfeed). Formfeeds in input files are preserved.
-T	Same as -t plus elimination of formfeeds in input files.
-v	Print unprintable characters in octal backslash notation.
-w PAGE_WIDTH	Set page width to PAGE_WIDTH characters (the default is 72).

File Summaries

The commands in this section generate information about files, such as line counts and checksums.

cksum

```
cksum [ OPTION ... ] [ FILE ... ]
```

cksum prints one line for each FILE, including standard input if no files are named or if FILE is -. Each line begins with the cyclic redundancy check (CRC) checksum for the file followed by the file's byte count and name, separated by spaces. Useful for checking files for data corruption due to transfer by unreliable means.

sum

```
sum [ OPTION ... ] [ FILE ... ]
```

sum prints 16-bit checksums and sizes for each named file, including standard input if no files are named or FILE is -. File sizes are in 1024-byte blocks (rounded up) by default. sum is provided for compatibility; the cksum command is recommended for new applications.

Option	Description
-r	Use the default (BSD compatible) algorithm. This option is included for compatibility with the System V sum. Unless -s was also given, it has no effect.
-s or --sysv	Compute checksums using an algorithm compatible with System V sum's default, and print file sizes in units of 512-byte blocks.

wc

wc [*OPTION* ...] [*FILE* ...]

wc counts the number of bytes, words, or lines for each named *FILE*, including standard input if no files are named or *FILE* is -. By default, wc prints all three counts for each file.

Option	Description
-c or --bytes or --chars	Print only byte counts.
-w or --words	Print only word counts.
-l or --lines	Print only line counts.

Sorting Data and Processing Sorted Data

The commands in this section sort files or operate on files that have been sorted.

comm

comm [*OPTION* ...] *FILE1 FILE2*

comm reads two sorted files (- indicates standard input) and outputs three columns containing lines that are unique to the first file (the first column), lines that are unique to the second file (the second column), and lines that are common to both files (the third column). The options -1, -2, and -3 can be used to suppress output of the corresponding columns. Columns are separated by tabs.

sort

sort [*OPTION* ...] [*FILE* ...]

sort sorts, merges, or compares all the lines from the given *FILE*s, including standard input if no files are given or *FILE* is -. sort has three modes of operation: sort (the default), merge, and a mode to determine whether the files are sorted.

Option	Description
-c	Determine whether files are sorted. Print an error message on standard error and exit with status 1 if not all files are sorted. Otherwise, exit successfully.
-m	Merge the given files. Input files must be sorted individually prior to merging.
-b	Ignore leading blanks when finding sort keys in each line.
-d	Ignore all characters except letters, digits, and blanks when sorting ("phone directory" order).
-f	Fold lowercase letters to uppercase when sorting.
-g	Sort numerically. The strtod library function is used internally to convert key values to double-precision floating point.
-i	Ignore characters outside the printable ASCII range 040–0176 octal (inclusive) when sorting.

continues >>

>>continued

Option	Description
-M	Interpret key fields containing initial whitespace followed by three letters as month abbreviations. The three letters are folded to uppercase and ordered chronologically (JAN, FEB, … DEC).
-n	Sort numerically. Each line begins with a number consisting of optional whitespace, an optional -, and zero or more digits, optionally followed by a decimal point and zero or more digits. If the data contains a leading + or exponential notation, the -g option must be used.
-r	Sort in reverse order.
-o OUTPUT-FILE	Write output to OUTPUT-FILE. One of the input files can be used for output.
-t SEPARATOR	Use SEPARATOR as the field separator. By default, fields are separated by the empty string between a non-whitespace character and a whitespace character.
-u	For the default case or the -m option, output only the first of a sequence of lines that compare equal. For the -c option, check that no pair of consecutive lines compares equal.
-k POS1[,POS2]	The recommended option for specifying a sort field. The field consists of the line between POS1 and POS2 (or the end of the line, if POS2 is omitted), inclusive. Fields and character positions are numbered starting with 1. See the sidebar "Position Descriptions" for information on how to specify POS1 and POS2.
-z	Input records separated by ASCII NULL (zero) characters instead of ASCII linefeeds.
+POS1[-POS2]	The obsolete option for specifying a sort field. The field consists of the line between POS1 and up to but not including POS2 (or the end of the line if POS2 is omitted). Fields and character positions are numbered starting with 0. See the sidebar "Position Descriptions" for information on how to specify POS1 and POS2.

Position Descriptions

A position has the form *f.c* where *f* is the number of the field to use and *c* is the number of the first character from the beginning of the field (for +POS) or from the end of the previous field (-POS). The .c part can be omitted, in which case it's taken to be the first character in the field. If the -b option has been given, the .c part of a field is counted from the first nonblank character of the field (for +POS) or from the first nonblank character following the previous field (for -POS).

A +POS or -POS argument can also have any of the global option letters M, b, d, f, i, n, or r appended. In these cases, the global ordering options are overridden for that specific field. Keys can span multiple fields.

uniq

uniq [OPTION ...] [INPUT [OUTPUT]]

uniq writes unique lines from the file INPUT or from standard input if INPUT is - or isn't specified. Output is written to the file OUTPUT or to standard output if OUTPUT isn't specified. Optionally, uniq can instead show only lines that appear exactly once, or lines that appear more than once. Input must be sorted.

Option	Description
-N or -f N or --skip-fields=N	Skip N fields on each line before checking for uniqueness. Fields are sequences of non-space or non-tab characters separated by sequences of tabs and/or spaces.
+N or -s N or --skip-chars=N	Skip N characters before checking for uniqueness. If both field- and character-skipping options are specified, the fields are skipped first.
-c or --count	Print the number of times each line occurred along with the line.
-i or --ignore-case	Ignore differences in case when comparing lines.
-d or --repeated	Print only duplicate lines.
-u or --unique	Print only unique lines.
-w N or --check-chars=N	After fields and characters are skipped, compare N characters. By default, the rest of the line is compared.

The following example illustrates the generation and use of sorted data.

Assuming that access_log is in Apache log file format, where each line of text represents one HTTP transfer and the seventh space-delimited field contains the name of the transferred file, the following shell pipeline can be used to obtain a report showing the frequency of transfers for each file. The most frequently requested files appear at the top of the output. gawk is used to extract the filenames. The filenames are then sorted so that they can be counted by uniq. The -c switch for uniq is used to obtain the frequency for each one. The second invocation of sort then generates the final output with the records ordered by descending frequency.

```
gawk '{print $7;}' < access_log ¦ sort ¦ uniq -c ¦ sort -r -k 1
```

Field-Oriented Processing

Lines of text are often used to represent logical data records that each contain one or more fields. The commands in this section operate on files that are structured in this way.

cut

```
cut [ OPTION ... ] [ FILE ... ]
```

cut writes selected parts of each line of each input file to standard output. The standard input file can be used if no files are specified or if - is specified. In the following table, BYTE-LIST, CHARACTER-LIST, and COLUMN-LIST are comma-separated numbers or comma-separated number ranges (two numbers separated by a hyphen). Bytes, characters, and fields are numbered starting at 1. Incomplete ranges can be given: -M means 1-M; N- means N through end of line or last field.

Option	Description
-b *BYTE-LIST* or --bytes=*BYTE-LIST*	Print only the bytes in positions listed in *BYTE-LIST*.
-c *CHARACTER-LIST* or --characters=*CHARACTER-LIST*	Same as -b for now but internationalization will introduce changes.
-f *FIELD-LIST* or --fields=*FIELD-LIST*	Print only the fields listed in *FIELD-LIST*.
-d *DELIM* or --delimiter=*DELIM*	Fields are separated by the first character in *DELIM* (tab by default).
-n	Don't split multi-byte characters. (This option is currently ignored.)
-s or --only-delimited	Don't print lines that don't contain the field separator.

join

```
join [ OPTION ... ] FILE1 FILE2
```

join writes to standard output a line for each pair of input lines that have matching values for specified fields. Either input file (but not both) can be -, which means standard input. Both input files should be sorted.

Option	Description
-a *FILE-NUMBER*	Print a line for each unpairable line in file *FILE-NUMBER* (either 1 or 2) in addition to normal output.
-e *STRING*	Replace output fields that are missing in the input with *STRING*.
-i or --ignore-case	Ignore case when comparing keys. Input files must be sorted the same way.
-1 *FIELD* or -j1 *FIELD*	Join on field *FIELD* (a positive integer) of file 1.
-2 *FIELD* or -j2 *FIELD*	Join on field *FIELD* (a positive integer) of file 2.
-j *FIELD*	Equivalent to -1 *FIELD* -2 *FIELD*.
-o *FIELD-LIST*	Format output line according to *FIELD-LIST*, which is a list of elements that are either 0 (the join field) or *M.N* where *M* is the file number (1 or 2) and *N* is a positive field number.
-t *CHAR*	Use the character *CHAR* as the input and output field separator.
-v *FILE-NUMBER*	Print a line for each unpairable line in file *FILE-NUMBER* (either 1 or 2) instead of normal output.

paste

```
paste [ OPTION ... ] [ FILE ... ]
```

paste outputs sequentially corresponding lines from each file to standard output. Standard input is used if - is specified as a filename or if no files are specified.

Option	Description
-s or --serial	Output lines one file at a time rather than one line from each file.
-d DELIM-LIST or --delimiters DELIM-LIST	Consecutively use the characters in DELIM-LIST instead of <TAB> to separate merged lines. When DELIM-LIST is exhausted, start again at its beginning.

Character Processing

The commands in this section perform character-level operations on input text. They perform translations, deletions, and conversions of individual characters.

expand

```
expand [ OPTION ... ] [ FILE ... ]
```

expand converts tabs in the input files to spaces and writes the result to standard output. Standard input is used if - is specified or if no files are specified.

Option	Description
- TAB1[,TAB2] ... or -t TAB1[,TAB2] ... or --tabs=TAB1[,TAB2] ...	Set tabs. If only one tab is given, set tabs TAB1 spaces apart (the default is 8). Otherwise, set tabs at positions TAB1, TAB2, and so on (numbered from 0). If -t or --tabs forms are used, column numbers can be separated by blanks as well as commas.
-i or --initial	Convert only the initial tabs on each line to spaces.

tr

```
tr [ options ] SET1 [ SET2 ]
```

tr translates, squeezes, and/or deletes characters from standard input and writes the result to standard output.

Option	Description
-c or --complement	Replace SET1 with its complement.
-d or --delete	Delete characters in SET1; don't translate.

continues >>

>>continued

Option	Description
-s or --squeeze-repeats	Replace the repetitions of characters in *SET1* with single occurrences of those characters. (See the example at the end of this section.)
-t or --truncate-set1	Truncate the length of *SET1* to the length of *SET2* before doing anything else.

*SET*s are specified as strings of characters. Most characters are represented by themselves. The following table describes interpreted characters.

Notation	Description
\NNN	Character with octal value *NNN* (one to three octal digits).
\\	Backslash.
\a	Audible BEL (beep).
\b	Backspace.
\f	Formfeed.
\n	Newline.
\r	Return.
\t	Horizontal tab.
\v	Vertical tab.
CHAR1-CHAR2	All characters from *CHAR1* to *CHAR2* in ascending order.
[*CHAR1-CHAR2*]	Same as *CHAR1-CHAR2* if both *SET1* and *SET2* use this.
[*CHAR**]	Copy *CHAR* into *SET2* until the length of *SET2* is equal to that of *SET1*.
[*CHAR*REPEAT*]	*REPEAT* copies of *CHAR*; *REPEAT* octal if starting with 0.
[:alnum:]	All letters and digits.
[:alpha:]	All letters.
[:blank:]	All horizontal whitespace.
[:cntrl:]	All control characters.
[:digit:]	All digits.
[:graph:]	All printable characters not including space.
[:lower:]	All lowercase letters.
[:print:]	All printable characters including space.
[:punct:]	All punctuation characters.
[:space:]	All horizontal and vertical whitespace.
[:upper:]	All uppercase characters.
[:xdigit:]	All hexadecimal digits.
[=*CHAR*=]	All characters equivalent to *CHAR* (at the moment, the same as *CHAR*).

The following example capitalizes its input:

```
tr [:lower:] [:upper:]
```

This example translates A   sstring to A string:

```
tr -s " s"
```

And this command deletes any characters that aren't digits:

```
tr -c -d [:digit:]
```

unexpand

```
unexpand [ OPTION ... ] [ FILE ... ]
```

unexpand writes the contents of each given *FILE* (or standard input if none are given or for a *FILE* of -) to standard output, with strings of two or more space or tab characters converted to as many tabs as possible followed by as many spaces as are needed to preserve the column alignment of the original text.

Option	Description
-*TAB1*[,*TAB2*] ... or -t *TAB1*[,*TAB2*] ... or --tabs=*TAB1*[,*TAB2*] ...	If only one tab stop is given, set the tabs *TAB1* spaces apart instead of the default 8. Otherwise, set the tabs at columns *TAB1*, *TAB2*, ... (numbered from 0), and leave spaces and tabs beyond the specified tab stops unchanged. If the tab stops are specified with the -t or --tabs option, they can be separated by blanks as well as by commas.
-a or --all	Convert all strings of two or more spaces or tabs, not just initial ones (the default) to tabs.

Advanced Text Processing

The section describes some of the more sophisticated text-processing utilities. These commands are useful if applications require pattern recognition and replacement or complex processing logic.

gawk

```
gawk [ OPTION ... ] PROGRAM [ FILE ... ]
gawk [ OPTION ... ] -f PROGRAM_FILE [ FILE ... ]
```

gawk is the GNU implementation of awk. Its basic function is to search text files for lines (or other units of text) that contain specified patterns. When matches are found, specified actions are performed on the corresponding line. Patterns and actions are either stated in the *PROGRAM* argument or are contained in the file *PROGRAM_FILE*.

The following table summarizes the command-line options accepted by gawk:

Option	Description
-F *FS* or --field-separator *FS*	Use *FS* as the field separator character and as the value for the predefined variable FS in the program.
-f *PROGRAM-FILE* or --file *PROGRAM-FILE*	Read the program from *PROGRAM_FILE*.
-mf *NNN* or -mr *NNN*	Set the maximum number of fields (-mf) or the maximum length of the record (-mr). These options are ignored by gawk and are included only for compatibility with the original awk.
-v *VAR=VAL* or --assign *VAR=VAL*	Assign the value *VAL* to the variable *VAR* prior to program execution.
-W traditional or -W compat or --traditional or --compat	Turn off gawk extensions. Compatibility mode.
-W copyleft or -W copyright or --copyleft or --copyright	Print the short version of the GNU General Public License and exit.
-W help or -W usage or --help or --usage	Print a short summary of the command options and exit.
-W lint or --lint	Print warnings concerning dubious or non-portable awk constructs.
-W posix or --posix	Use POSIX compatibility mode, which turns off gawk extensions.
-W re-interval or --re-interval	Allow interval expressions in regular expressions.
-W source=*PROGRAM-TEXT* or --source *PROGRAM-TEXT*	Use *PROGRAM-TEXT* as the awk program source. This enables mixing of command-line source code with source code from files.
-W version or --version	Print the gawk version information and exit.
--	Indicates end of options.

Language Summary

A gawk program consists of a series of statements of one of the following forms:

- *PATTERN*
- { *ACTIONS* }
- *PATTERN* { *ACTIONS* }
- function *FUNCTION*(*PARAMETERS*) { *ACTIONS* }

For each line of input, gawk executes *ACTIONS* if the line matches *PATTERN*. For statements that don't include *PATTERN*, gawk executes *ACTIONS* for each line of input. For statements that don't include *ACTIONS*, gawk prints each input line that matches *PATTERN*. function statements are used to create a user-defined function consisting of *ACTIONS* to be applied to values specified in *PARAMETERS*.

Patterns

Patterns used by gawk fall into several classes:

- */REGEXP/*—These patterns match when input-line text matches the regular expression *REGEXP*.

- *EXPRESSION*—These patterns match when *EXPRESSION* is nonzero (if numeric) or non-null (if a string).

- *PATTERN1,PATTERN2*—A pair of patterns is used to select ranges of consecutive input records. *PATTERN1* matches the first record in each range and *PATTERN2* matches the second record in each range.

- BEGIN and END—These are used to specify startup and cleanup actions. The associated actions for BEGIN are executed prior to any input records being read. The actions for END are executed after all input records have been read and processed.

Variables, Records, and Fields

Variables and *fields* may be floating-point numbers, strings, or both. They're typed dynamically depending on their context.

Records are normally separated by the character or regular expression contained in the RS variable. If RS is set to the null string, the records are separated by blank lines.

Fields are separated by the character or regular expression contained in the FS variable. If FS is the null string, each character is a separate field. The FIELDWIDTHS variable can be used to define fixed-width fields. In this case, the value of FS is ignored. Assigning a new value to FS overrides the use of FIELDWIDTHS.

Each field can be referenced by its position in the input record. The first field is $1 and the last field is $NF, since the variable NF indicates the number of fields in the current input record. The variable $0 refers to the entire input record. References to fields beyond NF are null strings but are assignable.

Assignments to fields beyond NF will increase the value of NF, assign the value to $NF, and assign null values to any intervening fields. The new intervening fields will be separated by the value of OFS.

Predefined Variables

The following table describes variables that are built into gawk and can be used in gawk scripts without being explicitly defined.

Variable	Description
ARGC	Number of command-line arguments.
ARGV	Array of command-line arguments.

continues >>

>>continued

Variable	Description
ARGIND	The index in ARGV of the current file being processed.
CONVFMT	Controls the conversion of numbers to strings. It's passed internally to sprintf. The default is "%.6g".
ENVIRON	Array of values of environment variables indexed by variable name.
ERRNO	If an error occurs during getline or close, ERRNO describes the error.
FIELDWIDTHS	Space-separated list of column widths that tells gawk how to split input.
FILENAME	Name of the file currently being processed.
FNR	Current record number in the current file.
FS	Field separator character or string. Its default is a single space.
IGNORECASE	A nonzero or non-null value indicates that regular-expression matching is case-independent. For more information on regular expression-based pattern matching, see Appendix A, "Regular Expressions."
NF	Number of fields in the current input record.
NR	Number of the current record.
OFMT	Controls the conversion of numbers to strings for printing with the print command. It's passed internally to sprintf. The default value is "%.6g".
OFS	Output field separator. The default value is a single space.
RLENGTH	Length of the substring matched by the match function.
RS	Record separator. The default value is a newline.
RSTART	Start index of characters of the substring matched by the match function.
RT	Contains input text that matches the text denoted by RS.
SUBSEP	Used to separate parts of indices of multidimensional arrays. The default is \034.

Arrays

Arrays are associative and can be indexed by any string expression. The index expression is contained in brackets ([ ]). Technically, gawk arrays are one-dimensional, but multidimensional arrays are emulated by separating the values of the subscripts with the value in the SUBSEP variable. For example, in the expression x["i","j"] the actual index used to retrieve the value from x is "i@j" if SUBSEP is set to "@".

Operators

The following table lists the operators in gawk in order of decreasing precedence.

Symbol	Description
(...)	Grouping.
$	Field reference.
++, --	Increment, decrement.
^ or **	Exponentiation.
+, -, !	Unary plus, unary minus, logical negation.
*, /, %	Multiplication, division, modulus.
+, -	Addition, subtraction.
space	String concatenation.
<, >, <=, >=, !=, ==	Relational tests.
~, !=	Regular expression match and negated match.
in	Array membership test.
&&	Logical AND.
!!	Logical OR.
?:	The C conditional expression.
=, +=, -=, *=, /=, %=, ^=	Absolute assignment and operator-assignment. Both pre- and post- forms are supported.

Statements

The following table describes statements that control the flow of execution in gawk scripts.

Syntax	Description
if (CONDITION) THEN-BODY [else ELSE-BODY]	Execute statements in THEN-BODY if CONDITION is true.
while (CONDITION) BODY	Repeatedly execute statements in BODY until CONDITION is false. CONDITION is checked before each iteration.
do BODY while CONDITION	Repeatedly execute statements in BODY until CONDITION is false. CONDITION is checked after each iteration. BODY is always executed at least once in the do statement.
for (INITIALIZATION ; CONDITION ; INCREMENT) BODY	After INITIALIZATION, BODY and INCREMENT execute until CONDITION is false.
break	Jumps out of the innermost for, while, or do loop that encloses it.
continue	Skips to the end of the innermost for, while, or do loop that encloses it.
next	Discontinue processing of the current input record.

continues >>

>>continued

Syntax	Description
nextfile	Discontinue processing of the current input file.
exit [RETURN_CODE]	Exit gawk with integer RETURN_CODE as the exit status code. If RETURN_CODE is omitted, gawk exits with 0.

Functions

The following table describes the functions that are built into gawk.

Function	Description
atan2(Y, X)	Arctangent of Y / X with X and Y in radians.
close(FILENAME)	Close the file FILENAME.
cos(X)	Cosine of X with X in radians.
exp(X)	Exponential of X.
fflush([FILENAME])	Flush any buffered output associated with FILENAME. If FILENAME is omitted, standard output will be flushed. If FILENAME is null, all open output files and pipes will be flushed.
index(IN, FIND)	Index of string FIND in the string IN. Returns zero if not found.
int(X)	Returns X truncated toward zero.
gensub(REGEXP, REPLACEMENT, HOW [, TARGET])	Same as sub and gsub except that TARGET isn't altered and the transformed string is the function's return. HOW beginning with g or G substitutes in the same manner as gsub. Otherwise, HOW is an integer indicating which match of REGEXP to replace.
gsub(REGEXP, REPLACEMENT [, TARGET])	Same as sub except that gsub replaces *all* the non-overlapping substrings it can find.
length([STRING])	Length of STRING. If STRING is omitted, length returns the length of variable $0, the current record.
log(X)	Natural logarithm of X.
match(STRING, REGEXP)	Position of the longest, leftmost substring in STRING matched by the regular expression REGEXP.
rand()	A random number.
sin(X)	Sine of X with X in radians.

Function	Description
split(STRING, ARRAY [, FIELDSEP])	Divides STRING into pieces separated by FIELDSEP and stores the pieces in ARRAY. FS is used if FIELDSEP is omitted.
sprintf(FORMAT, EXPRESSIONS)	Return, without printing, EXPRESSIONS formatted according to FORMAT.
sqrt(X)	Square root of X.
srand([X])	Set random number seed to X. If X is omitted, the seed is set to the current time and date. srand returns the value of the previous seed.
strftime([FORMAT [, TIMESTAMP]])	Return TIMESTAMP formatted according to FORMAT. If TIMESTAMP isn't supplied, the current system time is used. If FORMAT isn't supplied, "%a %b %d %H:%M:%S %Z %Y" is used.
sub(REGEXP, REPLACEMENT [, TARGET])	Replaces the leftmost longest substring in TARGET matched by REGEXP with REPLACEMENT, and places the resulting string back into TARGET. The variable $0 (the current record) is used if TARGET is omitted.
substr(STRING, START [, LENGTH])	Returns a LENGTH-character-long substring of STRING, starting at character number START. If LENGTH is omitted, the entire suffix from START to the end of the string is returned.
system(COMMAND)	Execute command COMMAND and return its exit status.
systime()	Return system time as the number of seconds since midnight of January 1, 1970, UTC.
tolower(STRING)	Return STRING converted to lowercase.
toupper(STRING)	Return STRING converted to uppercase.

The following command produces an alphabetically sorted list of user accounts. It uses gawk to extract the names from the /etc/passwd file. Note that the data values in /etc/passwd are delimited by the colon (:) character.

```
awk -F : '{print $1;}' < /etc/passwd | sort
```

The following gawk script assumes that the input file is in Apache log file format, where each line of text represents one HTTP transfer and the seventh space-delimited field contains the name of the transferred file. The script counts the number of GIF (extension .gif) and the number of JPEG (extension .jpg) files transferred. It also gives the total number of records at the end.

```
#!/usr/bin/gawk -f
#Initialize counters to zero and print report header. We also want to make
#pattern matching insensitive to upper or lower case.
BEGIN {gifs = 0; jpegs = 0;
  IGNORECASE=1;
  printf "GIFSs\tJPEGs\n";}

#Increment GIF counter if field 7 ends in ".gif".
match($7,/\.gif$/) {gifs++;}

#Increment JPEG counter if field 7 ends in ".jpg".
match($7,/\.jpg$/) {jpegs++;}

#Print report trailer.
END {
  printf "%d\t%d\n", gifs, jpegs;
  printf "Total Records: %d\n", NR;
}
```

The following **bash** script uses gawk to print a count of the lines, words, and characters in the files given as arguments. The format is similar to that of the output from wc.

```
#!/bin/bash

for i in $@; do
#Initialize counters
  gawk 'BEGIN {chars = 0; words = 0;} \
#Number of characters is line length
#plus one for the newline character.
  {chars += length($0)+1;} \
#Number of words in the line is the number of fields.
  {words += NF;} \
#Print summary for current file.
  END {printf "\t%d\t%d\t%d\t%s\n", NR, words, chars, FILENAME;}' $i;
done
```

grep

grep [*OPTION* ...] *PATTERN* [*FILE* ...]

grep searches the named input *FILE*s for lines containing *PATTERN*. Standard input is searched if no files are named or if - is named.

PATTERN is specified in one of three ways:

- *PATTERN* as command argument.

- *PATTERN* immediately following the -e command argument.

- The pattern is found in a file named *FILE* that immediately follows the -f argument.

For more information on patterns, see Appendix A.

grep accepts the following command options:

Option	Description
-G or --basic-regexp	Interpret *PATTERN* as a basic regular expression (the default).
-E or --extended-regexp	Interpret *PATTERN* as an extended regular expression.
-F or --fixed-strings	Interpret *PATTERN* as a list of fixed strings, separated by newlines, any of which is to be matched.
-*NUM*	Matches will be printed with *NUM* lines of leading and trailing context. grep will never print any given line more than once.
-A *NUM* or --after-context=*NUM*	Print *NUM* lines of trailing context after matching lines.
-B *NUM* or --before-context=*NUM*	Print *NUM* lines of leading context before matching lines.
-C or --context	Equivalent to -2.
-V or --version	Print the version number of grep to standard error.
-b or --byte-offset	Print the byte offset within the input file before each line of output.
-c or --count	Print the count of matching lines for each input file instead of normal output.
-e *PATTERN* or --regexp=*PATTERN*	Use *PATTERN* as the search pattern.
-f *FILE* or --file=*FILE*	Input the search pattern from *FILE*. This enables the use of multiple search patterns (one on each line in *FILE*).
-h or --no-filename	Don't print filenames on output.
-i or --ignore-case	Ignore case when matching patterns.
-L or --files-without-match	Print only the names of files that don't contain matching lines.
-l or --files-with-matches	Print only the names of files that contain matching lines.
-n or --line-number	Prefix output lines with corresponding input line numbers.
-q or --quiet	Suppress normal output and stop scanning on the first match.
-s or --silent	Suppress error messages about nonexistent or unreadable files.
-v or --revert-match	Select non-matching lines for output instead of matching lines.
-w or --word-regexp	Select only lines containing matches that form whole words.
-x or --line-regexp	Select only lines where the entire line is matched.
-y	Obsolete equivalent for -i.

sed

```
sed [ OPTION ... ] [ FILE ... ]
```

sed (the streams editor) reads input files (including standard input if no files are specified), edits the data according to one or more editing scripts, and writes the results to standard output.

Option	Description
-e *SCRIPT* or --expression=*SCRIPT*	Append one or more commands specified in *SCRIPT* to the list of editing commands. If there is just one -e option and no -f options, the -e flag can be omitted.
-f *SCRIPT-FILE* or --expression=*SCRIPT-FILE*	Append the editing commands contained in *SCRIPT-FILE* to the list of commands.
-h	Print usage summary (same as --help).
-n or --quiet or --silent	Suppress default output.
-V	Print the version number (same as --version).

Operations

sed operates on each line of input as follows:

- The line, not including its newline character, is copied into a temporary buffer known as a *pattern space*.

- All editing commands whose addresses match the pattern space are sequentially applied to the pattern space.

- When reaching the end of the command list, the pattern space is written to the standard output (except when the -n option is in effect) with an appended newline.

- The pattern space is cleared and the process is repeated with the next line of input.

sed leaves original files unchanged. In addition to the pattern space, some commands use a hold space for temporary storage of partial results.

Addresses

sed uses addresses to determine whether certain commands should be applied to an input line. Addresses take the following forms:

- A line number represented in decimal. Line numbers are cumulative across the entire set of input files and not reset.

- A regular expression.

- The $ that addresses the last line of input.

- *N~M*, which matches any line where the line number modulo *M* is *N*. If *M* is 0 or missing, 1 is used in its place.

The following rules apply to commands containing addresses:

- Commands with no addresses are applied to each input line.

- Commands with one address are applied to each line that matches the address.

- Commands with two addresses separated by commas select the lines starting with the first line matching the first address and ending with the first line matching the second address. If the second address starts before or is the same line as the first address, only the first line is selected.

- An address followed by ! selects all lines that don't match the address.

The following characters have special meaning only when used in replacement patterns:

\	Escapes the following character.
\N	Matches the Nth pattern previously saved by \ (and \ ), where N is a number from 0 to 9. Previously saved patterns are counted from the leftmost position on the line.
&	Prints the entire search pattern when used in a replacement string.

Commands

The following table summarizes 3ed commands. Typically there's only one command per line, but commands can also be concatenated on a single line with semicolons. Commands beginning with *ADDRESS* can be preceded by one address. Commands beginning with *ADDRESSES* can be preceded by one address or by two addresses separated by a comma (,). Multiple commands can be nested by using braces ({}). When nesting commands, the opening brace ({) must end a line and the closing brace (}) must be on a line by itself. The *TEXT* variable must begin on its own line and multiple lines in *TEXT* are separated by \ characters. For example, the following script uses the a command to append three lines of text to the end of a file:

```
$a\
This is the first line to be appended to the end of a file.\
This is the second line to be appended.\
This is the last line to be appended.
```

READ-FILENAME and *WRITE-FILENAME* arguments must terminate the command line and must be preceded by exactly one space.

Command	Description
# COMMENT	Comment line.
#n	Suppress output for the rest of the script.
:LABEL	Assign a label for use by control b or t control transfer commands. For example, the command $b last branches to the statement following :last when processing the last line of input.
[ADDRESS]=	Print the current line number to standard output.

continues >>

>>continued

Command	Description
[ADDRESS]a\TEXT	Append TEXT following each line matched by the address on the standard output before reading the next input line.
ADDRESSESb [LABEL]	Unconditionally transfer control to the : command bearing the LABEL. If no LABEL is specified, branch to the end of the script.
ADDRESSESc\TEXT	Replace the pattern with TEXT.
ADDRESSESd	Delete the pattern space.
ADDRESSESD	Delete the pattern space through the first newline.
ADDRESSESg	Replace the pattern space with hold space.
ADDRESSESG	Append the newline character followed by hold space to the pattern space.
ADDRESSESh	Replace the hold space with pattern space.
ADDRESSESH	Append the newline character followed by pattern space to the hold space.
[ADDRESS]i\TEXT	Insert TEXT by writing it to standard output.
ADDRESSESl	Write the pattern space to standard output in unambiguous form. Nonprinting characters are displayed as either three-digit octal values preceded by \ or as one of the following: \\ Backslash. \a Alert. \b Backspace. \f Formfeed. \n Newline. \r Carriage return. \t Horizontal tab. \v Vertical tab. Long lines are folded and the point of folding indicated by \ and a newline. Ends of lines are marked with $.
ADDRESSESn	Copy the pattern space to standard output. Replace the pattern space with the next input line.
ADDRESSESN	Append the next line of input to the pattern space with an embedded newline. The current line number changes.

Command	Description
ADDRESSESp	Print the pattern space to standard output.
ADDRESSESP	Copy the initial segment of the pattern space through the first newline to standard output.
ADDRESSq	Quit the current script and don't start a new cycle. Write the pattern space to standard output.
ADDRESSESr READ-FILENAME	Read the contents of READ-FILENAME and write it to standard output before reading the next input line.
ADDRESSESs/REGEXP/REPLACEMENT/FLAGS	Substitute the REPLACEMENT string with instances of the regular expression REGEXP in the pattern space. Any character can be substituted for /. FLAGS is zero or more of the following: N—Substitute for just the Nth occurrence of REGEXP. g—Globally substitute for all non-overlapping instances of REGEXP. P—Print the pattern space if a replacement was made. w WRITE-FILENAME—Append the pattern space to WRITE-FILENAME if a replacement was made.
ADDRESSESt LABEL	Transfer control to : marked with LABEL if any substitutions have been made since the most recent reading of an input line or execution of a t. If LABEL is empty, branch to the end of the script.
ADDRESSESw WRITE-FILENAME	Append the pattern space to WRITE-FILENAME.
ADDRESSESx	Exchange the pattern and hold spaces.
ADDRESSESy/STRING1/STRING2/	Replace all occurrences of characters in STRING1 with the corresponding characters in STRING2. STRING1 and STRING2 must be of equal length. Any other character except newline can be used in place of /. The delimiter character can be used in STRING1 or STRING2 if it's preceded by a backslash.

3
File Utilities

This chapter describes commands that manipulate files and that display and modify file characteristics.

Common Options

In addition to the options described in the following sections, each command can be invoked with the following options:

Option	Description
--help	Prints a usage message listing all available options and exits successfully.
--version	Prints the version number and exits successfully.

Backup Options

Some of the programs described in this section optionally make backup copies of files before writing new versions. The following table describes the options that control the implementation of these backups.

Option	Description
-b or --backup	Makes backups of files that are about to be overwritten or removed. Without this option, the original versions are destroyed.
-S SUFFIX or --suffix=SUFFIX	Appends SUFFIX to each backup file made with -b. If this option isn't specified, the value of the SIMPLE_BACKUP_SUFFIX environment variable is used. If SIMPLE_BACKUP_SUFFIX isn't set, the default is ~.

continues >>

>>continued

Option	Description
-V *METHOD* or --version-control=*METHOD*	Uses *METHOD* to determine the type of backups made with -b. If this option isn't specified, the value of the VERSION_CONTROL environment variable is used. If VERSION_CONTROL isn't set, the default backup type is existing. Valid values for *METHOD* (including unique abbreviations) are as follows:
	t or numbered—Always make numbered backups.
	nil or existing—Make numbered backups of files that already have backups, simple backups of the others.
	never or simple—Always make simple backups.

File Information

This section describes commands that list information about files.

dir

```
dir [ ARG ... ]
```

dir lists information about each file named on the command line. When invoked without arguments, dir is equivalent to ls -C. By default, files are listed in vertically sorted columns. For a complete description of the valid options for dir, see the description of the ls command.

dircolors

```
dircolors [ OPTION ... ] [ FILE ]
```

dircolors outputs a sequence of shell commands that can be used to set up the terminal so that the output from ls and the other directory-listing commands is color-coded. If *FILE* is specified, dircolors reads it to determine which colors to use for which file types and extensions. Otherwise, a precompiled database is used. The output is a shell command to set the LS_COLORS environment variable. The best way to use dircolors is to directly evaluate its output as in the bash command:

```
eval dircolors
```

A suggested addition to /etc/profile would be:

```
eval dircolors
alias ls=ls --color=auto
```

This would cause ls to display color-coded directory listings.

dircolors accepts the following options:

Option	Description
-b or --sh or --bourne-shell	Outputs Bourne shell commands. This is the default if the SHELL environment variable is set and doesn't end with csh or tcsh.
-c or --csh or --c-shell	Outputs C shell commands. This is the default if the SHELL environment variable ends with csh or tcsh.
-p or --print-database	Prints the compiled default color-configuration database. This output is itself a valid configuration file, and gives a readable example of color configuration.

ls

ls [ARG ...]

ls lists information about files (of any type, including directories). Options and file arguments can be mixed arbitrarily.

For non-option command-line arguments that are directories, by default ls lists the contents of directories, not recursively, and omitting files with names beginning with a period (.). For other non-option arguments, by default ls lists just the filename. If no non-option arguments are specified, ls lists the contents of the current directory.

By default, the output is sorted alphabetically. If standard output is a terminal, the output is in columns (sorted vertically); otherwise, they're listed one per line.

Selecting Files to List

The following table describes the ls command-line options that determine which files are listed.

Option	Description
-a or --all	List all files in directories including those that start with a period (.).
-A or --almost-all	List all files in directories (except for . and ..).
-B or --ignore-backups	Don't list files that end with a tilde (~) unless they're supplied on the command line.
-d or --directory	List just the names of directories as with other types of files, rather than listing their contents.

continues >>

>>continued

Option	Description
-I *PATTERN* or --ignore=*PATTERN*	Don't list files whose names match the shell pattern (not regular expression) *PATTERN* unless they're given on the command line. As in the shell, an initial period (.) in a filename doesn't match a wildcard at the start of *PATTERN*.
-L or --dereference	In a long listing, show file information for the targets of symbolic links rather than for the symbolic links themselves.
-R or --recursive	List the contents of all directories recursively.

Selecting File Information to List

The following table describes the `ls` command-line options that determine what file information will be listed.

Option	Description
-D or --dired	With the long listing (-1) format, print an additional line after the main output: `//DIRED// BEG1 END1 BEG2 END2 ...` *BEGN* and *ENDN* are unsigned integers that record the byte position of the beginning and end of each filename in the output. This makes it easy for Emacs to find the names—even when they contain unusual characters such as space or newline—without fancy searching. If directories are being listed recursively (-R), output a similar line after each subdirectory: `//SUBDIRED// BEG1 END1 ...`
-G or --no-group	Inhibit the display of group information in a long-format directory listing.
-i or --inode	Print the inode number (also called the *file serial number* and *index number*) of each file to the left of the filename.
-l or --format=long or --format=verbose	In addition to the name of each file, print the file type, permissions, number of hard links, owner name, group name, size in bytes, and timestamp (by default, the modification time). For files with a time more than six months old or more than one hour into the future, the timestamp contains the year instead of the time of day. For each directory listed, prefaces the files with a line `Total BLOCKS`, where *BLOCKS* is the total disk space used by all files in that directory. By default, 1024-byte blocks are used; if the environment variable `POSIXLY_CORRECT` is set, 512-byte blocks are used (unless the -k option is given). The *BLOCKS* computed counts each hard link separately; this is arguably a deficiency.

Option	Description
-o	Produce long-format directory listings, but don't display group information. Equivalent to using --format=long with --no-group.
-s or --size	Print the size of each file in 1024-byte blocks to the left of the filename. If the environment variable POSIXLY_CORRECT is set, 512-byte blocks are used instead, unless the -k option is given.

Sorting the Output

The following table describes the ls command-line options that determine how the file information is sorted.

Option	Description
-c or --time=ctime or --time=status	Sort according to the status change time (the ctime in the inode). If the long listing format (-1) is used, print the status change time instead of the modification time.
-f	Don't sort. List the files in the order by which they're stored in the directory. Also, enable -a (list all files) and disable -1, --color, and -s (if they were specified before the -f).
-r or --reverse	Reverse the sorting order.
-S or --sort=size	Sort by file size, largest first.
-t or --sort=time	Sort by modification time (the mtime in the inode), newest first.
-u or --time=atime or --time=access or --time=use	Sort by access time (the atime in the inode). If the long listing format is used, print the last access time.
-U or --sort=none	Don't sort. List the files in the order by which they're stored in the directory, but don't do any of the other unrelated things that -f does.
-X or --sort=extension	Sort directory contents alphabetically by file extension (characters after the last period). Files with no extension are sorted first.

General Output Formatting

The following table describes the ls command-line options that control the general appearance of the output.

Option	Description
-1 or --format=single-column	List one file per line. This is the default for ls when standard output isn't a terminal.
-C or --format=vertical	List files in columns, sorted vertically. This is the default for ls if standard output is a terminal.

continues >>

>>continued

Option	Description
`--color[=WHEN]`	Specify whether to use color for distinguishing file types. *WHEN* can be omitted, or can be one of the following: `none` Don't use color at all. This is the default. `auto` Use color only if the standard output is a terminal. `always` Always use color. Specifying `--color` and no *WHEN* is equivalent to `--color=always`.
`-F` or `--classify`	Append a character to each filename indicating the file type. Also, for regular files that are executable, append `*`. The file type indicators are / for directories, @ for symbolic links, ¦ for FIFOs, = for sockets, and nothing for regular files.
`--full-time`	List times in full, rather than using the standard abbreviation heuristics. The format is the same as `date`'s default. It's not possible to change this, but you can extract the date string with `cut` and then pass the result to `date -d`.
`-k` or `--kilobytes`	Print file sizes in kilobytes. This overrides the environment variable `POSIXLY_CORRECT`.
`-m` or `--format=commas`	List files horizontally, with as many as will fit on each line, separated by a comma and a space.
`-n` or `--numeric-uid-gid`	List the numeric UID and GID instead of the names.
`-p`	Append a character to each filename indicating the file type. This is the same as `-F` except that executables aren't marked.
`-x` or `--format=across` or `--format=horizontal`	List the files in columns, sorted horizontally.
`-T COLS` or `--tabsize=COLS`	Assume that each tab stop is *COLS* columns wide. The default is `8`. `ls` uses tabs where possible in the output, for efficiency. If *COLS* is zero, don't use tabs at all.
`-w COLS` or `--width=COLS`	Assume that the screen is *COLS* columns wide. The default is taken from the terminal settings if possible. Otherwise the environment variable `COLUMNS` is used if it's set. If neither the terminal settings nor the environment variable can be used, the default is `80`.

Formatting Filenames

The following table describes the `ls` command-line options that control how the filenames themselves are printed.

Option	Description
-b or --escape	Quote nongraphic characters in filenames using alphabetic and octal backslash sequences like those used in C.
-N or --literal	Don't quote filenames.
-q or --hide-control-chars	Print question marks instead of nongraphic characters in filenames. This is the default.
-Q or --quote-name	Enclose filenames in double quotes and quote nongraphic characters as in C.

vdir

```
vdir [ ARG ... ]
```

When invoked without arguments, `vdir` is equivalent to `ls -l`. By default, files are listed in columns, sorted vertically. For a more complete description of the capabilities of `vdir`, see the earlier description of `ls`.

Basic File Operations

This section describes commands that are used to copy, move, and delete files.

cp

```
cp [ OPTION ... ] SOURCE DEST
cp [ OPTION ... ] SOURCE ... DIRECTORY
```

`cp` copies files and directories. The first form copies the file *SOURCE* to the file *DEST*. The second form copies a single file or multiple files to the directory *DIRECTORY*.

`cp` won't copy a file onto itself. If the `--force-backup` option is specified with *SOURCE* and *DEST* identical, and referring to a regular file, `cp` will make a backup file, either regular or numbered, as specified in the earlier section "Backup Options."

Option	Description
-a or --archive	Preserve as much as possible of the structure and attributes of the original files in the copy (but don't preserve directory structure). Equivalent to -dpR.
-b or --backup	Make backups of files that are about to be overwritten or removed. See the earlier section "Backup Options" for more information.
-d or --no-dereference	Copy symbolic links as symbolic links rather than copying the files that they point to, and preserve hard links between source files in the copies.

continues >>

>>continued

Option	Description
-f or --force	Remove existing destination files.
-i or --interactive	Prompt whether to overwrite existing regular destination files.
-l or --link	Make hard links instead of copies of non-directories.
-p or --preserve	Preserve the original files' owner, group, permissions, and timestamps.
-P or --parents	Form the name of each destination file by appending to the target directory a slash (/) and the specified name of the source file. The last argument given to cp must be the name of an existing directory. For example, the following command: `cp --parents a/b/c existing_dir` copies the file a/b/c to existing_dir/a/b/c, creating any missing intermediate directories.
-r	Copy directories recursively, copying any non-directories and non-symbolic links (pipes, sockets and device files) as if they were regular files. This means trying to read the data in each source file and writing it to the destination.
-R or --recursive	Copy directories recursively.
--sparse=WHEN	A *sparse file* contains "holes"; that is, a sequence of zero bytes that doesn't occupy any physical disk blocks. The read system call reads these as zeroes. This can both save considerable disk space and increase speed, since many binary files contain lots of consecutive zero bytes. By default, cp detects holes in input source files via a crude heuristic and makes the corresponding output file sparse as well. Valid values for WHEN are as follows: auto The output file is sparse if the input file is sparse. This is the default. always Always make the output file sparse. This is useful when the input file resides on a filesystem that doesn't support sparse files but the output file is on another type of filesystem. never Never make the output file sparse.
-s or --symbolic-link	Make symbolic links instead of copies of non-directories. All source filenames must be absolute (starting with /) unless the destination files are in the current directory.
-S SUFFIX or --suffix=SUFFIX	Append SUFFIX to each backup file made with -b. See the "Backup Options" section for more information.
-u or --verbose	Print the name of each file before copying it.
-V METHOD or --version-control=METHOD	Change the type of backups made with -b. See the "Backup Options" section for more information.

Option	Description
-x or --one-file-system	Skip subdirectories that are on different filesystems from the one on which the copy started.

dd

dd [*OPTION* ...]

dd copies a file with a changeable I/O block size while optionally performing conversions on it. Standard input is copied to standard output by default.

Option	Description
if=*FILE*	Reads from *FILE* instead of standard input.
of=*FILE*	Writes to *FILE* instead of standard output.
ibs=*BYTES*	Specifies input block size (the number of bytes for each read operation) of *BYTES* bytes.
obs=*BYTES*	Specifies output block size (the number of bytes for each write operation) of *BYTES* bytes.
bs=*BYTES*	Both reads and writes *BYTES* bytes at a time. This overrides ibs and obs.
cbs=*BYTES*	Converts *BYTES* bytes at a time.
skip=*BLOCKS*	Skips *BLOCKS* blocks in the input file before copying. Block size is defined by the ibs option.
seek=*BLOCKS*	Skips *BLOCKS* blocks in the output file before copying. Block size is defined by the obs option.
count=*BLOCKS*	Copies *BLOCKS* blocks from the input file instead of everything until the end of the file. Block size is defined by the ibs option.
conv=*CONVERSIONS_LIST*	Applies the conversions in *CONVERSIONS_LIST*, which is a comma-separated list of the following: ascii Converts EBCDIC to ASCII. ebcdic Converts ASCII to EBCDIC. ibm Converts ASCII to alternate EBCDIC. block For each line in the input, outputs cbs bytes, replacing the input newline with a space and padding with spaces as necessary. unblock Replaces trailing spaces in each cbs-sized input block with a newline. lcase Changes uppercase letters to lowercase. ucase Changes lowercase letters to uppercase. swab Swaps every pair of input bytes. When an odd number of bytes are read, the last byte is simply copied.

continues >>

>>continued

Option	Description
	noerror Continue after read errors.
	notrunc Don't truncate the output file.
	sync Pads every input block to the size of ibs with trailing zero bytes.

install

```
install [ OPTION ... ] SOURCE DEST
install [ OPTION ... ] SOURCE ... DIRECTORY
install { -d ¦ --directory } [ OPTION ... ] DIRECTORY ...
```

install copies files while setting their permission modes and, if possible, their owner and group. In the first form, the *SOURCE* file is copied to the *DEST* target file. In the second form, each of the *SOURCE* files is copied to the destination *DIRECTORY*. In the third form, each *DIRECTORY* is created along with any missing parent directories.

install is similar to cp but enables you to control the attributes of destination files. It's typically used in Makefiles to copy programs into their destination directories. It refuses to copy files onto themselves.

Option	Description
-b or --backup	Makes backups of files that are about to be overwritten or removed. See the earlier section "Backup Options" for more information.
-c	Ignored but provided for compatibility with old UNIX versions of install.
-d or --directory	Creates each given directory and any missing parent directories, setting the owner, group, and mode as given on the command line or to the defaults. Also gives those attributes to any parent directories it creates.
-g GROUP or --group=GROUP	Sets the group ownership of installed files or directories to *GROUP*. The default is the process's current group. *GROUP* can be either a group name or a numeric group ID.
-m MODE or --mode=MODE	Sets the permissions for the installed file or directory to *MODE*, which can be either an octal number or a symbolic mode (as in chmod). The default mode is 0755: read, write, and execute for the owner, and read and execute for group and other.
-o OWNER or --owner=OWNER	If install is run as root, sets the ownership of installed files or directories to *OWNER*. The default is root. *OWNER* can be either a username or a numeric user ID.

Option	Description
-p or --preserve-timestamps	Retains creation and modification times of all files installed. The default behavior is to set these values to the current time.
-s or --strip	Strips the symbol tables from installed binary executables.
-S SUFFIX or --suffix=SUFFIX	Appends SUFFIX to each backup file made with -b. See the "Backup Options" section for more information.
-V METHOD or --version-control=METHOD	Changes the type of backups made with -b. See the "Backup Options" section for more information.

mv

```
mv [ OPTION ... ] SOURCE DEST
mv [ OPTION ... ] SOURCE ... DIRECTORY
```

mv moves or renames files or directories. If the last argument names an existing directory, mv moves each given file into a file with the same name in that directory. Otherwise, if only two files are given, it renames the first as the second. It's an error if the last argument is not a directory and more than two files are given.

If a destination file exists but is normally unwritable, standard input is a terminal, and the -f or --force option isn't given, mv prompts the user for whether to replace the file. (You might own the file or have write permission on its directory.) If the response doesn't begin with Y or y, the file is skipped.

Option	Description
-b or --backup	Makes backups of files that are about to be overwritten or removed. See the earlier section "Backup Options" for more information.
-f or --force	Removes existing destination files without prompting the user.
-i or --interactive	Prompts whether to overwrite each existing destination file, regardless of its permissions. If the response doesn't begin with Y or y, the file is skipped.
-u or --update	Don't move a nondirectory that has an existing destination with the same or newer modification time.
-v or --verbose	Prints the name of each file before moving it.

continues >>

>>continued

Option	Description
--suffix=*SUFFIX*	Appends *SUFFIX* to each backup file made with -b. See the "Backup Options" section for more information.
-V *METHOD* or --version-control=*METHOD*	Changes the type of backups made with -b. See the "Backup Options" section for more information.

rm

rm [*OPTION* ...] FILE [*FILE* ...]

rm removes each *FILE* given on the command line. By default, rm doesn't remove directories.

If a file is unwritable, standard input is a terminal, and the -f or --force option isn't given or the -i or --interactive option is given, rm prompts the user for whether to remove the file. If the response doesn't begin with Y or y, the file is skipped.

Option	Description
--	End of options. This is useful for removing files with names that start with -.
-d or --directory	Removes directories with unlink instead of rmdir and without requiring a directory to be empty before trying to unlink it. This works only if you have appropriate privileges. Because unlinking a directory causes any files in the deleted directory to become unreferenced, it's wise to fsck the filesystem after doing this.
-f or --force	Ignores nonexistent files and never prompts the user.
-i or --interactive	Prompts whether to remove each file. If the response doesn't begin with y or Y, the file is skipped.
-r or -R or --recursive	Removes the contents of directories recursively.
-v or --verbose	Prints the name of each file before removing it.

Special Files

This section describes commands used to create and delete directories, links, pipes, and device files.

ln

ln [*OPTION* ...] SOURCE [*DEST*]
ln [*OPTION* ...] SOURCE ... DIRECTORY

ln makes links between files. ln makes hard links by default and symbolic or "soft" links if the -s option is supplied.

If the last argument names an existing directory, ln links each *SOURCE* file into a file with the same name in that directory. If only one file is given, it links that file into the current directory. Otherwise, if only two files are given, it links the first onto the second. It's an error if the last argument is not a directory and more than two files are given. By default, it doesn't remove existing files.

Option	Description
-b or --backup	Makes backups of files that are about to be overwritten or removed.
-d or -F or --directory	Allows the superuser to make hard links to directories.
-f or --force	Removes existing destination files.
-i or --interactive	Prompts whether to remove existing destination files.
-n or --no-dereference	When given an explicit destination that's a symbolic link to a directory, treats that destination as if it were a normal file. The default is to treat a destination that's a symbolic link to a directory just like a directory.
-s or --symbolic	Makes symbolic links instead of hard links.
-v or --verbose	Prints the name of each file before linking it.
-S *SUFFIX* or --suffix=*SUFFIX*	Appends *SUFFIX* to each backup file made with -b. See the earlier section "Backup Options" for more information.
-V *METHOD* or --version-control=*METHOD*	Changes the type of backups made with -b. See the "Backup Options" section for more information.

mkdir

mkdir [*OPTION* ...] *NAME* ...

mkdir creates directories with the specified *NAME*s. It's not an error if any of the *NAME*s is already a directory. In these cases, mkdir continues operation. If a *NAME* exists and is not a directory, mkdir produces an error message and continues operation.

Option	Description
-m *MODE* or --mode=*MODE*	Sets the mode of created directories to *MODE*, which is specified as in chmod.
-p or --parents	Makes any missing parent directories for each argument. The mode for parent directories is set to the umask modified by u+wx.
--verbose	Prints a message for each created directory.

mkfifo

mkfifo [*OPTION*] *NAME* ...

mkfifo creates a FIFO ("First In First Out" or "named pipe") with the specified *NAME*s. A FIFO enables two independent processes to exchange data; it's the disk-resident counterpart of the anonymous pipes designated by the ¦ operator in shell scripts.

Option	Description
-m *MODE* or --mode=*MODE*	Sets the mode of created FIFOs to *MODE*, which is specified as in chmod.

mknod

mknod [*OPTION*] *NAME* *TYPE* [*MAJOR* *MINOR*]

mknod creates a special file named *NAME*. Valid values for *TYPE* are as follows:

p   A FIFO or named pipe.
b   A block special device. *MAJOR* and *MINOR* are also required.
c   A character special device. *MAJOR* and *MINOR* are also required.
u   An unbuffered special device. *MAJOR* and *MINOR* are also required.

Option	Description
-m *MODE* or --mode=*MODE*	Sets the mode of created files to *MODE*, which is specified as in chmod.

rmdir

rmdir [*OPTION*] *DIRECTORY* ...

rmdir removes empty directories. An error is reported for any *DIRECTORY* that isn't empty.

Option	Description
-p or --parents	Removes any parent directories that become empty after an argument *DIRECTORY* is removed.

Changing File Attributes

This section describes commands that change the ownership, access permissions, and timestamps of files.

chgrp

chgrp [*OPTION* ...] *GROUP* *FILE* ...

chgrp changes the group ownership of each given *FILE* to *GROUP*. *GROUP* can be either a group name or a numeric group ID.

Option	Description
-c or --changes	Verbosely describe the action for each *FILE* whose group was changed.
-f or --silent or --quiet	Don't print error messages about files whose group can't be changed.
-h or --no-dereference	Act on symbolic links themselves instead of what they point to.
-v or --verbose	Verbosely describe the action or non-action taken for every *FILE*.
-R or --recursive	Recursively change the group ownership of directories and their contents.

chmod

chmod [*OPTION* ...] *MODE FILE* ...

chmod changes the access permissions of the named *FILE*s. For *FILE*s that are symbolic links, chmod changes the permissions of the referenced files. *MODE* specifies the new permissions.

The *MODE* argument can be given in either a symbolic form or an octal numeric form. The format of the symbolic mode is one or multiple instances of the following, separated by commas:

[*USERS*][+|-|=][*PERMISSIONS*]

where *USERS* is any combination of the letters u, g, o, or a and *PERMISSIONS* is any combination of the letters r, w, x, X, s, t, u, g, or o.

The + operator causes the selected permissions to be added. The - causes them to be removed. = causes them to be the only permissions the file has.

USERS controls the selection of users whose access to the file will be changed:

u   The user who owns the file.
g   Other users in the file's group.
o   Other users not in the file's group.
a   All users.

If *USERS* isn't given, a is assumed but the bits that are set in the umask (in bash, umask -S will show this) are unaffected.

PERMISSIONS selects the new permissions for the affected users:

r   Read.
w   Write.
x   Execute for files, access for directories.
X   Execute only if the file is a directory or already has execute permission for some user.
s   Set user or group ID on execution.
t   Save program text on the swap device.
u   The permissions that the user who owns the file currently has for it.
g   The permissions that other users in the file's group have for it.
o   The permissions that other users not in the file's group have for it.

The numeric *MODE* is from one to four octal digits (0–7), derived by adding up the bits with values 4, 2, and 1. Any omitted digits are assumed to be leading zeroes. The first digit selects the set user ID (4) and set group ID (2) and save text image (1) attributes. The second digit selects permissions for the user who owns the file: read (4), write (2), and execute (1). The third selects permissions for other users in the file's group, with the same values. The fourth selects for other users not in the file's group, with the same values.

For example, the following adds execute capability to `file` for the file's owner:

```
chmod u+x file
```

The equivalent using a numeric *MODE* argument would be the following:

```
chmod 100 file
```

The following adds execute and read access to the owner of the file, copies the owner's access rights to the file's group, and sets access for other users to execute only:

```
chmod u+xr,g=u,o=x file
```

Option	Description
-c or --changes	Verbosely describe the action for each *FILE* whose permissions are changed.
-f or --silent or --quiet	Don't print error messages about files whose permissions can't be changed.
-v or --verbose	Verbosely describe the action or non-action taken for every *FILE*.
-R or --recursive	Recursively change permissions of directories and their contents.

chown

```
chown [ OPTION ... ] NEW-OWNER FILE ...
```

chown changes the user and/or group ownership of each *FILE* named on the command line. *NEW-OWNER* is the first non-option argument and is specified (without embedded whitespace) as follows:

```
[ OWNER ] [ {:|.} [ GROUP ] ]
```

Either the *OWNER* or *GROUP* can be omitted. The one that's omitted isn't changed. In addition, if *NEW-OWNER* is specified in one of the following forms, *OWNER* is made the owner of the files and the group of the files is changed to *OWNER*'s login group:

```
OWNER.
```

```
OWNER:
```

Option	Description
-c or --changes	Verbosely describe the action for each *FILE* whose ownership actually changes.
-f or --silent or --quiet	Don't print error messages about files whose ownership can't be changed.
-h or --no-dereference	Act on symbolic links themselves instead of the files to which they refer.

Option	Description
-v or --verbose	Verbosely describe the action or non-action taken for every *FILE*.
-R or --recursive	Recursively change ownership of directories and their contents.

touch

touch [*OPTION* ...] *FILE* ...

touch changes the access and/or modification times of the specified *FILEs*. By default, any *FILE* that doesn't exist is created empty.

If changing both the access and modification times to the current time, touch can change the timestamps for files that the user doesn't own but has write permission for. Otherwise, the user must own the files.

Option	Description
-a or --time=atime or --time=access or --time=use	Change the access time only.
-c or --no-create	Don't create files that don't exist.
-d or --date=*TIME*	Use *TIME* instead of the current time. It can contain month names, time zones, am and pm, and so on.
-f	Ignored; included for compatibility with BSD versions of touch.
-m or --time=mtime or --time=modify	Change the modification time only.
-r *FILE* or --reference=*FILE*	Use the times of the reference *FILE* instead of the current time.
-t *MMDDhhmm*[[*CC*]*YY*][.*ss*]	Use the argument (months, days, hours, minutes, optional century and years, optional seconds) instead of the current time.

4

Programming

This chapter describes tools used in developing and debugging binary files containing executable programs as well as relocatable and executable libraries.

Processing Source Files

This section describes the use of the C and C++ compilers.

gcc and g++

```
cc [ OPTION | FILENAME ] ...
gcc [ OPTION | FILENAME ] ...
g++ [ OPTION | FILENAME ] ...
```

gcc and g++ are, respectively, the C and C++ compilers. On Linux systems, gcc and cc (the "compiler controller") are synonyms. They process the files given using the *FILENAME* arguments through one or more of four stages:

- **Preprocessing.** Takes care of other files #included in *FILENAME* and expands any macros referenced in *FILENAME*.

- **Compilation.** Conversion of preprocessed C or C++ source to assembly language code.

- **Assembly.** Conversion of assembly code to relocatable binary object code.

- **Linking.** Relocatable binaries are combined to form executable programs or shared libraries.

Source-File Suffixes

The source-file suffixes indicate which type of processing should be done:

Suffix	Processing
.c or .C	Preprocesses, compiles, and assembles a C source.
.cc or .cxx	Preprocesses, compiles, and assembles a C++ source.
.m	Preprocesses, compiles, and assembles an Objective C source.

continues >>

>>continued

Suffix	Processing
.i	Compiles and assembles a C source that has previously been preprocessed.
.ii	Compiles and assembles a C++ source that has previously been preprocessed.
.s	Assembles an assembly language source that has already been preprocessed.
.S	Preprocesses and assembles an assembly language source.
.o	Links a relocatable object.
.a	Links an archive containing relocatable objects.

Command-Line Options

gcc and g++ accept many command-line options. Some of these options are architecture-specific. The following sections describe the command-line options that are useful for all Linux versions of gcc and g++.

General Options

Option	Description
-c	Compiles and assembles but doesn't link.
-E	Stops after preprocessing. The output is preprocessed source code that's sent to standard output.
-g	Includes debugging symbols for use by gdb.
-o FILE	Places the output in file FILE.
-pipe	Uses pipes instead of temporary files to pass data between stages.
-S	Compiles but doesn't assemble. This leaves behind a compiled source file with the .s suffix. The -o option can be used to specify another name.
-v	Verbose. Prints processing stages on standard error.
-x LANGUAGE	Specifies the input LANGUAGE rather than assuming it based on the file-name suffix. Valid values for LANGUAGE are c, objective-c, c-header, c++, cpp-output, assembler, and assembler-with-cpp.
-x none	Turns off any language specification set by -x LANGUAGE.

Language Options

Option	Description
-ansi	Assumes ANSI C input.
-fall-virtual	Treats all possible member functions as virtual, implicitly. All member functions (except for constructor functions and new or delete member operators) are treated as virtual functions of the class where they appear.
-fcond-mismatch	Allows conditional expressions with mismatched types in the second and third arguments. The value of such an expression is void.

Option	Description
-fdollars-in-identifiers	Permits the use of $ in identifiers (C++ only).
-fenum-int-equiv	Permits implicit conversion of int to enumeration types (C++ only).
-fexternal-templates	Produces smaller code for template declarations by generating only a single copy of each template function where it's defined (C++ only).
-fno-asm	Don't recognize asm, inline, or typeof as keywords. These words can then be used as identifiers. You can use __asm__, __inline__ and __typeof__ instead. -ansi implies -fno-asm.
-fno-builtin	Don't recognize built-in functions that don't begin with two leading underscores.
-fno-strict-prototype	Treats a function declaration with no arguments as C would treat it—that is, as saying nothing about the number of arguments or their types (C++ only).
-fsigned-char	Lets the type char be signed, like signed char.
-fthis-is-variable	Permits assignment to this (C++ only).
-fsigned-bitfields, -funsigned-bitfields, -fno-signed-bitfields, -fno-unsigned-bitfields	These options control whether a bit field is signed or unsigned when declared with no explicit signed or unsigned qualifier.
-funsigned-char	Lets the type char be unsigned, like unsigned char.
-fwritable-strings	Stores string constants in the writable data segment.
-traditional	Attempts to support some aspects of traditional C compilers. For details, see the GNU C Manual.
-traditional-cpp	Attempts to support some aspects of traditional C preprocessors.
-trigraphs	Supports ANSI C trigraphs. Implied by -ansi.

Preprocessor Options

Option	Description
-AQUESTION(ANSWER)	Asserts the answer ANSWER for QUESTION, in case it's tested with a preprocessor conditional such as #if #QUESTION(ANSWER).
DMACRO	Defines macro MACRO with 1 as its definition.
-DMACRO=DEFN	Defines MACRO as DEFN. All -D directives are processed before any -U directives.
-dD	Tells the preprocessor to pass all macro definitions in their proper sequence in the rest of the output.
-dM	Tells the preprocessor to output only a list of the macro definitions that are in effect at the end of preprocessing. Used with -E.
-dN	Like -dD except that the macro arguments and contents are omitted. Only #define NAME is included in the output.

continues >>

>>continued

Option	Description
-C	Tells the preprocessor not to discard comments. Used with -E.
-idirafter *DIR*	Adds the directory *DIR* to the second inclusion path. The directories on the second inclusion path are searched when a header file isn't found in any of the directories in the main inclusion path (the one that -I adds to).
-H	Prints the name of each header file used.
-imacros *FILE*	Processes *FILE* as input and discards the resulting output except for the retention of macro definitions.
-include *FILE*	Processes *FILE* as input before processing the regular input file.
-iprefix *PREFIX*	Specifies *PREFIX* as the prefix for subsequent -iwithprefix options.
-iwithprefix *DIR*	Adds a directory to the second inclusion path. The directory's name is made by concatenating *PREFIX* and *DIR*, where *PREFIX* was specified previously with -iprefix.
-M	Tells the preprocessor to output a rule suitable for make, describing the dependencies of each object file. For each source file, the preprocessor outputs one make rule whose target is the object filename for that source file and whose dependencies are all the files #included in it. The rules are printed on standard output. -E is implied.
-MD	Like -M but the dependency information is written to files with names made by replacing .o with .d at the end of the output filenames. -E is not implied.
-MG	Same as -M except that missing header files are treated as generated files and are assumed to exist in the same directory as the source file. -M must also be specified.
-MM	Like -M but the output mentions only the header files included with #include *FILE*. System header files included with #include <*FILE*> are omitted.
-MMD	Like -MD except that it mentions only user header files and not system header files.
-nostdinc	Don't search the standard system directories for header files.
-nostdinc++	Don't search for header files in the C++ specific standard directories, but search the other standard directories.
-P	Tells the preprocessor not to generate #line commands. Used with -E.
-U*MACRO*	Undefines the macro *MACRO*. -U options are evaluated after all -D options, but before any -include and -imacros options.
-undef	Don't predefine any nonstandard macros.

Assembler Options

Option	Description
-Wa,*OPTIONS*	*OPTIONS* is a comma-separated list of options to be passed to the assembler. *OPTIONS* are broken into separate arguments to be passed.

Linker Options

Option	Description
OBJECT_FILENAME	If a file is given whose name doesn't end with a recognized option, the file is assumed to be the name of an object file or library. If this is the case, *OBJECT_FILENAME* is passed to the linker if a link step is to be accomplished.
-l*LIBRARY*	Uses the library *LIBRARY* when linking. The actual file to be used will be named lib*LIBRARY*.a. The linker will search for the file in the standard list of directories plus those specified using the L option.
-lobjc	Required for linking Objective C programs.
-nostartfiles	Don't link with standard system startup files.
-nostdlib	Don't link with standard system libraries and startup files.
-static	Prevents linking with shared libraries.
-shared	Produces a shared object that can then be linked with other objects to form an executable.
-Xlinker *OPTION*	Passes *OPTION* to the linker.
-Wl,*OPTIONS*	*OPTIONS* is a comma-separated list of options to be passed to the linker. *OPTIONS* is broken into separate options before being passed.
-u *SYMBOL*	Pretends that *SYMBOL* is undefined in order to force linking of modules that contain it.

Directory Options

Option	Description
-I*DIR*	Appends the directory *DIR* to the list of directories searched for included files.
-I-	Subsequent -I*DIR* directives will be included in searches involving #include <*FILE*> as well as #include "*FILE*" searches. This option defers include operations based on its location on the command line. If -I- comes after -I, the directories specified with -I are only searched for #include *FILE* statements. If -I- comes before -I, directories specified with -I are searched for both #include *FILE* and #include <*FILE*> statements.
-L*DIR*	Adds the directory *DIR* to the list of directories to be searched for linking with the -l option.
-B*PREFIX*	Uses *PREFIX* as the prefix for the executables, libraries, and data files of the compiler itself.

Warning Options

Option	Description
-fsyntax-only	Checks code for syntax but doesn't generate any output.
-pedantic	Issues all the warnings demanded by strict ANSI standard C and rejects all programs that use forbidden extensions.
-pedantic-errors	Like -pedantic except that errors are produced rather than warnings.
-W	Prints extra warning messages in these situations: ■ A nonvolatile automatic variable might be changed by a call to longjump. ■ A function can return with or without a value. ■ An expression statement or the left side of a comma expression contains no side effects. ■ An unsigned value is compared against zero with > or <=.
-Waggregate-return	Warns if any functions that return structures or unions are defined or called.
-Wall	Enables all of the following: -W, -Wimplicit, -Wreturn-type, -Wunused, -Wswitch, -Wcomment, -Wtrigraphs, -Wformat, -Wchar-subscripts, -Wuninitialized, -Wparentheses, and -Wtemplate-debugging.
-Wcast-qual	Warns whenever a pointer is cast so as to remove a type qualifier from the target type.
-Wcast-align	Warns whenever a pointer is cast such that the required alignment of the target is increased.
-Wchar-subscripts	Warns if an array subscript has type char.
-Wcomment	Warns whenever the comment-start sequence /* appears in a comment.
-Wconversion	Warns if a prototype causes a type conversion that's different from what would happen to the same argument in the absence of a prototype.
-Wenum-clash	Warns about conversion between different enumerated types (C++ only).
-Werror	Treats warnings as errors and aborts compilation after any warning.
-Wformat	Checks calls to printf, scanf, and so on to make sure that the arguments are compatible with the format string.
-Wid-clash-*LEN*	Warns whenever two distinct identifiers are not unique within the first *LEN* characters.
-Wimplicit	Warns whenever a function or parameter is implicitly declared.
-Winline	Warns if a function can't be inlined and was declared as inline or the -finline-functions option was given.

Option	Description
-Wmissing-declarations	Warns if a global function is defined without a previous declaration.
-Wmissing-prototypes	Warns if a global function is defined without a previous prototype declaration.
-Wnested-externs	Warns if an extern declaration is encountered within a function.
-Wno-import	Inhibits warning messages about the use of #import.
-Woverloaded-virtual	Warns when a function has the same name as a virtual function in the base class but with a type signature that doesn't match any virtual functions from the base class (C++ only).
-Wparentheses	Warns if parentheses are omitted in certain contexts.
-Wpointer-arith	Warns about anything that depends on the "size of" a function type or of void.
-Wredundant-decls	Warns if anything is declared more than once in the same scope, even in cases where multiple declaration is valid and changes nothing.
-Wreturn-type	Warns whenever a function is defined with a return type that defaults to int. Also warns about any return statement with no return value in a function whose return type is not void.
-Wshadow	Warns whenever a local variable shadows another local variable.
-Wstrict-prototypes	Warns if a function is declared or defined without specifying the argument types.
-Wswitch	Warns whenever a switch statement has an enumerated index type and lacks a case for one or more of the possible values of that enumeration. The use of the default label suppresses the warning. case labels outside the enumeration range also provoke warnings when this option is used.
-Wtemplate-debugging	When using templates in a C++ program, warns if debugging isn't yet fully available.
-Wtraditional	Warns about certain constructs that behave differently between traditional and ANSI C: ■ Macro arguments occurring within string constants in the macro body. These would substitute the argument in traditional C, but are part of the constant in ANSI C. ■ A function declared external in one block and then used after the end of the block. ■ A switch statement has an operand of type long.
-Wtrigraphs	Warns if any trigraphs are encountered.
-Wuninitialized	Warns if an automatic variable is used without first being initialized.

continues >>

>>continued

Option	Description
-Wunused	Warns whenever a local variable is unused aside from its declaration, a function is declared static but never defined, or a statement computes a result that's not explicitly used.
-Wwrite-strings	Gives string constants the type const char[LENGTH] so that copying the address of one into a non-const char * pointer will get a warning.
-w	Inhibits all warning messages.

Debugging Options

The -g option can be used to support symbolic debugging (typically through gdb). In addition, -gFORMAT specifies the format expected by the debugger. Supported FORMATs include the following:

Format	Description
gdb	Produces debugging information for gdb.
gstabs	Produces debugging information in "stabs" format.
gstabs+	Produces debugging information in "stabs" format plus gdb extensions.
gdwarf	Produces debugging information in "dwarf" format.

-gFORMATLEVEL also indicates how much debugging information will be included. Valid values for LEVEL are as follows:

1   Descriptions of functions and external variables but no line numbers or local variables.
2   Default level. Level 1 information plus line numbers and local variables.
3   Includes extra information such as macro definitions.

The following table describes some additional debugging options. Some are used to debug the compiler itself.

Option	Description
-a	Generates extra code to write profile information for basic blocks, which will record the number of times each basic block is executed.
-da	Produces all dumps possible with the -d options except -dm and -dp.
-dc	Dumps after instruction combination to FILENAME.combine.
-dD	Dumps all macro definitions at the end of preprocessing, in addition to normal output.
-dd	Dumps after delayed branch scheduling to FILENAME.dbr.
-df	Dumps after flow analysis to FILENAME.flow.
-dg	Dumps after global register allocation to FILENAME.greg.

Option	Description
-dJ	Dumps after last jump optimization to *FILENAME*.jump2.
-dj	Dumps after first jump optimization to *FILENAME*.jump.
-dk	Dumps after conversion from registers to stack to *FILENAME*.stack.
-dL	Dumps after loop optimization to *FILENAME*.loop.
-dl	Dumps after local register allocation to *FILENAME*.lreg.
-dM	Dumps all macro definitions at the end of preprocessing, and writes no output.
-dm	Prints statistics on memory usage at the end of the run to standard error.
-dN	Dumps all macro names at the end of preprocessing.
-dp	Annotates the assembler output with a comment indicating which pattern and alternative was used.
-dR	Dumps after the second instruction scheduling pass to *FILENAME*.sched2.
-dr	Dumps after RTL (register transfer language) generation to *FILENAME*.rtl.
-dS	Dumps after the first instruction scheduling pass to *FILENAME*.sched.
-ds	Dumps afer CSE (common subexpression elimination, including the jump optimization that sometimes follows CSE) to *FILENAME*.cse.
-dt	Dumps after the second CSE pass to *FILENAME*.cse2.
-dx	Just generates RTL for a function instead of compiling it. Usually used with dr.
-dy	Dumps debugging information during parsing to standard error.
-fpretend-float	Produces floating-point format for the target machine when cross-compiling.
-p or -pg	Generates code that writes profile information. The resulting program generates data that can be analyzed using gprof.
-print-file-name=*LIBRARY*	Prints the full absolute name of the library file for *LIBRARY* that would be used for linking and doesn't do anything else.
-print-libgcc-file-name	Same as -print-file-name=libgcc.a.
-print-prog-name=*PROGRAM*	Like -print-file-name but searches for program files such as cpp.
-save-temps	Stores the usual "temporary" intermediate files permanently. Places them in the current directory and names them based on the source file.

Optimization Options

Option	Description
-fcaller-saves	Some values allocated to registers are saved and restored between function calls if function calls would overwrite them.
-fcse-follow-jumps	In common subexpression elimination (CSE), scans through jump instructions when the target of the jump isn't reached by any other path.
-fcse-skip-blocks	Similar to -fcse-follow-jumps, but causes CSE to follow jumps that conditionally skip over blocks.
-fdelayed-branch	If supported for the target machine, attempts to reorder instructions to exploit instruction slots available after delayed branch instructions.
-felide-constructors	Elides constructors when it seems safe to do so (C++ only).
-fexpensive-optimizations	Performs a number of minor optimizations that are relatively expensive.
-ffast-math	Allows the violation of some ANSI or IEEE rules/specifications in the interest of optimizing code for speed.
-ffloat-store	Don't store floating-point variables in registers.
-fforce-addr	Forces memory-address constants to be copied into registers before doing arithmetic on them.
-fforce-mem	Forces memory operands to be copied into registers before doing arithmetic on them.
-finline-functions	Code for simple functions is regenerated rather than called.
-fkeep-inline-functions	Even if all calls to a given function are integrated and the function is declared static, outputs a separate runtime callable version of the function.

Option	Description
`-fmemoize-lookups`, `-fsave-memoized`	Uses heuristics to compile faster (C++ only). These heuristics aren't enabled by default, since they're only effective for certain input files and may cause other input files to compile more slowly.
	The first time the compiler must build a call to a member function or reference to a data member, it must first determine whether the class implements member functions of the corresponding name. Then it must resolve which member function to call, which involves figuring out what sorts of type conversions need to be made. Finally, it must check the visibility of the member function to the caller. All of this adds up to slower compilation. Normally, the second member function call or reference to the same data member forces the compiler to go through the same lengthy process again. By using a software cache, a "hit" significantly reduces this cost. Unfortunately, using the cache introduces another layer of mechanisms that must be implemented, and so incurs its own overhead. `-fmemoize-lookups` enables the software cache.
	Because access privileges (visibility) to members and member functions may differ from one function context to the next, `g++` may need to flush the cache. With the `-fmemoize-lookups` flag, the cache is flushed after every function that's compiled. The `-fsave-memoized` flag enables the same software cache, but when the compiler determines that the context of the last function compiled would yield the same access privileges of the next function to compile, it preserves the cache. This is most helpful when defining many member functions for the same class. With the exception of member functions that are friends of other classes, each member function has exactly the same access privileges as every other, and the cache doesn't need to be flushed.

continues >>

>>continued

Option	Description
-fno-default-inline	Don't make member functions inline by default merely because they're defined inside the class scope (C++ only).
-fno-defer-pop	Always pop the arguments to each function call as soon as that function returns.
-fno-function-cse	Don't put function addresses in registers. Make each instruction that calls a constant function contain the function's address explicitly.
-fno-peephole	Disables any machine-specific peephole optimizations.
-fomit-frame-pointer	Don't keep the frame pointer in a register for functions that don't need one.
-frerun-cse-after-loop	Reruns common subexpression elimination (CSE) after loop optimization has been performed.
-fschedule-insns	If supported by the target machine, attempts instruction scheduling to eliminate or minimize pipeline stalls.
-fschedule-insns2	Similar to -fschedule-insns but requests an additional pass of instruction scheduling after register allocation has been done.
-fstrength-reduce	Performs the optimizations of loop strength reduction and elimination of iteration variables.
-fthread-jumps	Determines whether a jump branches to a location where another comparison subsumed by the first is found. If so, the first branch is redirected to either the destination of the second branch or a point immediately following it, depending on whether the condition is known to be true or false.
-funroll-all-loops	Unrolls all loops.
-funroll-loops	Unrolls loops whose iteration count can be determined at compile time or runtime.
O0	Don't optimize.
-O or -O1	Basic optimization; reduction of the cost of compilation while preserving statement independence for debugging.
-O2	All -O1 optimizations plus nearly all supported optimizations that don't involve space/speed tradeoffs.
-O3	All -O2 optimizations along with enabling -finline-functions.

Code-Generation Options

Option	Description
-finhibit-size-directive	Don't output a .size assembler directive or anything else that would cause trouble if the function is split in the middle and the two halves are placed at locations far apart in memory.
-fno-common	Allocates even uninitialized global variables in the bss section of the object file, rather than generating them as common blocks.
-fno-gnu-linker	Don't output global initializations (such as C++ constructors and destructors) in the form used by the GNU linker (on systems where the GNU linker is the standard method of handling them).
-fno-ident	Ignores the #ident directive.
-fnonnull-objects	Assumes that objects reached through references are not null (C++ only).
-fpcc-struct-return	Uses the same convention for returning struct and union values that's used by the usual C compiler on the system.
-fPIC	If supported for the target machine, emits position-independent code suitable for dynamic linking, even if branches need large displacements.
-fpic	If supported for the target machine, generates position-independent code suitable for use in a shared library.
-freg-struct-return	Uses the convention that struct and union values are returned in registers when possible.
-fshared-data	Requests that the data and non-const variables of this compilation be shared rather than private.
-fshort-double	Uses the same size for double as for float.
-fshort-enums	Allocates to an enum type only as many bytes as it needs for the declared range of possible values.
-fverbose-asm	Puts extra commentary information in the generated assembly code to make it more readable.
-fvolatile	Considers all memory references through pointers to be volatile.
-fvolatile-global	Considers all memory references to extern and global data items to be volatile.

Software Project Management

This section provides an introduction to management of software projects using make.

make

```
make [ OPTION ... ]
```

make is typically used to manage the building of programs with multiple source files. A file called a *makefile* is used to declare the dependencies between parts of the program and the steps needed to satisfy these dependencies. For example, a relocatable object file may be dependent on a C source file. In this case, make can be directed to invoke gcc to compile the source to generate the object. Typically, the timestamps on the files are used to determine whether the object needs to be regenerated.

Makefiles

The activities of make are directed by a makefile that's typically named makefile or Makefile, although other names can be specified using the -f or --file command option. The makefile can contain statements of several types:

- **Explicit rules.** An explicit rule lists the target file to be built, the files on which the target depends, and the commands used to build the target.

- **Implicit rules.** An implicit rule states when and how to remake a class of files based on their names.

- **Variable definitions.** A variable definition specifies a variable name and a text string to substitute for it when the name is referenced.

- **Directives.** Directives are special instructions for make. These include conditional statements, inclusions from other makefiles, and defining multiple-line values for variables.

- **Comments.** A # in a line starts a comment; it and the text that follows it are ignored.

Sample Makefile Statements

This explicit rule compiles source.c into object.o if either source.c or defs.h is newer than object.o:

```
object.o : source.c defs.h cc -c source.c -o object.o
```

The following example illustrates the use of an implicit rule:

```
prog : object1.o object2.o cc -o prog object1.o object2.o
```

If no other rules exist stating how to build object1.o and object2.o, these would typically be built from object.c and object2.c using the C compiler if they exist or can be built.

The preceding example could be rewritten using a variable definition:

```
OBJS = object1.o object2.o
prog : $(OBJS) cc -o prog $(OBJS)
```

A complete description of makefiles is beyond the scope of this book. For more information, consult the sources of information listed in Appendix C, "Web Resources."

Command-Line Options

The following table describes the command-line options for make.

Option	Description
--assume-new=*FILE*	Pretends that the target *FILE* has just been modified in order to force a remake of *FILE*.
--assume-old=*FILE*	Don't remake *FILE* regardless of its age or dependencies. Treat *FILE* as being very old.
-b	Ignored but included for compatibility with other versions of make.
-C *DIR*	Changes to the directory *DIR* before reading makefiles.
-d or --debug	Prints debugging information, which consists of information describing how make decides what to do.
--directory=*DIR*	Same as -C *DIR*.
-e or --environment-overrides	Gives variables taken from the environment precedence over variables from makefiles.
-f *FILE* or --file=*FILE*	Uses *FILE* as the makefile.
-h or --help	Prints a summary of make options and exits.
-I *DIR* or --include-dir=*DIR*	Searches *DIR* for included makefiles. If multiple -I options are used, the directories are searched in the order specified.
-i or --ignore-errors	Ignores all errors from commands executed by make.
-j [*JOBS*] or --jobs[=*JOBS*]	Allows *JOBS* jobs (commands) to run simultaneously. An infinite number are allowed if *JOBS* is omitted.
--just-print	Same as --dry-run.
-k or --keep-going	Continues as long as possible after an error.
-l [*LOAD*] or --load-average[=*LOAD*] or --max-load[=*LOAD*]	Specifies that no new jobs (commands) should be started if other jobs are running and the load average is at least *LOAD* (a floating-point number). With no argument, removes a previous load limit.
-m	Ignored but included for compatibility with other versions of make.
--makefile=*FILE*	Uses *FILE* as a makefile.
-n or --just-print or --dry-run or --recon	Prints the commands that would be executed but doesn't actually execute them.
--new-file=*FILE*	Same as --assume-new=*FILE*.
--no-builtin-rules	Disallows use of the built-in implicit rules.
--no-keep-going	Cancels the effect of the -k option.
--no-print-directory	Disables printing of the working directory under -w.
-o *FILE* --old-file=*FILE*	Same as --assume-old=*FILE*.
-p or --print-data-base	Prints the database (rules and variable values) resulting from reading the makefile before execution.

continues >>

>>continued

Option	Description
- -print-directory	Prints a message containing the working directory both before and after executing the makefile.
-q or - -question	Runs without executing any commands and returns an exit status that's 0 if the specified targets are already up to date, 1 if any remaking is required, or 2 if an error is encountered.
- -quiet	Silent operation. Don't print the commands as they're executed.
-r	Same as - -no-builtin-rules.
- -recon	Same as - -dry-run.
-S	Same as - -no-keep-going.
-s or - -silent	Same as - -quiet.
- -stop	Same as - -no-keep-going.
-t or - -touch	Touches files (marks them as being up to date without really changing them) instead of running their commands.
-v or - -version	Prints the make version information and exits.
-W FILE	Same as - -assume-new=FILE.
-w	Same as - -print-directory.
- -warn-undefined-variables	Issues a warning message whenever make sees a reference to an undefined variable.
- -what-if=FILE	Same as - -assume-new=FILE.

Processing Binary Files

Relocatable binary files are the direct result of source code compilation. The relocatable binaries are then combined to produce executable programs and libraries. This section describes the commands used to manipulate relocatable and executable binaries. These commands are often invoked from make scripts in the process of building software from source code.

ar

```
ar [-]P[MOD [REPOS]] ARCHIVE [ MEMBER ...]
ar -M
```

ar creates, modifies, and extracts from archives. An *archive* is a single file holding a collection of other files in a structure that makes it possible to retrieve the original individual files (called *members* of the archive). The attributes of each file such as ownership, timestamps, and so on are preserved in such a way that they can be restored upon extraction.

Archives can contain files of any type but are most often used as libraries of commonly used compiled subroutines.

ar can be used in two modes of operation. The first is controlled completely through the command-line options as in the first form above. The second is driven by standard input either interactively or from a script file. Note that the script file needs to be supplied using the < input redirection operator.

Command-Line Options

Each operation to be performed by ar is specified by a *P* operation code followed by optional *MOV* and *RELPOS* arguments. GNU ar allows you to mix the operation code *P* and modifier flags *MOD* in any order within the first command-line argument. The first command-line argument can begin with a hyphen (-).

The operation code *P* can be any of the following:

Code	Description
d	Delete *MEMBER*(s) from *ARCHIVE*.
m	Move *MEMBER* in *ARCHIVE*. The ordering of members in an archive can make a difference in how programs are linked using the library, if a symbol is defined in more than one member.
p	Print the specified members of the archive to the standard output file. If the v modifier is specified, show the member name before copying its contents to standard output. If no *MEMBER* is specified, all files in *ARCHIVE* are printed.
q	Quick append. Add the *MEMBER* files to the end of *ARCHIVE* without checking for replacement.
r	Insert the file *MEMBER* into *ARCHIVE* with replacement. If one of the *MEMBER* files doesn't exist, ar displays an error message and leaves undisturbed any existing members of the archive matching that name.
t	Display a table listing the contents of *ARCHIVE* or those of the files named as *MEMBER*(s) that are present in the archive. If you don't specify a *MEMBER*, all files in the archive are listed. If more than one file with the same name exists, only the first instance will be listed.
x	Extract members named *MEMBER* from the archive. If no *MEMBER*s are named, the entire archive is extracted.

Any number of modifiers (*MOD*) can immediately follow the *P* operation code. Valid modifiers are shown in the following table.

Modifier	Description
a *RELPOS*	Place after the member named *RELPOS*. For use with r.
b *RELPOS*	Place before the member named *RELPOS*. For use with r.
c	Creates the archive. The specified *ARCHIVE* is always created if it doesn't exist when you request an update. But a warning is issued unless you specify in advance that you expect to create it, by using this modifier.
f	Truncates names in the archive. ar will normally permit filenames of any length. This option causes it to create archives that are incompatible with the native ar program on some systems. If this is a concern, the f modifier can be used to truncate filenames when putting them in the archive.
i	Same as b.

continues >>

>>continued

Modifier	Description
l	Accepted but ignored.
o	Preserves the original dates of members when extracting them. If you don't specify this modifier, files extracted from the archive are stamped with the time of extraction.
s	Writes an object-file index into the archive or updates an existing one, even if no other change is made to the archive. You can use this modifier flag with any operation or alone. Running ar s on an archive is equivalent to running ranlib on it.
S	Don't generate an archive symbol table. This can speed up building a large library in several steps. To make the library usable by a linker, the symbol table should be built on the last step either by omitting S or running ranlib.
u	Replaces MEMBERs only if they're newer than the existing ones with the same names. The u modifier can only be used in combination with r.
v	Verbose operation.
V	Shows the version number of ar.

Using ar Scripts

When ar is invoked with the single option -M, its operation can be controlled with a rudimentary command language. This form of ar operates interactively if standard input is coming directly from a terminal. During interactive use, ar prompts for input (the prompt is AR >), and continues executing even after errors. If you redirect standard input to a script file, no prompts are issued, and ar abandons execution (with a nonzero exit code) on any error.

The following rules apply to ar commands:

- Commands are not case sensitive. LIST is the same as list.

- A single command appears on each line. The command is the first word on the line.

- Multiple-line commands are continued with +.

- Empty lines are allowed and have no effect.

- Arguments to commands are separated with either commas or blanks.

The following table describes commands that can be used in ar scripts.

Command	Description
addlib ARCHIVE [(MODULE ...)]	Adds the entire ARCHIVE or specified MODULE(s) from ARCHIVE to the current archive. Requires a prior open or create.
addmod MEMBER ...	Adds each named MEMBER as a module in the current archive. Requires a prior open or create.
clear	Discards the contents of the current archive.

Command	Description
create *ARCHIVE*	Creates an archive and makes it the current archive (required for many other commands). *ARCHIVE* may already exist and won't be replaced until **save** is executed.
delete *MODULE* ...	Deletes each *MODULE* from the current archive. Requires a prior **open** or **create**.
directory *ARCHIVE* (*MODULE* ...) [*OUTPUTFILE*]	Lists each named *MODULE* present in *ARCHIVE*. The listing is printed in *OUTPUTFILE* if specified; otherwise, it's printed on standard output.
end	Exits **ar** with a **0** exit code. Changes to the current archive, if any, aren't saved.
extract *MODULE* ...	Extracts each named *MODULE* from the current archive, writing them into the current directory as separate files. Requires a prior **open** or **create**.
list	Displays the full contents of the current archive in "verbose" style, regardless of the state of **verbose**. Requires a prior **open** or **create**.
open *ARCHIVE*	Opens an existing archive for use as the current archive (required for many other commands). Any changes as the result of subsequent commands won't affect *ARCHIVE* until **save** is executed.
replace *MODULE* ...	In the current archive, replaces each existing *MODULE* from files in the current working directory. To execute this without errors, both the file and the module in the current archive must exist. Requires a prior **open** or **create**.
save	Commits changes to the current archive and saves it as a file with the name specified in the last **create** or **end** command. Requires a prior **open** or **create**.
verbose	Toggles an internal flag governing the output from **directory**.

ld

ld [-o OUTPUT] OBJFILE ... [OPTION ...]

ld combines the OBJFILE(s) into a single executable program. OBJFILEs are relocatable object files typically created by gcc, g++, or some other language compiler. ld is usually invoked automatically by the compilers when executable output is requested.

Option	Description
-aKEYWORD	KEYWORD must be one of the strings archive, shared, or default. -archive is functionally equivalent to -Bstatic, and the other two keywords are functionally equivalent to -Bdynamic. This option can be used any number of times.
-b INPUT_FORMAT	Specifies the input format for the OBJFILE(s). By default, the most common format for the machine will be used. This can also be set using the GNUTARGET environment variable. A list of supported formats can be obtained with objdump -info.
-c MRI-COMMANDFILE or --mri-script=MRI-COMMANDFILE	Uses the MRI-compatible linker script MRI-COMMANDFILE.
-d or -dc or -dp	Assigns space to common symbols even if a relocatable output file is specified (with -r).
-e ENTRY	Uses ENTRY as the explicit symbol for beginning execution of the program, rather than the default entry point.
-E or --export-dynamic	When creating a dynamically linked ELF executable, adds all symbols to the dynamic symbol table. The dynamic symbol table is the set of symbols that are visible from dynamic objects at runtime.
-f or --auxiliary NAME	When creating an ELF shared object, sets the internal DT_AUXILIARY field to the specified NAME. This tells the dynamic linker that the symbol table of the shared object should be used as an auxiliary filter on the symbol table of the shared object NAME.
-F NAME or --filter NAME	When creating an ELF shared object, sets the internal DT_FILTER field to the specified NAME. This tells the dynamic linker that the symbol table of the shared object that's being created should be used as a filter on the symbol table of the shared object NAME.
--force-exe-suffix	Makes sure that an output file has an .exe suffix.
-g	Ignored but provided for compatibility with other tools.
-hNAME or -soname=NAME	When creating an ELF shared object, sets the internal DT_SONAME field to NAME.
-i	Performs an incremental link (same as -r).

Option	Description
-l*ARCHIVE* or --library=*ARCHIVE*	Adds the archive file *ARCHIVE* to the list of files to link.
-L*SEARCHDIR* or --library-path=*SEARCHDIR*	Adds *SEARCHDIR* to the list of paths to be searched for archive libraries and control scripts.
-m*EMULATION*	Emulates the *EMULATION* linker. The --verbose or -V options list the available emulations. This can also be controlled using the LDEMULATION environment variable.
-M or --print-map	Prints a link map to the standard output.
-n or --nmagic	Set the text segment to be read-only, and mark the output as NMAGIC.
-N or --omagic	Set the text and data sections to be readable and writable. Also, don't page-align the data segment. Mark the output as OMAGIC.
-o *OUTPUT* or --output=*OUTPUT*	Writes output to the file *OUTPUT*. The default is a.out.
-r or --relocatable	Generates relocatable rather than executable output. This option is equivalent to -i. This option won't resolve references to C++ constructors. -Ur should be used instead.
-R *FILENAME* or --just-symbols=*FILENAME*	Read symbol names and their addresses from *FILENAME*, but don't relocate it or include it in the output. This allows the output file to refer symbolically to absolute locations of memory defined in other programs.
-s or --strip-all	Omits all symbol information from the output.
-S or --strip-debug	Omits debugging symbols from the output.
-t or --trace	Prints names of input files as they're processed.
-T *COMMANDFILE* or --script=*COMMANDFILE*	Reads link commands from the file *COMMANDFILE*.
-u *SYMBOL* or --undefined=*SYMBOL*	Forces *SYMBOL* to be entered in the output file as an undefined symbol.
-v or --version or -V	Displays ld version information. The -V option also lists supported emulations.
-x or --discard-all	Deletes all local symbols.
-X or --discard-locals	Deletes all temporary local symbols. The names usually begin with L.
-y *SYMBOL* or --trace-symbol=*SYMBOL*	Prints the name of each linked file in which *SYMBOL* appears. This is useful for finding which files contain unresolved references.
-Y *PATH*	Adds *PATH* to the default library search path.
-z *KEYWORD*	Ignored but provided for Solaris compatibility.

continues >>

>>continued

Option	Description
-(ARCHIVES -) or --start-group ARCHIVES --end-group	The ARCHIVES should be a list of archive files. They can be either explicit filenames or -l options. The specified archives are searched repeatedly until no new undefined references are created. Normally, an archive is searched only once in the order in which it's specified on the command line. If a symbol in that archive is needed to resolve an undefined symbol referred to by an object in an archive that appears later on the command line, the linker wouldn't be able to resolve that reference. By grouping the archives, they can all be searched repeatedly until all possible references are resolved.
-assert KEYWORD	Ignored but provided for compatibility with SunOS.
-Bdynamic or -dy or -call_shared	Link against dynamic libraries.
-Bstatic or -dn or -non_shared or -static	Don't link against dynamic libraries.
-Bsymbolic	When creating a shared library, binds references to global symbols to the definition within the shared library, if any.
--cref	Outputs a cross-reference table.
--defsym SYMBOL=EXPRESSION	Creates a global symbol named SYMBOL in the output file, containing the absolute address given by EXPRESSION. EXPRESSION may be a hexadecimal constant or the name of an existing symbol, or use + and - to add or subtract hexadecimal constants or symbols.
--dynamic-linker FILE	Sets the name of the dynamic linker to FILE. This is only meaningful when generating dynamically linked ELF executables. The default dynamic linker is normally correct. Don't use this unless you know what you're doing.
-EB	Links big-endian objects. This affects the default output format.
-EL	Links little-endian objects. This affects the default output format.
--help	Prints a command-line option summary.
-Map MAPFILE	Prints the link map to MAPFILE.
--no-keep-memory	Optimizes for memory usage by rereading the symbol tables as necessary. This may be useful if ld runs out of memory while linking a large executable.
--no-warn-mismatch	Allows mismatched input files. This option should be used only in cases when action has been taken that ensures that the linker errors are inappropriate.
--no-whole-archive	Turns off the effect of the --whole-archive option for subsequent archive files.

Option	Description
--noinhibit-exec	Retains the executable output file whenever it's still usable, even if errors are encountered.
--oformat *OUTPUT-FORMAT*	Specifies the format of the output file. A list of supported formats can be obtained with objdump -info.
--retain-symbols-file *FILENAME*	Retains only the symbols listed in the file *FILENAME* and discards all others. *FILENAME* is simply a flat file, with one symbol name per line.
-rpath *DIR*	Adds the directory *DIR* to the runtime library search path. This is used when linking an ELF executable with shared objects.
-shared or -Bshareable	Creates a shared library.
--sort-common	Sorts the common symbols by size when it places them in the appropriate output sections.
--split-by-file	Creates a new output section for each input file.
--split-by-reloc *COUNT*	Attempts to create extra sections in the output file so that no single output section in the file contains more than *COUNT* relocations.
--stats	Computes and displays statistics about the operation of the linker, such as execution time and memory usage.
-Tbss *ORG* or -Tdata *ORG* or bss, -Ttext *ORG*	Uses *ORG* as the starting address for the data or text output file segments, respectively. *ORG* must be a single hexadecimal integer.
-Ur	Equivalent to -r for programs not written in C++. For C++ programs, it also resolves references to constructors.
--verbose	Displays the version number and lists the supported emulations.
--version-script=*VERSION-SCRIPTFILE*	Specifies the name of the version script file. This file supplies information about the version hierarchy of the library being built.
--warn-common	Warns when a common symbol is combined with another common symbol or with a symbol definition. This option enables you to find potential problems from combining global symbols.
--warn-constructors	Warns if any global constructors are used.
--warn-once	Only warns once for each undefined symbol instead of once per module referencing it.
--warn-section-align	Warns if the address of an output section is changed because of alignment.
--whole-archive	For each archive file mentioned after --whole-archive, the entire archive is included in the link instead of the required modules. This is usually used to convert archives into shared libraries.

continues >>

>>continued

Option	Description
--wrap *SYMBOL*	Uses a wrapper function for *SYMBOL*. Any undefined reference to *SYMBOL* will be resolved to __wrap_*SYMBOL*. Any undefined reference to __real_*SYMBOL* will be resolved to *SYMBOL*.

nm

nm [*OPTION* ...] [*OBJFILE* ...]

nm lists the symbols from the object file(s) **OBJFILE** .... If no object files are listed as arguments, nm assumes **a.out**.

For each symbol, nm shows the symbol's value, type, and name. The symbol's value is shown in hexadecimal by default but another radix can be selected by using the -t or --radix= option. Symbol types include—but are not limited to—the following list (others are possible depending on the object file format):

Symbol	Description
A	The symbol's value is absolute and won't be changed by further linking.
B	The symbol is in the uninitialized data section (known as **bss**).
C	The symbol is common. Common symbols are uninitialized data. When linking, multiple common symbols may appear with the same name.
D	The symbol is in the initialized data section.
G	The symbol is in an initialized data section for small objects. Some object file formats permit more efficient access to small data objects, such as a global int variable as opposed to a large global array.
I	The symbol is an indirect reference to another symbol.
N	The symbol is a debugging symbol.
R	The symbol is in the read-only data section.
S	The symbol is in the uninitialized data section for small objects.
T	The symbol is in the text (code) section.
U	The symbol is referenced but undefined.
W	The symbol is weak. When a weak defined symbol is linked with a normal defined symbol, the normal defined symbol is used with no error. When a weak undefined symbol is linked and the symbol is undefined, the value of the weak symbol becomes **0** with no error.
–	The symbol is a "stabs" symbol in an **a.out** object file. In this case, the next values printed are the "stabs" other field, the "stabs" descriptor field, and the "stabs" type. "Stabs" symbols are needed to support symbolic debugging.
?	The symbol type is unknown or specific to the object-file format.

The following table describes nm command-line options:

Option	Description
-A or -o or --print-file-name	Precedes each symbol with the name of the input file or archive element in which it was found. Otherwise, nm only identifies the filename once before listing its symbols.
-a or --debug-syms	Displays all symbols, even debugger-only symbols that normally aren't listed.
-B	Same as --format=bsd.
-C or --demangle	Decodes ("demangles") low-level symbol names into user-level names. In addition to removing any initial underscore prepended by the system, this makes C++ function names readable.
--no-demangle	Don't demangle low-level symbol names. This is the default.
-D or --dynamic	Displays the dynamic symbols rather than the normal symbols. This is meaningful only for dynamic objects, such as certain types of shared libraries.
-f FORMAT or --format=FORMAT	Uses the output format FORMAT, which can be bsd, sysv, or posix. The default is bsd. Only the first character of FORMAT is significant; it can be either uppercase or lowercase.
-g or --extern-only	Displays only external symbols.
-l or --line-numbers	For each symbol, uses debugging information to try to find a filename and line number. For a defined symbol, looks for the line number of the address of the symbol. For an undefined symbol, looks for the line number of a relocation entry that refers to the symbol. If line number information is found, it's printed in the form SOURCE_FILENAME:LINE after the other symbol information.
-n or -v or --numeric-sort	Sorts symbols numerically by address rather than alphabetically by name.
-p or --no-sort	Don't sort symbols. Print them in order of appearance.
-P or --portability	Uses the POSIX.2 standard output format instead of the default format. Same as -f posix.
-s or --print-armap	When listing archives, includes an index showing which modules contain definitions for which names.
-r or --reverse-sort	Reverses the order of sorting.
--size-sort	Sorts symbols by size. The size is computed as the difference between the value of the symbol and the value of the symbol with the next higher value. The size of the symbol is printed, rather than the value.

continues >>

>>continued

Option	Description
-t *RADIX* or --radix=*RADIX*	Uses *RADIX* as the radix for printing the symbol values: d for decimal, o for octal, or x for hexadecimal.
--target=*BFDNAME*	Specifies an object code format other than the system's default format. A list of supported formats can be obtained with objdump -info.
-u or --undefined-only	Displays only symbols that are referenced but not defined.
--defined-only	Displays only defined symbols for each object file.
-V or --version	Shows the nm version number and exits.
--help	Shows the nm options summary.

ranlib

```
ranlib ARCHIVE
ranlib [ OPTION ]
```

ranlib generates an index to the contents of an archive and stores it in the archive. The index lists each symbol defined by a member of an archive that's a relocatable object file. The index can be printed using nm -s or nm --print-armap.

An archive with such an index speeds up linking to the library and allows routines in the library to call each other without regard to their placement in the archive.

Option	Description
-v or -V	Shows the version and copyright information.
--help	Shows the command syntax and list of supported relocatable object targets.

strip

```
strip [ OPTION ... ] OBJFILE ...
```

strip discards all symbols from object file(s) *OBJFILE* .... The list of object files can include archives. At least one object file must be given.

Option	Description
-F *BFDNAME* or --target=*BFDNAME*	Treats the original *OBJFILE* as a file with the object code format *BFDNAME* and rewrites it in the same format. A list of supported formats can be obtained with objdump-info.
--help	Shows a summary of the options to strip and exits.
-I *BFDNAME* or --input-target=*BFDNAME*	Treats the original *OBJFILE* as a file with the object code format *BFDNAME*. A list of supported formats can be obtained with objdump -info.

Option	Description
-O *BFDNAME* or --output-target=*BFDNAME*	Replaces *OBJFILE* with a file in the output format *BFDNAME*. A list of supported formats can be obtained with objdump -info.
-R *SECTIONNAME* or --remove-section=*SECTIONNAME*	Removes any section named *SECTIONNAME* from the output file. This option can be given more than once. Using this option inappropriately may make the output file unusable.
-s or --strip-all	Removes all symbols.
-g or -S	Removes debugging symbols only.
--strip-unneeded	Removes all symbols that aren't needed for relocation processing.
-K *SYMBOLNAME* or --keep-symbol=*SYMBOLNAME*	Keeps only the symbol *SYMBOLNAME* from the source file. This option can be given more than once.
-N *SYMBOLNAME* or --strip-symbol-*SYMBOLNAME*	Removes the symbol *SYMBOLNAME* from the source file. This option can be given more than once and can be combined with strip options other than -K.
-o *FILE*	Puts the stripped output in *FILE* rather than replacing the existing file. When this argument is used, only one *OBJFILE* argument can be specified.
-p or --preserve-dates	Preserves the access and modification dates of the file.
-x or --discard-all	Removes all non-global symbols.
-X or --discard-locals	Removes compiler-generated local symbols. These usually start with L or ..
-V or --version	Shows the version number for strip.
-v or --verbose	Verbose output. Lists all object files and archive members modified.

Debugging and Program Information

This section describes commands that can be used to debug programs and to find information about them.

gdb

```
gdb [ OPTION ... ] [ PROGRAM [ CORE ¦ PID ] ]
```

gdb is a symbolic debugger, used to provide source-level isolation of problems with C and C++ programs. Partial support is available for Modula-2, Chill, Pascal, and Fortran. For programs written in unsupported languages or ones for which no source is available, gdb can be used to provide assembly-language-level support.

gdb can be used in four ways:

- Starting and debugging a new process.

- "Post mortem" debugging of a process that has failed and has left a core dump file.

- Debugging a process that's already running.

- As a back end for debugging facilities such as xxgdb and the emacs debugger.

PROGRAM is an executable binary program linked with symbolic data included. Some programs leave a *CORE* file behind (typically named core) when errors such as segmentation faults are encountered. The purpose of this file is to support debugging of the failed process. The *CORE* file contains data describing the process state at the time of the failure.

Supplying *PID* enables debugging of a process that's already running.

Command-Line Options for gdb

The following command-line options can be used:

Option	Description
-b *BPS*	Sets the line speed (baud rate or bits per second) of any serial interface used by gdb for remote debugging.
-batch	Runs in batch mode. Exits with status 0 after processing all the command files specified with -x.
-cd *DIRECTORY*	Runs gdb using *DIRECTORY* as its working directory, instead of the current directory.
-command *FILE*	Executes gdb commands from the file *FILE*.
-core *FILE* or -c *FILE*	Uses the file *FILE* as a core dump to examine.
-c *NUMBER*	Connects to the process ID *NUMBER*. If a file named *NUMBER* exists in core dump format, uses *NUMBER* as a core file instead.
-directory *DIRECTORY* or -d *DIRECTORY*	Adds *DIRECTORY* to the path to search for source files.
-exec *FILE* or -e *FILE*	Uses the file *FILE* as the executable file to execute when appropriate and for examining pure data in conjunction with a core dump file.
-fullname or -f	Outputs the full filename and line number in a standard, recognizable fashion each time a stack frame is displayed (which includes each time a program stops).
-nx or -n	Don't execute commands from any initialization files (normally called .gdbinit).
-quiet or -q	Don't print the introductory and copyright messages.
-r or -readnow	Reads each symbol file's entire symbol table immediately.

Option	Description
-se *FILE*	Reads the symbol table from the file *FILE* and uses it as the executable file.
-symbols *FILE* or -s *FILE*	Reads the symbol table from the file *FILE*.
-tty *DEVICE*	Uses *DEVICE* for the program's standard input and output.
-x *FILE*	Same as -command *FILE*.

Interactive gdb Commands

gdb commands contain only one line but the line can be of any length. Each command starts with the command name and is followed by arguments that depend on the command being used. Many commands can be repeated by pressing Return or Enter. Any text from # to the end of the line is ignored and treated as comment data. This is mainly useful for running gdb in batches using command files.

There are too many gdb commands to list them all here. The online help facility provides complete information on available commands:

Command	Description
help or h	Lists classes of commands along with a description of each class.
help *CLASS*	Lists the commands belong to *CLASS* along with a description of each command.
help *COMMAND*	Provides a short paragraph on how to use *COMMAND*.

ldd

ldd [*OPTION* ...] *FILE* ...

ldd prints shared library dependencies for each *FILE*. Each *FILE* must be a program or a shared ELF library. For each library on which *FILE* depends, ldd prints a line containing the library name, an arrow (=>), and the full pathname to the library file that satisfies the reference (or a message indicating that the library can't be found).

Option	Description
-d	Performs relocations and reports any missing functions (ELF only).
-r	Performs relocations for both data objects and functions and reports any missing objects (ELF only).
-V	Prints the version of the dynamic linker ld.so.
-v	Prints the version number of ldd.

ltrace

ltrace [*OPTION* ...] [*COMMAND* [*ARG* ...]]

ltrace shows a process's system calls and calls made to dynamic libraries. It either runs *COMMAND* with optional *ARG* or can monitor an existing process using the -p command-line options. By default, ltrace write its output to standard error. At the time of this writing, ltrace only works on i386 architectures.

Option	Description
`-a` or `--align` *COLUMN*	Aligns return values in a specific column (the default value is **50**).
`-C` or `--demangle`	Decodes (demangles) low-level symbol names into user-level names. In addition to removing any initial underscore prepended by the system, this makes C++ function names readable.
`-d` or `--debug`	Increases the debugging level.
`-e` *EXPR*	*EXPR* is an expression that modifies which events to trace. The expression is a comma-separated list of functions. Placing ! in front of the list negates the set of values. For example, `-e printf` means to trace only the `printf` library call. By contrast, `-e !printf` means to trace every library call except `printf`.
`-f`	Traces child processes as they're created by currently traced processes as a result of the `fork()` or `clone()` system calls. The new process is attached as soon as its process ID is known.
`-h` or `--help`	Shows a summary of `ltrace` options and exits.
`-i`	Prints the instruction pointer at the time of the library call.
`-L`	Don't display library calls. This should be used with the `-S` option.
`-o` or `--output` *FILENAME*	Writes the trace output to *FILENAME* instead of standard error.
`-p` *PID*	Attaches to process *PID* and begins tracing.
`-S`	Displays system calls as well as library calls.
`-s` *SIZE*	Specifies the maximum string size to print (the default is **32**).
`-t`	Prefixes each line of the trace with the time of day.
`-tt`	Prefixes each line of the trace with the time of day, including the microseconds.
`-ttt`	Prefixes each line of the trace with the time of day, including the microseconds. The leading portion will be printed as the number of seconds since the epoch.
`-u` *USERNAME*	Runs the command with the user ID, group ID, and supplementary groups of *USERNAME*. This option is only useful when running as root and enables the correct execution of `setuid` and/or `setgid` binaries.
`-V` or `--version`	Shows the version number of `ltrace` and exits.

size

```
size [ OPTION ... ] [ OBJFILE ... ]
```

size lists the section sizes and the total size for each of the object or archive files
OBJFILE ... in its argument list. If no OBJFILEs are given, the file a.out will be
used.

Option	Description
-A or -B or --format=COMPATIBILITY	Sets the format of the output:
	System V: --format=sysv or -A
	Berkeley: --format=berkeley or -B
--help	Shows the option summary.
-d or -o or -x or --radix=NUMBER	Specifies the radix for the output of each section:
	Decimal: -d or --radix=10
	Octal: -o or --radix=8
	Hexadecimal: -x or --radix=16
	The total size is always given in two radices: decimal and hexadecimal for -d or -x output, or octal and hexadecimal if using -o.
--target=BFDNAME	Specifies that the object-code format for OBJFILE is BFDNAME. This option may not be necessary, since size can automatically recognize many formats. A list of supported formats can be obtained with objdump -info.

strace

```
strace [ OPTION ... ] [ COMMAND [ ARG ... ] ]
strace -c [ OPTION ... ] [ COMMAND [ ARG ... ] ]
```

strace intercepts and records the system calls that are called by a process and the
signals received by a process. The name of each system call and a formatted argument
list and return value are printed on standard error or to the file specified using the
-o option.

The primary function of strace is to provide information concerning the interactions between user processes and the kernel. It's valuable both as a diagnostic tool
(especially when dealing with programs for which no source is available) and as an
educational aid for investigating user/kernel interactions.

strace has two basic modes of operation, as the forms of invocation indicate. The first
shows detailed traces with one output line for each system call or signal detected. The
second shows counts for the time and number of calls and errors for each system call.

Option	Description
-a *COLUMN*	Aligns return values in a specific column. The default is column 40.
-c	Prints a summary of system call activity.
-d	Shows the debugging output for strace itself on standard error.
-e *EXPR*	*EXPR* is a qualifying expression that specifies which events to trace and how to trace them. The format for *EXPR* is [*QUALIFIER*][!]*VALUELIST*, where *VALUELIST* is a comma-separated list of values dependent on the *QUALIFIER* used. The ! can be used to negate the set of values specified by *EXPR*. For example, -e trace=!open means to trace every system call except open. *QUALIFIER* is one of the following:
	trace=*SET* Traces only the specified system calls. For example, trace=open,close traces only open and close calls.
	trace=file Traces all system calls that take a filename as an argument.
	trace=process Traces all process management calls.
	trace=network Traces all network-related system calls.
	trace=signal Traces all signal-related system calls.
	trace=ipc Traces all IPC-related system calls.
	abbrev=*SET* Abbreviates output for each system call in *SET*. The default is abbrev=all.
	verbose=*SET* Dereferences structures for the system calls in *SET*. The default is verbose=all.
	raw=*SET* Prints raw data values for the arguments of the calls in *SET*.
	signal=*SET* Traces only the specified subset of signals. The default is signal=all.
	read=*SET* Dumps all data read from file descriptors in *SET* in hexadecimal or ASCII format.
	write=*SET* Dumps all data written to file descriptors in *SET* in hexadecimal or ASCII format.
-f	Traces child processes as they're created by currently traced processes as a result of the fork system call. strace attaches to the new process as soon as its PID is known.
-ff	If the -o *FILENAME* option is in effect, each process's trace is written to *FILENAME*.*PID*, where *PID* is the numeric process ID of each process.
-h	Prints the help summary.
-i	Prints the instruction pointer at the time of the system call.
-O *OVERHEAD*	Sets the overhead for tracing system calls to *OVERHEAD* microseconds. This is useful for overriding the default heuristic for guessing how much time is spent in mere measuring when timing system calls using the -c option.
-o *FILENAME*	Writes the trace output to the file *FILENAME* rather than to standard error.

Option	Description
-p *PID*	Attaches to the process with the process ID *PID* and begins tracing. The trace can be terminated at any time by the keyboard interrupt signal (Ctrl+C), which will cause strace to detach itself from the processes being traced and let the process continue running. Multiple -p options can be used to attach up to 32 processes in addition to *COMMAND*. *COMMAND* is optional if -p is used.
-q	Suppresses messages about attaching, detaching, etc. This happens automatically when output is redirected to a file and the command is run directly instead of attaching.
-r	Prints a relative timestamp on entry to each system call. This records the time difference between the beginnings of successive system calls.
-S *SORTBY*	Sorts the output of the histogram printed when -c is used. Legal values for *SORTBY* are time, calls, name, and nothing.
-s *STRSIZE*	Specifies the maximum string size to print (the default is 32). Filenames aren't considered strings and are always printed in full.
-t	Prefixes each line of the trace with the time of day.
-tt	Prefixes each line of the trace with the time of day, including the microseconds.
-ttt	Prefixes each line of the trace with the time of day, including the microseconds, and with the leading portion printed as the number of seconds since the epoch.
-T	Shows the time spent in each system call. This records the time difference between the beginning and the end of each system call.
-u *USERNAME*	Runs *COMMAND* with the user ID, group ID, and supplementary groups of *USERNAME*. This option is only useful when running as root and enables the correct execution of setuid and/or setgid binaries. Unless this option is used, setuid and setgid programs are executed without effective privileges.
-v	Prints the unabbreviated version of some of the more complex call arguments. The default behavior displays a reasonable subset of structure members. This option should be used to get all the details.
-V	Prints the version number of strace.
-x	Prints all non-ASCII strings in hexadecimal string format.
-xx	Prints all strings in hexadecimal string format.

strings

```
strings [ OPTION ... ] FILE ...
```

For each *FILE* named on the command line, strings prints sequences of printable characters that are at least four characters long (or the number given using options) and are followed by an unprintable character. By default, strings only prints the strings from the initialized and loaded sections of object files. For other types of files, it prints the strings from the whole file. It's useful mainly for investigating the contents of non-text files.

Option	Description
-a or --all	For object files, scans the entire file rather than just the initialized and loaded sections.
-f or --print-file-name	Prints the name of the file before each string.
--help	Prints a summary of command-line options and exits.
-MIN-LEN or -n *MIN-LEN* or -bytes=*MIN-LEN*	Prints sequences of characters that are at least *MIN-LEN* characters long, instead of the default four characters.
-o	Same as -t o.
-t *RADIX* or --radix=*RADIX*	Prints the offset in *RADIX* within the file before each string. Valid values for *RADIX* are -o for octal, -x for hexadecimal, and -d for decimal.
--target=*BFDNAME*	Specifies an object code format other than the system's default format. A list of supported formats can be obtained using objdump -info.
-v or --version	Prints the program version number on the standard output and exits.

5

Network Clients

This chapter describes programs that provide access to network services. These services enable network information, network file and data transfer, and remote command execution.

Information Utilities

This section describes commands that provide network information services. These services enable users to see who is logged onto remote hosts and to query the status of those hosts.

finger

```
finger [ OPTION ... ] [ USER ... ]
```

finger displays information about remote or local users. USERs can refer to users local to the system or users on a remote system through use of the form USER@HOST. If no users are specified, finger shows information about every user logged onto the local system. If no options are specified, the -l format is used.

Option	Description
-s	Displays the user's login name, real name, terminal name and write status, idle time, login time, office location, and office phone number.
-l	Displays all the information from the -s option plus the user's home directory, home phone number, login shell, mail status, and the contents of .plan, .project, and .forward files in the user's home directory.
-p	Prevents the -l option from displaying the .plan and .project files.
-m	Prevents matching of usernames. If -m is not specified, matching is done on the users' real names as well as usernames.

rstat

rstat *HOST*

rstat displays a summary of the current status of *HOST*. The output shows the current time of day, how long the system has been up, and the load averages. The load average numbers give the number of jobs in the run queue averaged over 1, 5, and 15 minutes.

rup

rup [*OPTION* ...] [*HOST* ...]

rup displays a summary of the current status of a particular *HOST* or all hosts on a network. The output shows the current time of day, how long the system has been up, and the load averages. The load average numbers give the number of jobs in the run queue averaged over 1, 5, and 15 minutes.

Option	Description
-d	Reports the local time for each host.
-h	Sorts the display alphabetically by hostname.
-l	Sorts the display by load average.
-t	Sorts the display by up time.

ruptime

ruptime [*OPTION* ...]

ruptime shows status lines for each machine on the local network. These are formed from packets broadcast by each host on the network once a minute. If no *OPTION*s are given, the listing is sorted by hostname.

Option	Description
-a	Users idle an hour or more aren't counted unless the -a flag is given.
-l	Sorts by load average.
-r	Reverses the sort order.
-t	Sorts by uptime.
-u	Sorts by the number of users.

rusers

rusers [*OPTIONS* ...] [*HOST* ...]

rusers prints a listing similar to that produced by who but for the list of *HOST* arguments.

Option	Description
-a	Prints all machines responding, even if no one is logged in.
-l	Prints a long format listing. This includes the username, hostname, the user's controlling TTY, date and time the user logged in, idle time, and the remote host from which the user logged in (if applicable).

rwho

```
rwho [ -a ]
```

rwho produces output similar to that produced by who but for all machines on the local network. Users with more than an hour of idle time are omitted from the listing unless the -a flag is used.

File and Data Transfers

This section describes commands that provide network file and data transfers.

fromport

```
fromport [ -v ] PORT
```

fromport is a simple client that reads data from the selected TCP/IP *PORT*. Typically the data will be generated by the companion client toport. The -v option selects verbose mode, which is intended for debugging.

ftp

```
ftp [ OPTION ... ] [ HOST ]
```

ftp is an interactive client that uses the ARPANET standard File Transfer Protocol (FTP) to transfer files between the local host and a remote host specified by *HOST*.

Options for ftp

ftp accepts the following command-line *OPTION*s:

Option	Description
-d	Enables debugging.
-g	Disables filename globbing.
-i	Turns off interactive prompting during multiple file transfers.
-n	Disables "auto-login" on initial connection to the host.
-v	Verbose mode. This forces ftp to show all responses from the remote server as well as report data-transfer statistics.

ftp Commands

In addition to command-line *OPTIONS*s, the following commands can be executed from within ftp:

Command	Description
![COMMAND [ARG ...]]	Executes *COMMAND* locally with the argument(s) *ARG*(s). If *COMMAND* isn't given, invokes an interactive shell on the local machine.
$MACRO_NAME [ARG ...]	Executes the macro *MACRO_NAME* that was previously defined using the macdef command.

continues >>

>>continued

Command	Description
account[*PASSWD*]	Supplies a supplemental password required by the remote system. The user will be prompted in non-echoing mode if no *PASSWD* is specified.
append *LOCAL_FILE* [*REMOTE_FILE*]	Appends *LOCAL_FILE* on the local machine to *REMOTE_FILE* on the remote machine. If *REMOTE_FILE* isn't specified, *LOCAL_FILE* is appended to a file of the same name on the remote machine.
ascii	Sets the transfer type to ASCII.
bell	Turns on the sounding of the bell on completion of each file transfer.
binary	Sets the transfer type to binary.
bye	Terminates the ftp session.
case	Toggles the filename case mapping during mget commands.
cd *REMOTE_DIRECTORY*	Changes the working directory on the remote machine to *REMOTE_DIRECTORY*.
cdup	Changes the working directory on the remote machine to the parent of that directory.
chmod *MODE FILENAME*	Changes the permission modes of the file *FILENAME* on the remote system to *MODE*.
close	Terminates the session with the current remote server. Any defined macros are erased.
cr	Toggles carriage return stripping during ASCII file transfers.
delete *REMOTE_FILE*	Deletes the file *REMOTE_FILE* from the remote machine.
debug [*DEBUG_VALUE*]	Toggles debugging mode.
dir [*REMOTE_DIRECTORY*] [*LOCAL_FILE*]	Prints a directory listing of *REMOTE_DIRECTORY* (or the current working directory if not specified) to *LOCAL_FILE* (standard output if not specified).
disconnect	Synonym for close.
form *FORMAT*	Sets the file transfer form to *FORMAT*.
get *REMOTE_FILE* [*LOCAL_FILE*]	Transfers *REMOTE_FILE* on the remote machine to *LOCAL_FILE* on the local machine. If *LOCAL_FILE* isn't specified, *REMOTE_FILE* is simply transferred to the local machine.
glob	Toggles filename expansion for mdelete, mget, and mput.

Command	Description
hash	Toggles hash-sign (#) printing for each data block (1024 bytes) transferred.
help [COMMAND]	Prints a description of the command COMMAND. If COMMAND isn't given, a list of available commands is printed.
idle [SECONDS]	Sets the inactivity timer on the remote server to SECONDS. If SECONDS isn't given, the current setting is printed.
lcd [DIRECTORY]	Changes the working directory on the local machine. If DIRECTORY isn't specified, the user's home directory is used.
ls [REMOTE_DIRECTORY] [LOCAL_FILE]	Prints a directory list of the REMOTE_DIRECTORY on the remote machine (or the current directory if REMOTE_DIRECTORY isn't given) to LOCAL_FILE (standard output if not given).
macdef MACRO NAME	Defines a macro. Subsequent lines are stored as a macro named MACRO_NAME. A null line terminates macro input mode. The following special characters are used in macro definitions: $N refers to macro argument N. $i loops the macro for each macro argument. \ enables $ to be treated literally.
mdelete REMOTE_FILES	Expands REMOTE_FILES to the filename list on the remote machine and deletes each file in the resulting list.
mdir REMOTE_FILES LOCAL_FILE	Like dir except that you can specify multiple remote files.
mget REMOTE_FILES	Expands REMOTE_FILES to the filename list on the remote machine and transfers each file in the resulting list to the local machine.
mkdir DIRECTORY_NAME	Creates the directory DIRECTORY_NAME on the remote machine.
mls REMOTE_FILES LOCAL_FILE	Like nlist except that you can specify multiple remote files.
mode [MODE_NAME]	Sets the file transfer mode to MODE_NAME ("stream" by default).
mput LOCAL_FILES	Expands wildcards in LOCAL_FILES to the filename list on the local machine and transfers each file in the resulting list to the remote machine.

continues >>

>>*continued*

Command	Description
newer *FILENAME* [*LOCAL_FILE*]	Transfers the file *FILENAME* from the remote machine if its modification timestamp is more recent than that of *LOCAL_FILE* (same as *FILENAME* if not specified). If *LOCAL_FILE* doesn't exist, the remote file is considered newer.
nlist [*REMOTE_DIRECTORY*] [*LOCAL_FILE*]	Prints a list of the files in *REMOTE_DIRECTORY* (or the current working directory if *REMOTE_DIRECTORY* isn't specified) on the remote machine to *LOCAL_FILE* (standard output if not specified).
nmap [*INPATTERN OUTPATTERN*]	Sets or unsets the filename mapping mechanism. If no arguments are specified, the filename mapping mechanism is unset. The mapping follows the pattern set by *INPATTERN* and *OUTPATTERN*. *INPATTERN* is a template for incoming filenames. Variable templating is accomplished by including the sequences $1, $2, ..., $9 in *INPATTERN*. Use \ to prevent this special treatment of the $ character. All other characters are treated literally, and are used to determine the nmap *INPATTERN* variable values. The *OUTPATTERN* determines the resulting mapped filename. The sequences $1, $2, ..., $9 are replaced by any value resulting from the *INPATTERN* template. The sequence $0 is replaced by the original filename. Also, the sequence [*SEQ1*, *SEQ2*] is replaced by *SEQ1* if *SEQ1* is not a null string; otherwise, it's replaced by *SEQ2*. For example, the command nmap $1.$2.$3 [$1,$2].[$2,file] yields the output filename myfile.data for input filenames myfile.data and myfile.data.old, the output filename myfile.file for the input filename myfile, and the output filename myfile.myfile for the input filename .myfile. Spaces can be included in *OUTPATTERN*. Use the \ character to prevent special treatment of the $, [,], and , characters.

Command	Description
ntrans [*INCHARS* [*OUTCHARS*]]	Sets or unsets the filename character-translation mechanism. If no arguments are specified, the filename character-translation mechanism is unset. If arguments are specified, characters in remote filenames are translated during mput commands and put commands issued without a specified remote target filename. Characters in a filename matching a character in *INCHARS* are replaced with the corresponding characters in *OUTCHARS*. If the character's position in *INCHARS* is longer than the length of *OUTCHARS*, the character is deleted from the filename.
open *HOST* [*PORT*]	Establishes a connection with the *HOST* FTP server at TCP port *PORT* (standard port 21 if not specified).
prompt	Toggles interactive prompting.
proxy *FTP COMMAND*	Executes an ftp command on a secondary control connection. This command allows simultaneous connections to two remote FTP servers for transferring files between two servers. The first proxy should be an open to establish the secondary control connections. The host on the secondary control connection takes the place of the local host when the get, mget, put, mput, and append commands are executed.
put *LOCAL_FILE* [*REMOTE_FILE*]	Stores *LOCAL_FILE* on the remote machine as *REMOTE_FILE*. If *REMOTE_FILE* isn't specified, *LOCAL_FILE* will be used.
pwd	Prints the name of the current working directory on the remote machine.
quit	Synonym for bye.
quote *ARG* ...	The arguments specified are sent verbatim to the remote FTP server.
recv *REMOTE_FILE* [*LOCAL_FILE*]	Synonym for get.
reget *REMOTE_FILE* [*LOCAL_FILE*]	reget acts like get except that, if *LOCAL_FILE* exists and is smaller than *REMOTE_FILE*, *LOCAL_FILE* is presumed to be partially transferred. The transfer is continued from the apparent point of failure. If *LOCAL_FILE* doesn't exist, ftp won't transfer the file. This is useful for transferring large files over unreliable connections.
remotehelp [*COMMAND_NAME*]	Requests help from the remote FTP server.

continues >>

>>*continued*

Command	Description
remotestatus [*FILENAME*]	With no arguments, shows the status of the remote machine. If *FILENAME* is specified, shows the status of the file *FILENAME* on the remote machine.
rename [*FROM_FILE*] [*TO_FILE*]	Renames *FROM_FILE* on the remote server to *TO_FILE* on the remote server.
reset	Clears the reply queue. Re-synchronizes the command/reply sequence with the remote FTP server.
restart *BYTE_COUNT*	Restarts the immediately following get or put at the indicated *BYTE_COUNT*.
rmdir *DIRECTORY*	Removes *DIRECTORY* from the remote server.
runique	Toggles unique-name generation for local files that already exist. By default, get and mget overwrite local files with name conflicts. When runique is on, a suffix is generated for each conflicting file. These suffixes begin with .1 and continue incrementally until a unique name is found or .99 is reached, whichever comes first. If a unique name can't be generated in this way, an error is reported and the transfer is canceled. Generated unique filenames are reported.
send *LOCAL_FILE* [*REMOTE_FILE*]	A synonym for put.
sendport	Toggles the use of the FTP protocol PORT commands.
site *ARG* ...	The arguments are sent, verbatim, to the remote FTP server as a SITE command.
size *FILENAME*	Returns the size of the file *FILENAME* on the remote machine.
status	Shows the current status of ftp.
struct [*STRUCT_NAME*]	Sets the file transfer structure to *STRUCT_NAME*. By default, "stream" structure is used.
sunique	Toggles the storing of remote files under unique names.
system	Shows the type of operating system running on the remote host.
tenex	Sets the file transfer type to that required for TENEX machines.
trace	Toggles packet tracing.
type [*TYPE_NAME*]	Sets the file transfer type to *TYPE_NAME*. If no *TYPE_NAME* is given, the current type is printed. The default type is network ASCII.

Command	Description
umask [NEWMASK]	Sets the default umask on the remote server to UMASK. If NEWMASK is omitted, the current mask is printed.
user USER_NAME [PASSWORD] [ACCOUNT]	Identifies ftp as USER_NAME to the remote host. The PASSWORD and ACCOUNT arguments, if required but not specified, are prompted. This command is executed automatically when the connection to the server is established, unless "auto-login" is disabled.
verbose	Toggles verbose mode. In verbose mode, all responses from the server are displayed along with file-transfer efficiency statistics. Verbose mode is on by default.
? [COMMAND]	A synonym for help.

rcp

rcp [OPTION ...] FILE1 FILE2
rcp [OPTION ...] FILE ... DIRECTORY

rcp copies files between machines. Each file or directory is either a local filename or a remote filename of the form FILE@HOST:PATH.

Option	Description
-k REALM	Obtains tickets for the remote host in realm REALM instead of the remote host's realm as determined by krb_realmofhost.
-p	Preserves or duplicates modification times and modes of source files.
-r	Recursive copy. rcp copies subtrees of any source files that are directories. The destination must be a directory.
-x	Turns on DES encryption for all data transferred.

tftp

tftp [HOST]

tftp is the user interface to the Trivial File Transfer Protocol (TFTP). If HOST is specified, tftp uses it as the default host for transfers. Within tftp, several commands are accepted:

Command	Description
? COMMAND_NAME ...	Prints the help information for COMMAND_NAME.
ascii	Switches the transfer mode to ASCII.
binary	Switches the transfer mode to binary.

continues >>

>>continued

Command	Description
connect *HOST* [*PORT*]	Sets the *HOST* (and optionally *PORT*) for transfers. Note that the TFTP protocol, unlike the FTP protocol, doesn't maintain connections between transfers. Thus, the connect command doesn't actually create a connection, but merely remembers what host is to be used for transfers.
get *FILENAME* or get *REMOTENAME LOCALNAME* or get *FILENAME* ...	Gets a file or set of files from the specified *SOURCE*s. *SOURCE* can be in one of two forms: a filename on the remote host if the host has already been specified, or a string of the form *HOST:FILENAME* to specify both a host and filename at the same time. If the latter form is used, the last hostname specified becomes the default for future transfers.
mode *TRANSFER_MODE*	Sets the transfer mode to *TRANSFER_MODE*, which can be either ascii or binary. The default is ascii.
put *FILE* or put *LOCALFILE REMOTEFILE* or put *FILE* ... *REMOTE_DIRECTORY*	Puts a file or set of files into the specified remote file or directory. The destination can be in one of two forms: a filename on the remote host if the host has already been specified, or a string of the form *HOST:FILENAME* to specify both a host and filename at the same time. If the latter form is used, the hostname specified becomes the default for future transfers.
quit	Exits tftp.
rexmt *RETRANSMISSION_TIMEOUT*	Sets the per-packet retransmission timeout in seconds.
status	Shows the current status.
timeout *TOTAL_TRANSMISSION_TIMEOUT*	Sets the total transmission timeout in seconds.
trace	Toggles packet tracing.
verbose	Toggles verbose mode.

toport

toport [*OPTION* ...] *HOST PORT*

toport sends data to *HOST* at TCP port *PORT*. toport is typically used in conjunction with fromport running on *HOST* and listening on port *PORT*.

Option	Description
-b *BLOCKSIZE*	Sets the size of the I/O buffers. The default is 1024.
-p	Prints the IP address in dotted-decimal notation instead of the hostname.
-t	Prints transfer statistics.
-v	Verbose mode. Useful for debugging.

Remote Command Execution

This section describes commands that execute commands and establish sessions on remote hosts.

rexec

`rexec [ OPTION ... ] HOST COMMAND`

`rexec` executes *COMMAND* on *HOST* using username/password authentication. The username and password can be supplied on the command line, although this isn't recommended due to security implications. Instead, the password should be predefined on the remote host in either the **REXEC_USER** or **REXEC_PASS** environment variable in the $HOME/.netrc file.

Option	Description
-a	By default, `rexec` sets up a separate channel for diagnostic output from the remote command. If -a is specified, the remote standard error and output are both returned on the local standard output.
-b	Use signal handling as in BSD `rsh`. Only the signals **SIGINT**, **SIGQUIT**, and **SIGTERM** are echoed to the remote process and don't remain raised locally. Also, Ctrl+Z only suspends execution locally and the remote command can continue to run.
-c	Don't close the remote standard input when the local standard input closes.
-h	Prints a usage message.
-l *USERNAME*	Sets the login name for the remote host to *USERNAME*.
-p *PASSWORD*	Provides a *PASSWORD* to the remote host.
-s	Don't echo signals received by `rexec` to the remote process.

rlogin

`rlogin [ OPTION ... ] HOST`

`rlogin` starts a terminal session on the remote host *HOST*. `rlogin` first attempts to use Kerberos authorization. If Kerberos isn't supported on the remote host, the Berkeley `rhosts` authorization is used.

Option	Description
-8	Allows 8-bit data input at all times. Otherwise, parity bits are stripped except when the remote side's stop and start characters are other than Ctrl+S/Ctrl+Q.
-d	Turns on socket debugging.
-E	Stops any character from being recognized as an escape character. When used with the -8 option, this provides a completely transparent connection.
-e *C*	Defines *C* as the escape character—a literal character or an octal value in the form *NNN*.
-K	Turns off Kerberos authentication.
-k *REALM*	Obtains tickets from the remote host in *REALM* instead of the remote host's realm as determined by `krb_realmofhost`.
-L	Allows an `rlogin` session to run without any output postprocessing (`litout` mode).
-x	Turns on DES encryption for all data exchange.

rsh

`rsh [ OPTION ... ] HOST [ COMMAND ]`

`rsh` executes *COMMAND* on *HOST*. If *COMMAND* isn't specified, a session is established on *HOST* using `rlogin`.

Option	Description
-d	Turns on socket debugging.
-K	Turns off Kerberos authentication.
-k *REALM*	Obtains tickets from the remote host in *REALM* instead of the remote host's realm as determined by `krb_realmofhost`.
-l *USERNAME*	Executes a command or establishes a session as *USERNAME*. By default, the remote user is the same as the local user.
-n	Redirects input from the /dev/null device. This option is typically used when running `rsh` in the background.
-x	Turns on DES encryption for all data exchange.

rwall

`rwall HOST [ FILE ]`

`rwall` broadcasts the message in *FILE* to all users logged onto *HOST*. If *FILE* isn't specified, the message is read from standard input and terminated with EOF.

talk

`talk PERSON [ TTYNAME ]`

`talk` is an interactive communications program that enables users to type messages to each other. *PERSON* is either a local username or a remote user of the form *USER@HOST*. *TTYNAME* is used to identify the user's terminal if the person is logged in more than once. If user *USERA* executes `talk` *USERB*, user *USERB* must respond with `talk` *USERA* to "answer the call" and complete the connection. An interrupt character can be used to exit the conversation.

telnet

telnet [*OPTIONS* ...] [*HOST* [*PORT*]]

`telnet` enables the user to establish and maintain a session on a remote host using the Telnet protocol. If invoked without options, it enters its command mode. If *HOST* is specified, it performs an **open** command implicitly. The *PORT* argument is used if connection to a nonstandard TCP port is required. The standard port is 23.

Command-Line Options

`telnet` accepts the following options from the command line:

Option	Description
-8	Requests 8-bit operation.
-a	Attempts automatic login. This sends the username via the USER variable of the ENVIRON option if supported by the remote system. The username is retrieved via `getlogin`.
-d	Turns on socket-level debugging.
-E	Disables the escape character.
-e *ESCAPECHAR*	Sets the escape character to *ESCAPECHAR*. Entering the escape character causes `telnet` to drop into command mode.
-L	Specifies 8-bit data path on output.
-l *USER*	Specifies *USER* as the user of the remote session.
-n *TRACEFILE*	Opens *TRACEFILE* for recording trace information.
-r	Emulates `rlogin`.
-S *TOS*	Sets the IP type-of-service (TOS) option for the connection to *TOS*.

Interactive Commands

`telnet` accepts the following commands in interactive mode:

Command	Description
! [*COMMAND*]	Executes a *COMMAND* in a subshell on the local system. If *COMMAND* is omitted, an interactive subshell is invoked.
? [*COMMAND*]	Get help. With no arguments, `telnet` prints a help summary. If *COMMAND* is specified, `telnet` prints the help information just for *COMMAND*.
close	Closes the connection to the remote host (if any) and returns to command mode.
display *ARGUMENT* ...	Displays `set` and `toggle` values.

continues >>

>>continued

Command	Description
environ *ARGUMENT* ...	environ is used to propagate environment variables to the remote session. Valid *ARGUMENT*s are as follows: define *VARIABLE VALUE* sets *VARIABLE* to *VALUE*. undefine *VARIABLE* removes the definition of *VARIABLE*. export *VARIABLE* marks *VARIABLE* for export to the remote host. unexport *VARIABLE* indicates not to mark *VARIABLE* for propagation to the remote host. The remote host can still ask explicitly for variables that aren't exported. list lists the current set of environment variables. ? prints help information on the environ command.
logout	Sends the TELNET LOGOUT protocol option to the remote host. If the remote host supports the LOGOUT option, this closes the connection.
mode *TYPE*	telnet asks the remote host to go into the requested mode. Valid options for *TYPE*, depending on the state of the session, are as follows: character disables the TELNET LINEMODE option. If the remote side doesn't understand the LINEMODE option, this enters "character at a time" mode. line enables the TELNET LINEMODE option, or, if the remote side doesn't understand the LINEMODE option, attempts to enter "line-by-line" mode. isig or -isig attempts to enable or disable the TRAPSIG mode of the LINEMODE option. This requires that the LINEMODE option be enabled. edit or -edit attempts to enable or disable the EDIT mode of the LINEMODE option. This requires that the LINEMODE option be enabled. softtabs or -softtabs attempts to enable or disable the SOFT_TAB mode of the LINEMODE option. This requires that the LINEMODE option be enabled. litecho or -litecho attempts to enable or disable the LIT_ECHO mode of the LINEMODE option. This requires that the LINEMODE option be enabled. ? prints help information for the mode command.

Command	Description
open *HOST* [[-l] *USER*] [[-]*PORT*]	Opens a connection to the named *HOST*. If no port number is specified, `telnet` uses the standard port (23). The host specification can be a hostname or IP address. The -l option can be used to specify a username to be passed to the remote system. When connecting to ports other than the standard port, `telnet` doesn't attempt Telnet protocol negotiations. The optional hyphen (-) before the port number forces Telnet protocol negotiations. After establishing a connection, any commands associated with the remote host in the user's `.telnetrc` file are executed. The format of the `.telnetrc` file is as follows: Blank lines and lines beginning with # are ignored. The rest of the file should consist of hostnames and sequences of `telnet` commands to use with that host. Commands should be one per line, indented by whitespace; lines beginning without whitespace are interpreted as hostnames. On connecting to a particular host, the commands associated with that host are executed.
quit	Closes any open sessions and exits `telnet`.
send *ARGUMENT* ...	Sends one or more special `telnet` protocol character sequences to the remote host. The following are valid codes for *ARGUMENT*:
	abort sends the TELNET ABORT (Abort Processes) sequence.
	ao sends the TELNET AO (Abort Output) sequence, which should cause the remote system to flush all output from the remote system to the user's terminal.
	ayt sends the TELNET AYT (Are You There?) sequence. The remote system may or may not choose to respond.
	brk sends the TELNET BRK (Break) sequence, which may have significance to the remote system.
	ec sends the TELNET EC (Erase Character) sequence, which should cause the remote system to erase the last character entered.
	el sends the TELNET EL (Erase Line) sequence, which should cause the remote system to erase the line currently being entered.
	eof sends the TELNET EOF (End of File) sequence.
	eor sends the TELNET EOR (End of Record) sequence.
	escape sends the current `telnet` escape character.

continues >>

>>*continued*

Command	Description
	ga sends the TELNET GA (Go Ahead) sequence, which probably has no significance to the remote system.
	getstatus sends the subnegotiation to request that the server send its current option status, if the remote side supports the TELNET STATUS command.
	ip sends the TELNET IP (Interrupt Process) sequence, which should cause the remote system to abort the currently running process.
	nop sends the TELNET NOP (No Operation) sequence.
	susp sends the TELNET SUSP (Suspend Process) sequence.
	synch sends the TELNET SYNCH sequence. This sequence causes the remote system to discard all previously typed (but not yet read) input. This sequence is sent as TCP urgent data.
	do *CMD*, dont *CMD*, will *CMD*, or wont *CMD* sends the TELNET DO *CMD* sequence. *CMD* can be either a decimal number between 0 and 255 or a symbolic name for a specific Telnet command. *CMD* can also be either help or ? to print out help information, including a list of known symbolic names.
	? prints help information for the send command.
set *ARGUMENT VALUE* or unset *ARGUMENT VALUE*	The set command sets any one of a number of telnet variables to a specific value or to TRUE. The special value off turns off the function associated with the variable. This is equivalent to using the unset command. The unset command disables or sets to FALSE any of the specified variables. The values of variables can be interrogated with the display command. The variables—which can be set or unset but not toggled—are listed here. In addition, any of the variables for the toggle command can be explicitly set or unset:
	ayt If telnet is in localchars mode or LINEMODE is enabled and the status character is typed, a TELNET AYT sequence is sent to the remote host. The initial value for the "Are You There" character is the terminal's status character.
	echo This is the value (initially Ctrl+E) that, when in "line by line" mode, toggles between doing local echoing of entered characters (for normal processing), and suppressing echoing of entered characters (for entering a password, for example).

Command	Description
	eof If telnet is operating in LINEMODE or "line-by-line" mode, entering this character as the first character on a line causes this character to be sent to the remote system. The initial value of the eof character is taken to be the terminal's eof character.
	erase If telnet is in localchars mode (see toggle) and operating in "character at a time" mode, when this character is typed a TELNET EC sequence (see send) is sent to the remote system. The initial value for the erase character is taken to be the terminal's erase character.
	escape This is the telnet escape character (initially Ctrl+[) that causes entry into telnet command mode (when connected to a remote system).
	flushoutput If telnet is in localchars mode (see toggle) and the flushoutput character is typed, a TELNET AO sequence (see send) is sent to the remote host. The initial value for the flush character is taken to be the terminal's flush character.
	fors1 or forw2 If telnet is operating in LINEMODE, these are the characters that, when typed, cause partial lines to be forwarded to the remote system. The initial value for the forwarding characters are taken from the terminal's eol and eol2 characters.
	interrupt If telnet is in localchars mode (see toggle) and the interrupt character is typed, a TELNET IP sequence (see send) is sent to the remote host. The initial value for the interrupt character is taken to be the terminal's intr character.
	kill If telnet is in localchars mode (see toggle) and operating in "character at a time" mode, when this character is typed a TELNET EL sequence (see send) is sent to the remote system. The initial value for the kill character is taken to be the terminal's kill character.
	lnext If telnet is operating in LINEMODE or "line-by-line" mode, this character is taken to be the terminal's lnext character. The initial value for the lnext character is taken to be the terminal's lnext character.
	quit If telnet is in localchars mode (see toggle) and the quit character is typed, a TELNET BRK sequence (see send) is sent to the remote host. The initial value for the quit character is taken to be the terminal's quit character.

continues >>

>>*continued*

Command	Description
	reprint If telnet is operating in LINEMODE or "line-by-line" mode, this character is taken to be the terminal's reprint character. The initial value for the reprint character is taken to be the terminal's reprint character.
	rlogin This is the rlogin mode escape character. Setting it enables rlogin mode, as with the -r command-line option.
	start If the TELNET TOGGLE-FLOW-CONTROL option has been enabled, this character is taken to be the terminal's start character. The initial value for the start character is taken to be the terminal's start character.
	stop If the TELNET TOGGLE-FLOW-CONTROL option has been enabled, this character is taken to be the terminal's stop character. The initial value for the stop character is taken to be the terminal's stop character.
	tracefile This is the file to which the output will be written if netdata or option tracing is TRUE. If it's set to -, tracing information will be written to standard output (the default).
	worderase If telnet is operating in LINEMODE or "line-by-line" mode, this character is taken to be the terminal's worderase character. The initial value for the worderase character is taken to be the terminal's worderase character.
	? Displays the set of legal set or unset commands.
slc *STATE*	Set Local Characters. Used to set or change the state of the special characters when the TELNET LINEMODE option has been enabled. Special characters are characters that get mapped to TELNET command sequences (such as ip or quit) or line-editing characters (such as erase or kill). The local special characters are exported by default. The following are valid values for *STATE*:
	check Verifies the current settings for the current special characters. The remote side is requested to send all the current special-character settings. If there are any discrepancies with the local side, the local side switches to the remote values.
	export Switches to the local defaults for the special characters. The local default characters are the local terminal characters at the time when telnet was started.

Command	Description
	import Switches to the remote defaults for the special characters. The remote default characters are those of the remote system at the time when the Telnet connection was established.
	? Prints help for the slc command.
status	Shows the status of the telnet process. This includes the name of the remote host, if any, as well as the current mode.
toggle FLAG ...	Toggles between TRUE and FALSE the various flags that control how telnet responds to events. These flags can also be set explicitly to TRUE or FALSE by using the set and unset commands. More than one flag can be toggled at once. The state of these flags can be examined with the display command. Valid values for FLAG are as follows:
	? displays the legal toggle commands.
	autoflush If autoflush and localchars are both TRUE, when the ao or quit characters are recognized and transformed into Telnet sequences, telnet refuses to display any data on the user's terminal until the remote system acknowledges (via a TELNET TIMING MARK option) that it has processed those Telnet sequences. The initial value for this toggle is TRUE if the terminal user had not done an stty noflsh; otherwise FALSE (see the stty command in Chapter 1, "Shell Utilities").
	autosync If autosync and localchars are both TRUE, when either the intr or quit characters are typed the resulting telnet sequence sent is followed by the TELNET SYNCH sequence. This procedure should cause the remote system to begin throwing away all previously typed input until both of the telnet sequences have been read and acted on. This toggle is initially set to FALSE.
	binary Enables or disables the TELNET BINARY option for both input and output.
	crlf If this is TRUE, carriage returns will be sent as <CR><LF>. If this is FALSE, carriage returns will be sent as <CR><NUL>. The toggle is initially set to FALSE.

continues >>

>>continued

Command	Description
	`crmod` Toggles carriage return mode. When this mode is enabled, most carriage return characters received from the remote host are mapped into a carriage return followed by a linefeed. This mode doesn't affect those characters typed by the user—only those received from the remote host. This mode is only useful if the remote host sends carriage returns without linefeeds. The initial value for this toggle is `FALSE`.
	`debug` Toggles socket-level debugging. This toggle is initially set to `FALSE`.
	`localchars` If this is `TRUE`, the `flush`, `interrupt`, `quit`, `erase`, and `kill` characters are recognized locally and transformed into the appropriate TELNET control sequences (`ao`, `ip`, `brk`, `ec`, and `el`, respectively). The initial value for this toggle is `TRUE` in "line-by-line" mode and `FALSE` in "character at a time" mode. When the `LINEMODE` option is enabled, the value of `localchars` is ignored, and assumed to always be `TRUE`. If `LINEMODE` has ever been enabled, `quit` is sent as `abort` and `eof` is sent as `eof` and `susp`.
	`inbinary` Enables or disables the TELNET `BINARY` option for input.
	`netdata` Toggles the display of all network data (in hexadecimal format). The initial value for this toggle is `FALSE`.
	`options` Toggles the display of some internal telnet protocol processing. The initial value for this toggle is `FALSE`.
	`prettydump` When the `netdata` toggle is enabled, if `prettydump` is enabled the output from the `netdata` command is formatted in a more user-readable format. Spaces separate characters in the output, and the beginnings of TELNET escape sequences are preceded by * to aid in locating them.
	`outbinary` Enables or disables the TELNET `BINARY` option for output.
	`skiprc` When the `skiprc` toggle is `TRUE`, the `.telnetrc` file isn't processed. The initial value for this toggle is `FALSE`.
	`termdata` Toggles the display of all terminal data (in hexadecimal format). The initial value for this toggle is `FALSE`.
z	Suspends `telnet`.

6

bash

bash is one of several shells (command interpreters) available for use with Linux distributions. Typical distributions include several shells, but bash is generally designated as the default. The name is an acronym for "Bourne-Again SHell," a pun on the name of Steve Bourne. Steve Bourne was the author of the shell sh, which was the standard UNIX shell.

bash is fully compatible with sh and also offers many extensions, including useful features from the Korn shell ksh and the C shell csh. It's ultimately intended to be a conformant implementation of the IEEE POSIX Shell and Tools specification (IEEE Working Group 1003.2).

Invoking bash

```
bash [LONG_OPT] [-ir] [-abefhkmnptuvxdBCDHP] [-o OPTION] [ARGUMENT ...]
bash [LONG_OPT] [-abefhkmnptuvxdBCDHP] [-o OPTION] -c STRING [ARGUMENT ...]
bash [LONG_OPT] -s [-abefhkmnptuvxdBCDHP] [-o OPTION] [ARGUMENT ...]
```

The single letter options (-a, -b, and so on) and the -o OPTION are the same as the options enabled using the set built-in command. The following table describes the other command-line options for bash.

Option	Description
-c STRING	Reads and executes commands from STRING after processing the options, and then exits. Any remaining arguments are assigned to the positional parameters, starting with $0.
-D	A list of all double-quoted strings preceded by $ is printed on the standard output. This implies the -n option. No commands are executed.
--dump-strings	Equivalent to -D.
--help	Displays a usage message on standard output and exits successfully.
-i	Forces the shell to run interactively.

continues >>

>>continued

Option	Description
`--login`	Makes this shell act as if it were directly invoked by login. This is equivalent to `exec -l bash` but can be issued from another shell. If you want to replace your current login shell with a `bash` login shell, you would use `exec bash --login`.
`--noediting`	Don't use the GNU `readline` library to read interactive command lines.
`--noprofile`	Don't load the system-wide startup file `/etc/profile` or any of the personal initialization files `~/.bash_profile`, `~/.bash_login`, or `~/.profile` when `bash` is invoked as a login shell.
`--norc`	Don't read the `~/.bashrc` initialization file in an interactive shell. This is on by default if the shell is invoked as `sh`.
`--posix`	Changes the behavior of `bash` to match the POSIX 1003.2 standard whenever the default operation differs from this standard. This is intended to make `bash` behave as a strict superset of that standard.
`-r` or `--restricted`	Makes the shell a restricted shell.
`--rcfile FILENAME`	Executes initialization commands from `FILENAME` (instead of `~/.bashrc`) in an interactive shell.
`-s`	If this flag is present or if no arguments remain after option processing, commands are read from the standard input. This option allows the positional parameters to be set when invoking an interactive shell.
`--verbose`	Equivalent to `-v`.
`--version`	Shows version information for the currently running `bash` on the standard output and exits successfully.

If arguments remain after option processing and neither the `-c` nor the `-s` option has been supplied, the first argument is assumed to be the name of a file containing shell commands. When `bash` is invoked in this fashion, `$0` is set to the name of the file, and the positional parameters are set to the remaining arguments. `bash` reads and executes commands from this file and exits. `bash`'s exit status is the exit status of the last command executed in the script. If no commands are executed, the exit status is `0`.

Basic Commands

This section describes commands that every `bash` user needs to know.

cd

```
cd [ -PL ] [ DIR ]
```

`cd` changes the current working directory to `DIR`. The variable `HOME` is the default `DIR`. The variable `CDPATH` defines the search path for the directory containing `DIR`. Alternate directory names in `CDPATH` are separated by colons (:). A null directory name is the same as the current directory (.). If the *DIR* isn't found and the shell option cdable_vars is set, bash will try to use *DIR* as a variable name. If that variable has a value, the value of that variable will become the new current working directory.

Option	Description
-P	Uses the physical directory structure instead of following symbolic links.
-L	Follows symbolic links.

exit

```
exit [ N ]
```

exit exits the shell with status *N*. If *N* is omitted, the exit status is that of the last command executed.

help

```
help [ PATTERN ... ]
```

help displays helpful information about built-in commands. If *PATTERN* is specified, help gives detailed help on all commands matching *PATTERN*; otherwise, it prints a list of the built-ins.

logout

```
logout
```

logout logs out from a login shell.

pwd

```
pwd [ -PL ]
```

pwd prints the current working directory. With the -P option, pwd prints the physical directory, without any symbolic links. The -L option makes pwd follow symbolic links.

time

```
time [-p] PIPELINE
```

time executes a *PIPELINE* (any number of commands using pipes and/or I/O redirection) and prints a summary of the real time, user CPU time, and system CPU time spent executing *PIPELINE* when it terminates. The -p option causes time to print the timing summary format according to the TIMEFORMAT variable.

times

```
times
```

times prints the cumulative user and system times for processes run from the current shell.

type

```
type [ -all ] [ -type ¦ -path] [ NAME ... ]
```

For each *NAME*, type indicates how it would be interpreted if used as a command name (shell built-in, executable, and so on).

Option	Description
-all	Shows all places where *NAME* can be found. This includes aliases and functions if and only if the -path flag is not also used.
-path	Returns the name of the disk file that would be executed, or does nothing if -type would not return file.
-type	Returns the single word alias, function, builtin, file, or keyword, if *NAME* is an alias, shell function, shell built-in, disk file, or shell reserved word, respectively. If *NAME* isn't found, nothing prints, and type returns a failure status.

Variables for bash

This is the most basic form of variable reference:

$NAME

The following table shows other forms of variable references.

Expression	Description
${NAME:-WORD}	Returns *NAME* if it's defined. Otherwise, returns *WORD*.
${NAME:=WORD}	Returns *NAME* if it's defined and isn't null. Otherwise, returns *WORD*.
${NAME:?MESSAGE}	Returns *NAME* if it's defined and isn't null. Otherwise, prints *NAME* followed by *MESSAGE* and aborts the current command or script.
${NAME:+WORD}	If *NAME* exists and isn't null, returns *WORD*. Otherwise, returns null.
${NAME#PATTERN}	If *PATTERN* matches the beginning of *NAME*'s value, deletes the shortest part that matches and returns.
${NAME##PATTERN}	If *PATTERN* matches the beginning of *NAME*'s value, deletes the longest part that matches and returns the rest.
${NAME%PATTERN}	If *PATTERN* matches the end of *NAME*'s value, deletes the shortest part that matches and returns.
${NAME%%PATTERN}	If *PATTERN* matches the end of *NAME*'s value, deletes the longest part that matches and returns the rest.

When a **bash** script is run, a set of variables represent the arguments that were given on the command line:

Variable	Description
0	This variable holds the name by which the script was invoked.
#	This variable holds the number of arguments that were passed.
N	This variable holds the value of the *N*th argument.

Variable	Description
*	This is a single-character string that consists of all the positional parameters, separated by the first character in the environment variable IFS.
@	This is a single-character string consisting of N separate double-quoted strings "$1" "$2" ... "$N", where N is the number of positional parameters.

For example, this script prints the number of arguments passed to it followed by the their values, each on a separate line ($@ is assumed in the for statement):

```
echo $# arguments:
for i do echo $i; done
```

Special Characters for bash

Some characters have special meanings in bash. The following table lists these characters and describes how bash interprets them.

Character	Description
~	The user's home directory.
`	Command substitution. `COMMAND` is treated as an expression, with standard output from COMMAND as the expression's value.
#	The text after # is ignored and treated as a comment.
$	Variable substitution. The value of the expression $NAME is the value of the environment variable NAME. The value is null if NAME is undefined.
&	COMMAND & runs COMMAND in the background.
*	Filename expansion wildcard. See Appendix A, "Regular Expressions."
(and)	Begin and end a subshell. The text between (and) is executed as a script under a separate bash process.
\	Quote the next character. Useful if the next character is a special character but needs to be interpreted literally. Also used as a line-continuation character: \ at the end of a line causes bash to interpret the following line as part of the same command.
|	Pipe. COMMAND1 | COMMAND2 takes standard output from COMMAND1 and passes it as standard input to COMMAND2.
[and]	Begin and end a character set. See Appendix A.
{ and }	Begin and end a command block. The text between { and } is executed as a nameless function.
;	Command separator. Useful for entering two or more commands on one line.
'	Strong quote. Text between two ' characters is treated as a literal string.
"	Weak quote. Same as a strong quote except that parameter substitution, command substitution, and arithmetic expression evaluation are carried out.
<	Input redirection. COMMAND < FILE executes COMMAND with standard input coming from FILE.

continues >>

>>continued

Character	Description
>	Output redirection. *COMMAND* > *FILE* executes *COMMAND* with standard output written to *FILE*.
/	Used to separate directory components from pathnames.

Command History and Editing

The history mechanism in **bash** can save users time by enabling them to recall and edit previously issued commands and command sequences.

bind

```
bind [-m KEYMAP] [-lpsvPSV] [-q NAME] [-r KEYSEQ]
bind [-m KEYMAP] -f FILENAME
bind [-m KEYMAP] KEYSEQ:FUNCTION-NAME
```

bind displays current **readline** key and function bindings, or binds a key sequence to a **readline** function or macro.

Option	Description
-m *KEYMAP*	Use *KEYMAP* as the keymap to be affected by the subsequent bindings. Acceptable *KEYMAP* names are emacs, emacs-standard, emacs-meta, emacs-ctlx, vi, vi-command, and vi-insert. vi is equivalent to vi-command; emacs is equivalent to emacs-standard.
-l	Lists the names of all **readline** functions.
-p	Displays **readline** function names and bindings in such a way that they can be reread.
-P	Lists current **readline** function names and bindings.
-v	Displays **readline** variable names and values in such a way that they can be reread.
-V	Lists current **readline** variable names and values.
-s	Displays **readline** key sequences bound to macros and the strings they output in such a way that they can be reread.
-S	Displays **readline** key sequences bound to macros and the strings they output.
-f *FILENAME*	Reads key bindings from *FILENAME*.
-q *NAME*	Queries which keys invoke the function *NAME*.
-r *KEYSEQ*	Removes any current binding for *KEYSEQ*.

fc

```
fc [-e ENAME] [-nlr] [FIRST] [LAST]
fc -s [OLD=NEW] [COMMAND]
```

fc recalls, edits, and re-executes a group of commands. With the first form, *FIRST* and *LAST* can be numbers specifying the range, or *FIRST* can be a string, which means the most recent command beginning with that string. With the second format, *COMMAND* is re-executed after the substitution *OLD=NEW* is performed.

Option	Description
-e *ENAME*	*ENAME* selects which editor to use. The default is FCEDIT, then EDITOR, then the editor that corresponds to the current readline editing mode, and finally vi.
-l	Lists lines instead of editing.
-n	No line numbers are listed.
-r	Reverses the order of the lines.

history

```
history [-c] [N]
history -awrn [FILENAME]
history -ps ARG [ARG ...]
```

history displays the history list with line numbers. Lines listed with * have been modified. When *N* is given, history lists only the last *N* lines. If *FILENAME* is given, that file is used as the history file unless the HISTFILE environment variable has a value. If HISTFILE has a value, that value is used as the name of the history file. If neither of the above is true, ~/.bash_history is used as the history file.

Option	Description
-a	Appends history lines from this session to the history file.
-c	Clears the history list.
-n	Reads all history lines not already read from the history file and appends them to the history list.
-p	Performs history expansion on each *ARG* and displays the result, without storing anything in the history list.
-r	Reads the file and appends the contents to the history list.
-s	Appends the non-option *ARG*s to the history list as a single entry.
-w	Writes out the current history to the history file.

Environment Control

This section describes commands used to alter the working context within bash.

alias

```
alias [-p] [ NAME[=VALUE] ... ]
```

Without arguments or with the -p option, alias prints the list of aliases on the standard output in a form that allows them to be reused as input. If arguments are supplied, an alias is defined for each *NAME* whose *VALUE* is given. If no *VALUE* is given, the name and value of the alias are printed.

export

```
export [-fn] [-p] [ NAME[=VALUE] ... ]
```

export marks each *NAME* to be passed to child processes in the environment and optionally sets the value of *NAME* to *VALUE*.

Option	Description
-f	*NAME*s refer to shell functions.
-n	*NAME* can no longer be exported.
-p	If -p is given or no *NAMES* are given, prints a list of exported names.

set

```
set [-abefhkmnptuvxBCHP] [-o OPTION] [ ARGUMENT ... ]
```

set provides general environment control. Using + rather than - causes flags to be turned off. The flags can also be used on invocation of the shell. The current set of flags can be found in $-.

Option	Description
-a	Marks variables that are modified or created for export.
-b	Causes the status of terminated background jobs to be reported immediately, rather than before printing the next primary prompt.
-e	Exits immediately if a simple command exits with a nonzero status.
-f	Disables filename generation (globbing).
-h	Locates and remembers (hash) commands as they're looked up for execution.
-k	All arguments in the form of assignment statements are placed in the environment for a command, not just those that precede the command name.
-m	Enables job control.
-n	Reads commands but doesn't execute them.
-o OPTION	Sets the flag corresponding to *OPTION*. Valid values for *OPTION* are as follows: allexport Same as -a. braceexpand Same as -B. emacs Uses emacs–style line editing. errexit Same as -e. hashall Same as -h. histexpand Same as -H. history Enables command history. ignoreeof The shell won't exit upon reading EOF.

Option	Description
	keyword Same as -k.
	monitor Same as -m.
	noclobber Same as -C.
	noexec Same as -n.
	noglob Same as -f.
	notify Same as -b.
	nounset Same as -u.
	onecmd Same as -t.
	physical Same as -P.
	posix Changes the behavior of **bash** to match the POSIX 1003.2 standard when the default operation differs from the standard. This is intended to make **bash** behave as a strict superset of that standard.
	privileged Same as -p.
	verbose Same as -v.
	vi Uses a vi-style line-editing interface.
	xtrace Same as -x.
-p	Turns on privileged mode. In this mode, the **BASH_ENV** file is not processed, and shell functions are not inherited from the environment. This is enabled automatically on startup if the effective user (group) ID isn't equal to the real user (group) ID. Turning this option off causes the effective user and group IDs to be set to the real user and group IDs.
-t	Exits after reading and executing one command.
-u	Treats unset variables as errors when substituting.
-v	Prints shell input lines as they're read.
-x	Prints commands and their arguments as they're executed.
-B	The shell performs brace expansion.
-C	Disallows output redirection to existing files.
-H	Enables !-style history substitution. This flag is on by default for interactive shells.
-P	If set, don't follow symbolic links when performing commands such as cd that change the current directory.
--	If no arguments follow this flag, the positional parameters are unset. Otherwise, the positional parameters are set to the *ARGUMENTs*, even if some begin with -.
-	Signals the end of options, causing all remaining *ARGUMENTs* to be assigned to the positional parameters. The -x and -v options are turned off. If there are no arguments, the positional parameters remain unchanged.

shopt

shopt [-pqsu] [-o] [*OPTNAME* ...]

shopt toggles the values of variables controlling optional shell behavior. With no options or with the -p option, a list of all settable options is displayed, with an indication of whether each option is set. Other options have the following meanings:

Option	Description
-o	Restricts the values of *OPTNAME* to those defined for the -o option to the **set** built-in.
-p *PROMPT*	Displays *PROMPT*, without a trailing newline, before attempting to read any input. The prompt is displayed only if input is coming from a terminal.
-q	Suppresses normal output. The return status indicates whether the *OPTNAME* is set or unset. If multiple *OPTNAME* arguments are given with -q, the return status is zero if all *OPTNAME*s are enabled and nonzero otherwise.
-s	Enables (sets) each *OPTNAME*.
-u	Disables (unsets) each *OPTNAME*.

The following table shows a list of **shopt** options.

Option	Description
cdable_vars	If set, an argument to the **cd** built-in command that isn't a directory is assumed to be the name of a variable. The value of that variable becomes the current working directory.
cdspell	If set, minor errors in the spelling of a directory component in a **cd** command are corrected.
checkhash	If set, checks that a command found in the hash table exists before trying to execute it.
checkwinsize	If set, checks the window size after each command and, if necessary, updates the values of **LINES** and **COLUMNS**.
cmdhist	If set, attempts to save all lines of a multiple-line command in the same history entry.
dotglob	If set, includes filenames beginning with . (period) in the results of the filename expansion.
execfail	If set, a non-interactive shell won't exit if it can't execute the file specified as an argument to the **exec** built-in command.
histappend	If set, the history list is appended to the file named by the value of the **HISTFILE** variable when the shell exits, rather than overwriting the file.
histreedit	If set, and **readline** is being used, a user is given the opportunity to re-edit a failed history substitution.
histverify	If set, and **readline** is being used, the results of history substitution aren't passed immediately to the shell parser. Instead, the resulting line is loaded into the **readline** editing buffer, allowing further modification.
hostcomplete	If set, and **readline** is being used, attempts to perform hostname completion when a word beginning with @ is being completed.

GEORGE MASON UNIVERSITY FAIRFAX CAMPUS

2080 CASH-1   3085 0366 003

978073570852 TRADE
Linux Essential Re   MDS 1   24.95
            SUBTOTAL   24.95
    4.5% SALES TAX   1.12
              TOTAL   26.07

  Cash   26.07
All textbook sales are final

                    3/22/00 7:24 PM

price. Cash back on merchandise credits will not exceed $10. All merchandise must be in original condition. Exceptions: Custom course materials, outlines, study guides, magazines and prepaid phone cards. Software must be unopened for exchange or refund. Open software may be exchanged for the identical item only.

How to get a refund.

We will be happy to issue a textbook refund for books returned with a valid receipt within the first two weeks of classes (or the first week of summer terms).

- Special course sessions may have unique refund time frames; please see the Store Manager for details.
- Outside this time frame, a signed add/drop slip is required in addition to the valid receipt.
- Textbooks must be in original condition.
- Refunds will be given in original form of payment.

We are sorry that we cannot issue textbook refunds without a valid bookstore receipt.

All merchandise other than textbooks may be refunded anytime with a valid receipt. Without a receipt, a merchandise credit will be issued at the current selling price. Cash back on merchandise credits will not exceed $10. All merchandise must be in original condition.

Option	Description
interactive_comments	Allows a word beginning with # to cause that word and all remaining characters on that line to be ignored in an interactive shell.
lithist	If enabled, and the cmdhist option is enabled, multiline commands are saved to the history with embedded newlines rather than using semicolon separators (where possible).
mailwarn	If set, and a file that bash is checking for mail has been accessed since the last time it was checked, displays the message The mail in MAILFILE has been read.
nullglob	If set, bash allows filename patterns that match no files to expand to a null string, rather than themselves.
promptvars	If set, prompt strings undergo variable and parameter expansion after being expanded.
shift_verbose	If set, the shift built-in prints an error message when the shift count exceeds the number of positional parameters.
sourcepath	If set, the source built-in uses the value of PATH to find the directory containing the file supplied as an argument.

ulimit

ulimit [-acdflmnpstuvSH] [*LIMIT*]

ulimit provides control over the resources available to processes started by the shell. If *LIMIT* is given, it's the new value of the specified resource. Otherwise, ulimit prints the current value of the soft limit for the specified resource, unless the -H option is supplied. Options are interpreted as follows:

Option	Description
-a	Reports all current limits.
-c	Maximum size of core files created.
-d	Maximum size of a process's data segment.
-f	Maximum size of files created by the shell.
-H	Hard limit associated with a resource.
-l	Maximum size that can be locked into memory.
-m	Maximum resident set size.
-n	Maximum number of open file descriptors.
-p	Pipe buffer size. Prints the number of blocks where each block is 512 bytes. This variable can't be changed.
-S	Soft limit associated with a resource.
-s	Maximum stack size.
-t	Maximum amount of CPU time in seconds.
-u	Maximum number of processes available to a single user.
-v	Maximum amount of virtual memory available to the process.

umask

umask [-S] [*MODE*]

umask sets the shell process's file-creation mask to *MODE*. If *MODE* begins with a digit, it's interpreted as an octal number. If not, it's interpreted as a symbolic mode mask similar to that accepted by the chmod command. If *MODE* is omitted, umask prints the current value of the mask. If the -S option is supplied without a *MODE* argument, the mask is printed in a symbolic format.

unalias

unalias [-a] [*NAME* ...]

unalias removes each *NAME* from the list of aliases. If -a is supplied, unalias removes all aliases.

unset

unset [-fv] [*NAME*]

With unset, each variable or function *NAME* becomes undefined. If no options are supplied or the -v option is given, each *NAME* refers to a shell variable. If the -f option is given, the *NAME*s refer to shell functions, and the function definition is removed. Read-only variables and functions can't be unset.

bash Programming

bash has built-in commands that support the automation of complex command sequences. This section describes these commands.

. (period)

. *FILENAME*

Same as source *FILENAME*.

[(bracket)

[*ARG* ...]

Evaluates the set of *ARG*s as a conditional expression. For example, the following script checks for the existence of the file given as the first argument:

```
if [ -e $1 ]; then
  echo $1 exists;
fi
```

break

break [*N*]

break exits from the current for, while, until, or select loop. If *N* is supplied, break exits *N* levels up.

builtin

```
builtin [ COMMAND [ ARGS ] ]
```

builtin runs *COMMAND* as a built-in shell command. This is used if *COMMAND* is currently user-defined.

case

```
case WORD in [ PATTERN_LIST ) COMMANDS ;; ] ... esac
```

case executes *COMMANDS* if *WORD* is matched by *PATTERN_LIST*, where *PATTERN_LIST* is a list of one or more patterns separated by vertical bars (¦). Note that the double semicolon (;;) is used to separate each execution branch from the next. See Appendix A for more information on patterns.

For example, this script fragment:

```
case $1 in
  horse ¦ dog ¦ cat) echo -n "four";;
  man ¦ kangaroo ) echo -n "two";;
  ant ¦ beetle ) echo -n "six";;
  spider ) echo -n "eight";;
  *) echo -n "an unknown number of";;
esac
echo " legs."
```

will output this:

```
The man has two legs
```

when invoked this way:

```
script man
```

Note that $1 is bound to the first script argument and that the -n echo switch is used to suppress the carriage returns.

continue

```
continue [ N ]
```

continue resumes the next iteration of an enclosing for, while, until, or select loop. If *N* is supplied, the execution of the *N*th enclosing loop is resumed.

declare

```
declare [ OPTION ... ] [ NAME[=VALUE] ] ...
```

declare declares variables and gives them attributes. If no *NAME*s are given, declare displays the values of variables instead.

Option	Description
a	Each *NAME* is an array variable.
-f or -F	Prints function declarations only.
-i	The variable is to be treated as an integer. Arithmetic evaluation is performed when the variable is assigned a value.
-r	Makes each *NAME* read-only.
-x	Exports each *NAME*.

dirs

dirs [*OPTION* ...]

dirs displays directories currently on the directory stack.

Option	Description
+*N*	Displays the *N*th directory (counting from the left of the list printed by dirs when invoked without options), starting with zero.
-*N*	Displays the *N*th directory (counting from the right of the list printed by dirs when invoked without options), starting with zero.
-c	Clears the directory stack.
-l	Produces a listing of full names. The default listing format uses ˜ (tilde) to denote the home directory.
-p	Prints the directory stack with one entry per line.
-v	Prints the directory stack with one entry per line and includes each entry's index in the stack.

echo

echo [*OPTION* ..] [*ARG* ..]

echo outputs the *ARG*s separated by a space and terminated with a newline.

Option	Description
-E	Disables the interpretation of escape characters.
-e	Interprets backslash-escaped characters as in the echo shell utility. See the "echo" section in Chapter 1, "Shell Utilities."
-n	Suppresses the trailing newline character.

enable

enable [-n] [-p] [-f *FILENAME*] [-ads] [*NAME* ...]

enable enables or disables built-in shell commands.

Option	Description
-a	Lists each built-in with an indication of whether or not it's enabled.
-d	Deletes a built-in loaded with -f.
-f *FILENAME*	Loads the new built-in command *NAME* from the shared object *FILENAME*.
-n	Disables *NAME*s. Otherwise, *NAME*s are enabled. If no *NAME*s are given, the names of disabled built-ins are printed.
-p	With -p or with no *NAME* arguments, a list of shell built-ins is printed. With no other arguments, the list consists of all enabled shell built-ins.
-s	If used with -f, the new built-in becomes a special built-in. Restricts enable to POSIX.2 special built-ins.

eval

```
eval [ ARG ... ]
```

With eval, ARGs are concatenated together and then executed as a single command.

exec

```
exec [ -cl ] [ -a NAME ] [ COMMAND ] [ ARG ... ]
```

exec executes COMMAND, replacing the current shell with the specified program. If COMMAND isn't specified, the redirections take effect in this shell.

Option	Description
-a NAME	The shell passes NAME the zero[th] argument to COMMAND.
-c	COMMAND is executed with an empty environment.
-l	The shell places a hyphen in the zero[th] ARG passed to COMMAND. This is what the login program does.

false

```
false
```

false returns an unsuccessful result.

for

```
for NAME [in WORDLIST ]; do COMMANDS; done
```

for executes COMMANDS for each element of WORDLIST. For each iteration, NAME takes on the value of the current element of WORDLIST.

For example, this for loop prints the line counts of all the files with a .txt extension in the current working directory:

```
for name in *.txt; do
  wc -l < $name;
done
```

function

```
[ function ] NAME () { COMMAND-LIST; }
```

This construct defines a shell function named NAME. Within the body of the function, the variable # is the number of arguments passed. The 0 parameter is unchanged but the other parameters are named after their positions.

For example:

```
function myfunc () {
  echo I was passed $# parameters.
  echo My first parameter was $1
}

echo Before myfunc
myfunc 1 2 3
echo After myfunc'
```

This fragment produces the following output:

```
Before myfunc
I was passed 3 parameters.
My first parameter was 1
After myfunc
```

getopts

getopts *OPTSTRING NAME [ARGS]*

getopts is used by shell scripts to parse positional parameters.

OPTSTRING contains the option letters to be recognized. If a letter is followed by a colon, the option is expected to have an argument that should be separated from it by whitespace. Each time it's invoked, the next option is placed in the shell variable NAME, initializing NAME if it doesn't exist, and the index of the next argument to be processed is placed in the variable OPTIND. OPTIND is initialized to 1 each time the shell or a shell script is invoked. When an option requires an argument, **getopts** places that argument into the variable OPTARG. The shell doesn't reset OPTIND automatically. It must be manually reset between multiple calls to **getopts** within the same shell invocation if a new set of parameters is to be used.

getopts can report errors in two ways. If the first character of OPTSTRING is a colon, SILENT error reporting is used. In normal operation, diagnostic messages are printed when illegal options or missing option arguments are encountered. If the variable OPTERR is set to 0, no error message will be displayed, even if the first character of OPTSTRING isn't a colon.

If an illegal option is seen and **getopts** is not silent, it places ? in *NAME*, prints an error message, and unsets OPTARG. If **getopts** is silent, the option character found is placed in OPTARG and the diagnostic message isn't printed.

If a required argument is not found and **getopts** isn't silent, a question mark (?) is placed in NAME, OPTARG is unset, and a diagnostic message is printed. If **getopts** is silent, a colon (:) is placed in NAME and OPTARG is set to the option character found.

For example:

```
while getopts ":ab:c" option; do
  case $option in
    a ) echo Processing -a option;;
    b ) echo Processing -b option echo $OPTARG is option -b argument;;
    c ) echo Processing -c option;;
    ? ) echo Error in command line;;
  esac
done
```

This fragment will output the following:

```
Processing -c option
Processing -b option
boption is option -b argument
```

when invoked with this command line:

```
script -c -b boption
```

if

```
if CONDITION_COMMANDS; then
    CONSEQUENT_COMMANDS;
  [elif CONDITION_COMMANDS; then
    CONSEQUENT_COMMANDS;]
  [else ALTERNATE_CONSEQUENTS>;]
  fi
```

if provides bash with a typical if-then-else conditional flow-control mechanism. The first set of *CONDITION_COMMANDS* with zero exit status triggers the corresponding set of *CONSEQUENT_COMMANDS*. *ALTERNATE_CONSEQUENTS* are executed if no *CONSEQUENT_COMMANDS* are successful.

let

```
let EXPRESSION [EXPRESSION]
```

let allows arithmetic to be performed on shell variables. If the last *EXPRESSION* evaluates to 0, let returns 1; otherwise it returns 0. See the later section "Arithmetic Operators" for more information.

local

```
local NAME[=VALUE]
```

local is used within a function to declare a local variable named *NAME* and assign it to *VALUE*.

popd

```
popd [+N ¦ -N] [-n]
```

popd pops the directory stack and cds to the new top directory. When no arguments are given, popd removes the top directory from the stack and performs a cd to the new top directory. The elements are numbered from 0, starting at the first directory listed with dirs.

Option	Description
+N	Removes the Nth directory (counting from the left of the list printed by dirs), starting with zero.
-N	Removes the Nth directory (counting from the right of the list printed by dirs), starting with zero.
-n	Suppresses the cd operation. Only the directory stack is changed.

pushd

pushd [DIR ¦ +N ¦ -N] [-n]

pushd pushes the current directory onto the directory stack and then cds to DIR. With no arguments, the top two directories are exchanged.

Option	Description
DIR	cds to DIR after pushing the current directory onto the top of the stack.
+N	Brings the Nth directory (counting from the left of the list printed by dirs, starting with zero) to the top of the list by rotating the stack.
-N	Brings the Nth directory (counting from the right of the list printed by dirs, starting with zero) to the top of the list by rotating the stack.
-n	Suppresses the cd operation. Only the directory is changed.

read

read [OPTION ...] [NAME ...]

read reads a line from standard input and sets the first NAME to the first word, the second NAME to the second word, and so on. Leftover words are assigned to the last NAME. Only the characters in the value of the IFS variable are recognized as word delimiters. If no names are supplied, the line read is assigned to the variable REPLY. The return code is 0 unless EOF is encountered.

Option	Description
-a ANAME	The words are assigned to sequential indices of the array variable ANAME, starting at 0.
-e	The readline library routine is used to obtain the line.
-p PROMPT	Displays PROMPT (without a trailing newline) before attempting to read any input. The prompt is displayed only if input is coming from a terminal.
-r	If this option is given, a backslash-newline pair is not ignored, and the backslash is considered to be part of the line.

readonly

readonly [OPTION ...] [NAME ...]

readonly marks each NAME as unchangeable. The values of these names can't be changed by subsequent assignment.

Option	Description
-a	Each NAME refers to an array.
-f	Each NAME refers to a shell function.
-p	If -p is given or if no NAMEs are given, readonly prints a list of all read-only names.

return

```
return [ N ]
```

return causes a shell function to return exit status *N*. This can also be used to terminate execution of a script being executed with the . built-in.

select

```
select NAME [in WORDS ... ;] do COMMANDS ; done
```

With select, the set of expanded *WORDS* is printed on the standard error, each preceded by a number. If in *WORDS* isn't present, in "$@" is assumed. The PS3 prompt is then displayed and a line read from the standard input. If the line consists of the number corresponding to one of the displayed words, *NAME* is set to that word. If the line is empty, *WORDS* and the prompt are redisplayed. If EOF is read, the command completes. Any other value read causes *NAME* to be set to null. The line read is saved in the variable *REPLY*. *COMMANDS* are executed after each selection until a break or return command is executed.

For example,

```
PS3=You would like a line count for which file?'
select name in *.c;
  do wc -l $name;
done
```

produces output similar to the following:

```
1) antlr.c         6) egman.c      11) gen.c        16) misc.c
2) bits.c          7) err.c        12) globals.c    17) mrhoist.c
3) build.c         8) fcache.c     13) hash.c       18) pred.c
4) dumpcycles.c    9) fset.c       14) lex.c        19) scan.c
5) dumpnode.c     10) fset2.c      15) main.c
You would like a line count for which file?1
   3202 antlr.c
1) antlr.c         6) egman.c      11) gen.c        16) misc.c
2) bits.c          7) err.c        12) globals.c    17) mrhoist.c
3) build.c         8) fcache.c     13) hash.c       18) pred.c
4) dumpcycles.c    9) fset.c       14) lex.c        19) scan.c
5) dumpnode.c     10) fset2.c      15) main.c
You would like a line count for which file?
```

shift

```
shift [ N ]
```

shift shifts positional parameters to the left by *N*. *N* must be a non-negative number less than or equal to $#.

source

```
source FILENAME
```

source reads and executes the commands in *FILENAME* in the current shell context.

test

```
test ARG ...
```

test evaluates the set of *ARG*s as a conditional expression. For example, this script will print myfile exists if the first argument is the name of an existing disk file:

```
if test -e $1; then
  echo $1 exists;
fi
```

trap

```
trap [ OPTION ... ] [ARG] [SIGSPEC ...]
```

With trap, the commands in *ARG* are to be read and executed when the shell receives the signal *SIGSPEC*. If *ARG* is absent or equal to -, all specified signals are reset to the values they had when the shell was started. If *ARG* is the null string, the signal specified by each *SIGSPEC* is ignored by the shell and commands it invokes. Each *SIGSPEC* is either a signal name such as SIGINT (with or without the SIG prefix) or a signal number. If a *SIGSPEC* is 0 or EXIT, *ARG* is executed when the shell exits. For more information on signals, see the section "Signals" in Chapter 7, "Process Control."

Option	Description
-l	Prints a list of signal names and their corresponding numbers.
-p	Lists commands associated with each *SIGSPEC*. If no *SIGSPEC* is given, lists signal handling commands for all signals.

true

```
true
```

true returns a true condition.

typeset

typeset has been deprecated. Use declare instead.

until

```
until TEST_COMMANDS ; do CONSEQUENT_COMMANDS ; done
```

until executes *CONSEQUENT_COMMANDS* as long as the final command in *TEST_COMMANDS* has an exit status that isn't zero.

The following example counts from 1 to 3:

```
let i=1
until [ $i -gt 3 ];do
  echo $i;
  let i=$i+1;
done
```

while

```
while TEST_COMMANDS ; do CONSEQUENT_COMMANDS ; done
```

while executes *CONSEQUENT_COMMANDS* as long as the final command in *TEST_COMMANDS* has an exit status of zero.

The following example counts from 1 to 3:

```
let i=1
while [ $i -le 3 ];do
  echo $i;
  let i=$i+1;
done
```

Arithmetic Operators

The following table describes bash arithmetic operators in order of increasing precedence. Evaluation is done in long integers with no check for overflow, although division by zero is trapped and flagged as an error.

Operator	Description
– and +	Unary minus and plus.
! and ~	Logical and bitwise negation.
*, /, and %	Multiplication, division, and remainder or mod.
+ and –	Addition and subtraction.
<< and >>	Left and right bitwise shifts.
<=, >=, and < >	Comparison.
== and !=	Equality and inequality.
&	Bitwise AND.
^	Bitwise XOR.
|	Bitwise OR.
&&	Logical AND.
||	Logical OR.
=, *=, /=, %=, +=, -=, <<=, >>=, &=, ^=, and |=	Assignment.

Conditional Expressions

Conditional expressions are used by the test and [built-ins. The following table summarizes bash conditional expressions.

Expression	True If...
-b *FILE*	*FILE* exists and is a block special file.
-c *FILE*	*FILE* exists and is a character special file.
-d *FILE*	*FILE* exists and is a directory.
-e *FILE*	*FILE* exists.
-f *FILE*	*FILE* exists and is a regular file.
-g *FILE*	*FILE* exists and is set-group-ID.

continues >>

>>continued

Expression	True If...
-k *FILE*	*FILE* has its "sticky bit" set.
-L *FILE*	*FILE* exists and is a symbolic link.
-p *FILE*	*FILE* exists and is a named pipe.
-r *FILE*	*FILE* exists and is readable.
-s *FILE*	*FILE* exists and has a size greater than zero.
-S *FILE*	*FILE* exists and is a socket.
-t *FD*	*FD* is opened on a terminal.
-u *FILE*	*FILE* exists and its set-user-ID bit is set.
-w *FILE*	*FILE* exists and is writable.
-x *FILE*	*FILE* exists and is executable.
-O *FILE*	*FILE* exists and is owned by the effective user ID.
-G *FILE*	*FILE* exists and is owned by the effective group ID.
FILE1 -nt *FILE2*	*FILE1* is newer (according to modification date) than *FILE2*.
FILE1 -ot *FILE2*	*FILE1* is older than *FILE2*.
FILE1 -ef *FILE2*	*FILE1* and *FILE2* have the same device and inode numbers.
-o *OPTNAME*	The shell option *OPTNAME* is enabled. The list of options appears in the description of the -o option to the **set** built-in.
-z *STRING*	The length of *STRING* is zero.
-n *STRING* or *STRING*	The length of *STRING* is nonzero.
STRING1 = *STRING2* or *STRING1* == *STRING*	The strings are equal.
STRING1 != *STRING2*	The strings are not equal.
STRING1 < *STRING2*	*STRING1* is lexicographically less than *STRING2*.
STRING1 > *STRING2*	*STRING1* is lexicographically greater than *STRING2*.
! *EXPR*	*EXPR* is false.
EXPR1 -a *EXPR2*	Both *EXPR1* and *EXPR2* are true.
EXPR1 -o *EXPR2*	Either *EXPR1* or *EXPR2* is true.
EXPR1 *OP* *EXPR2*	*EXPR1* and *EXPR2* are positive or negative integers. *OP* can be one of the following: -eq Equal. -ne Not equal to. -lt Less than. -le Less than or equal to. -gt Greater than. -ge Greater than or equal to.

Job Control

Job control refers to the ability to selectively suspend the execution of processes and resume their execution at a later time. This section describes the job control commands accepted by bash.

%

```
%[DIGITS ¦ WORD] [&]
```

% resumes a stopped or background job. If *DIGITS* is given, that job is used. If *WORD* is given, the job whose name begins with *WORD* is used. Following the job specification with & places the job in the background.

bg

```
bg [JOBSPEC]
```

bg places *JOBSPEC* in the background. If *JOBSPEC* isn't given, the current job is used.

disown

```
disown [-h] [JOBSPEC ...]
```

disown removes each *JOBSPEC* from the table of active jobs. If the -h option is given, the job isn't removed from the table, but is marked so that SIGHUP isn't sent to the job if the shell receives a SIGHUP.

fg

```
fg [JOBSPEC]
```

fg places *JOBSPEC* in the foreground. If *JOBSPEC* isn't given, the current job is used.

jobs

```
jobs [-lnprs] [JOBSPEC ...]
jobs -x COMMAND [JOBSPEC ...]
```

jobs shows information on active jobs.

Option	Description
-l	Includes process IDs in the listing.
-n	Shows only processes that have changed status since the last notification.
-p	Lists process IDs only.
-r	Shows only running jobs.
-s	Shows only stopped jobs.
-x COMMAND	Runs *COMMAND* with the process IDs of the process group leaders of the jobs given by the *JOBSPEC*s.

Background jobs can be referred to in several of the previously mentioned commands (such as jobs) using the following references:

Reference	Description
%N	Job number *N*.
%STRING	Job whose command begins with *STRING*.
%?STRING	Job whose command contains *STRING*.

continues >>

>>continued

Reference	Description
%+	Most recently invoked background job.
%%	Same as %+.
%-	Second most recently invoked background job.

Process Handling

This section describes commands used by bash processes when interacting with other processes.

kill

```
kill [-s SIGSPEC ¦ -n SIGNUM ¦ -SIGSPEC] [PID ¦ JOB] ...
kill -l [SIGSPEC ... ]
```

kill sends the processes named by PID (or JOB) the signal SIGSPEC or SIGNUM. SIGSPEC is a symbolic signal name; SIGNUM is a signal number. The -n or -s switch can be used to indicate to kill which form is being used. If SIGSPEC isn't present, SIGTERM is assumed. An argument of -l lists the signal names. Arguments following -l are assumed to be signal numbers for which names should be listed. kill is a shell built-in for two reasons: It allows job IDs to be used instead of process IDs, and if the limit on processes that can be created has been reached, a new process doesn't have to be started to kill another one. For more information on signals, see the section "Signals" in Chapter 7.

suspend

```
suspend [-f]
```

suspend suspends the execution of this shell until it receives a SIGCONT signal. The -f indicates not to complain about this being a login shell and suspend anyway.

wait

```
wait [ N ]
```

wait waits for the specified process and reports its termination status. If N isn't given, all currently active child processes are waited for, and the return code is 0. N can be a process ID or a job specification. If a job spec is given, all processes in the job's pipeline are waited for.

7

Process Control

This chapter describes commands and utilities for managing user processes and for examining their status.

Signals

Signals are frequently used for interprocess communication and process management. Logically, a signal is an integer value transmitted from a sender process to a receiver process. A signal can also be sent to a process by the kernel when certain internal conditions are encountered. For example, the system administrator can use a signal to indicate to a daemon that it should reset its configuration, or a process can receive a signal from the kernel when it tries to execute an illegal instruction.

On receiving the signal, the receiving process can either ignore the signal or execute a subroutine called a *signal handler*. The signal handler is specified for the given signal value using the `signal` system call, which takes the signal value and the signal handler's address as arguments. If no signal handler is specified for a signal value, the receiving process will execute the default action defined for that signal. If a signal is to be ignored, the constant `SIG_IGN` can be passed to `signal` as the signal handler. See the `signal(2)` manual page for more information on the `signal` system call.

Signals are sent by either the `kill` system call or the `kill` command. When sending signals using the `kill` command, the integer value can be given or the signal's name can be used. The following table lists the names and values of signals, their meanings, and the default actions to be taken when received. Some of the signals have more than one value. In these cases, the first is for Alpha and Sparc systems, the second for Intel and PowerPC, and the third for Mips. A minus sign (-) indicates that the signal isn't defined for the corresponding architecture.

Name	Value(s)	Default Action	Description
SIGHUP	1	Terminate process.	Hangup detected on controlling terminal.
SIGINT	2	Terminate process.	Interrupt from keyboard.
SIGQUIT	3	Terminate process.	Quit from keyboard.
SIGILL	4	Terminate process.	Illegal instruction.

continues >>

>>continued

Name	Value(s)	Default Action	Description
SIGABRT	6	Dump core.	Abort signal from abort(3).
SIGFPE	8	Dump core.	Floating-point exception.
SIGKILL	9	Terminate process.	Kill signal. This signal can't be ignored and no signal handler can be defined.
SIGSEGV	11	Dump core.	Invalid memory reference.
SIGPIPE	13	Terminate process.	Broken pipe. This is generated when a write to a pipe with no readers is attempted.
SIGALRM	14	Terminate process.	Time signal from alarm(2).
SIGTERM	15	Terminate process.	Termination signal.
SIGUSR1	30, 10, 16	Terminate process.	User-defined signal 1.
SIGUSR2	31, 12, 17	Terminate process.	User-defined signal 2.
SIGCHLD	20, 17, 18	Ignore.	Child stopped or terminated.
SIGCONT	19, 18, 25	Ignore.	Stopped process has continued.
SIGSTOP	17, 19, 23	Process is stopped.	Stop the process. This signal can't be ignored and no signal handler can be defined.
SIGTSTP	18, 20, 24	Process is stopped.	Stop typed at TTY.
SIGTTIN	21, 21, 26	Process is stopped.	TTY input for background process.
SIGTTOU	22, 22, 27	Process is stopped.	TTY output for background process.
SIGTRAP	5	Dump core.	Trace/breakpoint trap.
SIGIOT	6	Dump core.	I/O trap. A synonym for SIGABRT.
SIGEMT	7, -, 7	Dump core.	Emulation trap.
SIGBUS	10, 7, 10	Terminate process.	Bus error.
SIGSYS	12, -, 12	Dump core.	Bad system call argument.
SIGSTKFLT	-, 16, -	Terminate process.	Stack fault on coprocessor.
SIGURG	16, 23, 21	Ignore.	Urgent condition on socket.
SIGIO	23, 29, 22	Terminate process.	I/O now possible.
SIGPOLL	23, 29, 22	Terminate process.	Synonym for SIGIO.
SIGCLD	-, -, 18	Ignore.	Synonym for SIGCHLD.
SIGXCPU	24, 24, 30	Terminate process.	CPU time limit exceeded.
SIGXFSZ	25, 25, 31	Terminate process.	File size limit exceeded.
SIGVTALRM	26, 26, 28	Terminate process.	Virtual alarm clock.
SIGPROF	27, 27, 29	Terminate process.	Profile alarm clock.
SIGPWR	29, 30, 19	Terminate process.	Power failure.
SIGINFO	29, -, -	Terminate process.	Synonym for SIGPWR.
SIGWINCH	28, 28, 20	Ignore.	Window resize signal.

General Process Control

This section describes commands that send signals to processes, change scheduling priorities, and display the system's load status.

kill

```
kill [ -SIGNAL ] PID ...
kill [ -l ]
```

kill sends a signal to processes specified by the *PID* arguments. *SIGNAL* can be either a symbolic signal name or a signal number. A list of valid signal names and numbers can be obtained using the -l flag. If no signal is specified, kill will send SIGTERM (software termination).

The kill command is often used to terminate processes that are out of control and don't exit by themselves. Although SIGTERM is the default, SIGKILL can be used when SIGTERM doesn't work. Because SIGKILL can't be caught or ignored, it will always terminate the process. However, for the same reason, it can cause processes to exit without performing cleanup operations such as removing temporary work files or saving work in progress. Therefore, SIGKILL should be used only if the process doesn't respond to SIGTERM.

Another common use for the kill command is to tell daemons to reinitialize themselves. Daemons often use SIGHUP by convention to indicate that their configurations should be reloaded.

See the earlier section "Signals" for more information on signals and their meanings.

renice

```
renice PRIORITY [ PROCESS ... ]
```

renice alters the scheduling priority of one or more running processes. *PROCESS* is one of the following:

ID ...	Interpret *ID* as a process ID.
-g *ID* ...	Interpret *ID* as a group ID.
-p *ID* ...	Interpret *ID* as a process ID.
-u *ID* ...	Interpret *ID* as a user ID.

ID and -p *ID* are the same. If the flag isn't given, the ID is interpreted as a process ID.

skill

```
skill [ -SIGNAL ] [ -OPTIONS ] { CATEGORIES }
skill -l
```

skill sends a signal to processes specified by the *CATEGORIES* arguments. A list of valid signal names and numbers can be obtained using the -l flag. If no signal is specified, kill will send SIGTERM (software termination). *CATEGORIES* is one or more of the following:

-c *COMMAND*	Select processes running *COMMAND*.
-u *USER*	Select processes being run by *USER*.
-t *TTY*	Select processes whose controlling terminal is *TTY*.
-p *PID*	Select process *PID*.

The -c, -u, -t, and -p switches can be omitted if *TTY*, *USER*, *COMMAND*, and *PID* are specified in the order just given.

The options in the following table can be specified in any combination.

Option	Description
-i	Interactive mode. The user is prompted with each process that's a candidate for action.
-v	Verbose mode. The ID is displayed for each process successfully acted upon.
-f	In fast mode, the machine-dependent code responsible for reading processes is allowed to make decisions to improve speed at the expense of error reporting.
-w	Displays warning messages for unreachable processes.
-n	Displays process IDs but doesn't act on them.

snice

```
snice [ {-¦+}PRIORITY ] [ OPTIONS ] [ CATEGORIES ]
```

snice alters the scheduling priorities to processes selected as they would be with skill (*OPTIONS* and *CATEGORIES* are interpreted as they are in skill). By default, the new priority is +4, but an argument of the form +N or -N can be used to specify different values. An invalid priority is quietly rounded down (or up) to the first acceptable value.

uptime

```
uptime [ -V ]
```

uptime gives a one-line display of the following information:

- The current time.
- How long the system has been running.
- How many users are currently logged on.
- The system load averages for the past 1, 5, and 15 minutes.

uptime -V shows version information.

Process Status

This section describes commands that can be used to view the status of processes.

ps

```
ps [ OPTION ... ] [ PID ... ]
```

ps gives a snapshot of the status of processes currently running. If repetitive display is needed, use top. If *PID*(s) are specified, only the status information for the specified processes will be shown.

Field Descriptions for ps Output

The following table describes the status values shown by ps.

Field	Description
PRI	The counter field in the kernel task structure for the process. The time in HZ of the process's possible time slice.
NI	Standard UNIX nice value. A positive value means less CPU time.
SIZE	Virtual image size: text+data+stack.
RSS	Resident set size. Number of kilobytes of the program in memory.
WCHAN	Name of the kernel function where the process is sleeping, with the sys_ stripped from the function name. A hexadecimal address if /etc/psdatabase doesn't exist.
STAT	Three characters describing the process state: R for ready, S for sleeping, D for uninterruptible sleep, T for stopped or traced, Z for zombie. The second character contains W if the process has no resident pages. The third character is N if the process has a positive nice value (NI field).
TT	The controlling TTY for the process.
PAGEIN	Number of major page faults (page faults that cause pages to be read from disk, including pages read from the buffer cache).
TRS	Text resident size.
SWAP	Kilobytes (or pages if the p option is used) on the swap device.
SHARE	Shared memory.

Sort Keys

The output from ps can be sorted on a number of different fields. The following table provides the long and short key names and their descriptions.

Short	Long	Description
c	cmd	Name of executable.
C	cmdline	Full command name.
f	flags	Flags as in the long format F field.
g	pgrp	Process group ID.
G	tpgid	Controlling TTY of the process group.
j	cutime	Cumulative user time.

continues >>

>>continued

Short	Long	Description
J	cstime	Cumulative system time.
k	utime	User time.
K	stime	System time.
m	min_flt	Number of minor page faults.
M	maj_flt	Number of major page faults.
n	cmin_flt	Cumulative minor page faults.
N	cmaj_flt	Cumulative major page faults.
o	session	Session ID.
p	pid	Process ID.
P	ppid	Parent process ID.
r	rss	Resident set size.
R	resident	Resident pages.
s	size	Memory size in kilobytes.
S	share	Amount of shared pages.
t	tty	Minor device number of the TTY.
T	start_time	Time the process was started.
U	uid	User ID number.
u	user	Username.
v	vsize	Total virtual memory size in bytes.
y	priority	Kernel scheduling priority.

Command-Line Options for ps

The following table describes the command-line options for ps.

Option	Description
l	Long format.
u	User format. Gives username and start time.
j	Jobs format.
s	Signal format.
v	Virtual memory format.
m	Displays memory info (combine with the p flag to show the number of pages).
f	"Forest" or process family tree format.
a	Show processes of other users as well as that of the invoking user.
x	Show processes with the controlling terminal.
S	Add child CPU time and page faults.
c	Show command name without arguments.
e	Show environment.
w	Wide output. Don't truncate command lines to fit on one line. Each w given makes each line longer by the number of characters in a line without w. Up to 100 w characters can be used.

Option	Description
h	Leave out column headings.
r	Running processes only.
n	Numeric output for USER and WCHAN.
t*XX*	Show only processes with controlling TTY *XX*. For *XX*, you can use either the name of a device file under /dev or that name with either tty or cu sliced off.
O*KEYLIST*	Order the process listing according to the multilevel sort specified by *KEYLIST*. *KEYLIST* is a concatenated, separated list of keys. Each key can be preceded by + or -. The + makes no difference; - reverses the direction of the sort. Valid key values can be obtained using the --help option.
--sort*KEYLIST*	Equivalent to O*KEYLIST*.
--version	Display the ps version number.

top

```
top [ OPTION ... ]
```

top provides a periodically updating display of the most CPU-intensive processes on the system. top also provides an interactive interface for manipulating processes. For a description of the information provided by top, see the earlier section "Field Descriptions for ps Output."

Command-Line Options for top

The following table describes command-line options for top.

Option	Description
d	Specifies the delay between screen updates (in seconds).
q	Causes top to refresh without any delay.
S	Specifies cumulative mode, where each process is listed with the CPU time spent by the process as well as its dead children.
s	Runs in secure mode. This disables the potentially dangerous use of the interactive commands.
i	Ignores any idle or zombie processes.
c	Displays the command line instead of the command name only.

Interactive Commands for top

The following table describes interactive commands for use within top.

Command	Description
space	Pressing the spacebar immediately updates the display.
Ctrl+L	Erases and redraws the screen.
h or ?	Displays a help screen giving a brief summary of commands and the status of secure and cumulative modes.
k	Kills a process. Prompts for a PID and a signal to send.

continues >>

>>continued

Command	Description
i	Toggles ignoring of idle and zombie processes.
n or #	Changes the number of processes to be displayed.
q	Quits.
r	Re-nices a process. Prompts for PID and a value to which to nice it.
S	Toggles cumulative mode.
s	Changes the delay between updates.
f or F	Adds or removes fields from the display.
o or O	Changes the order of displayed fields.
l	Toggles display of load average and uptime.
m	Toggles display of memory information.
t	Toggles display of processes and CPU states information.
c	Toggles between full command line and command name only.
M	Sorts tasks by resident memory usage.
P	Sorts tasks by CPU usage (the default).
T	Sorts tasks by time and cumulative time.
W	Writes the current setup to ~/.toprc. This is the recommended way to set up a top configuration file.

Scheduling and Managing Batch Jobs

This section describes commands used in the execution of batch jobs.

at

at [OPTION ...] TIME at -c JOB ...

at schedules jobs to be run at TIME. The commands to be executed are read from standard input or a disk file.

at allows fairly complex TIME specifications, extending the POSIX.2 standard. It accepts times of the form HH:MM to run a job at a specific time of day. (If that time is already past, the next day is assumed.) You also can specify midnight, noon, or teatime (4 p.m.) and a time of day suffixed with AM or PM for running in the morning or the evening. Specify what day the job will be run by giving a date in the form MONTH-NAME DAY with an optional YEAR, or giving a date of the form MMDDYY or MM/DD/YY or DD.MM.YY. The specification of a date must follow the specification of the time of day. Times are stated in the form now + COUNT TIME-UNITS, where COUNT is a number and TIME-UNITS is minutes, hours, days, or weeks. You also can tell at to run the job today by suffixing the time with today or run the job tomorrow by suffixing the time with tomorrow.

The job inherits the working directory, the environment (except for TERM, DISPLAY, and _) and the umask from the process that invoked at.

Option	Description
-c	Prints the jobs listed on the command line to standard output.
-d *JOB*	Deletes job *JOB* from the schedule. *JOB* is a number assigned at the time the job was scheduled.
-f *FILE*	Reads the job from *FILE* rather than standard input.
-l	Lists the scheduled jobs. at -l is an alias for atq.
-m	Sends mail to the user when the job has completed, even if there was no output.
-q *QUEUE*	Uses the specified *QUEUE*. A queue designation consists of a single letter. Valid queue designations range from a to z and A to Z. The a queue is the default for at and the b queue for batch. Queues with higher letters run with increased niceness. The special queue = is reserved for jobs that are currently running.
-V	Prints the version number.

atq

atq [-V] [-q *QUEUE*]

atq prints the job numbers, execution times, and queues for queue *QUEUE*. It lists the user's pending jobs (or all if the user is root). If no queue is specified, atq shows all jobs scheduled. The -V flag shows the at version number. atq is a symbolic link to at.

atrm

atrm [-V] *JOB* ...

atrm removes the specified *JOB*(s) from the schedule. The -V flag shows the at version number. atrm is a symbolic link to at.

batch

batch [*OPTION* ...]

batch executes commands when the system load average drops below 0.8 or the value specified in the invocation of atrun or atd. The -V flag also shows the at version number.

Option	Description
-f *FILE*	Reads the job from *FILE* rather than standard input.
-m	Sends mail to the user when the job has completed, even if there was no output.
-V	Prints the version number.

crontab

```
crontab [ -u USER ] FILE
crontab [ -u USER ] { -l ¦ -r ¦ -e }
```

crontab is used to maintain periodic job schedules. Each line in the periodic schedule is either an environment variable setting of the form *NAME=ENVIRONMENT* or a cron command. cron commands are of the following form:

DATE_AND_TIME COMMAND

DATE_AND_TIME, a set of five space-separated fields, sets the schedule for the execution of *COMMAND*:

MINUTE HOUR DAY_OF_MONTH MONTH DAY_OF_WEEK

The following table describes the allowable values for these fields.

Field	Valid Values
MINUTE	0 to 59
HOUR	0 to 23
DAY_OF_MONTH	1 to 31
MONTH	1 to 12
DAY_OF_WEEK	0 to 6 (Sunday is 0)

The following are also allowed:

- * indicates "all" or "any."
- Comma-separated lists such as 5,10,15.
- Hyphen-separated ranges such as 1-10.
- First three letters of the month or day (case doesn't matter, and ranges aren't allowed with names).
- Lines that begin with # are ignored and can be used as comments.

For example:

```
# run somejob at 10 pm on weekdays
0 22 * * 1-5 /home/epetron/somejob.sh
```

The following is equivalent to the preceding example:

```
0 22 * * 1,2,3,4,5 /home/epetron/somejob.sh
```

Command-Line Options for crontab

Option	Description
-e	Edit the current schedule using the editor specified by the VISUAL or EDITOR environment variable. The schedule is installed automatically after exiting the editor.
FILE	Update the schedule from *FILE*.
-l	List the current schedule to standard output.
-r	Remove the schedule.
-u *USER*	Alter the schedule for user *USER*. Only the superuser can use the -u option. Without -u, the schedule of the invoking user is altered.

II

Administration

8

User Management

This chapter describes the commands used to maintain user and group accounts.

Password Maintenance

This section describes the commands used to delete and change passwords for users and groups.

chpasswd

```
chpasswd [ -e ]
```

chpasswd provides batch update of user passwords. It reads a file of username and password pairs from standard input and uses the data to update the corresponding user passwords. Without the -e switch the passwords are assumed to be clear text; with the -e switch the passwords are expected to be encrypted. Each line is of the form USER:PASSWORD. The specified USER must exist. PASSWORD will be encrypted if necessary.

dpasswd

```
dpasswd [ -a ¦ -d ] SHELL
```

dpasswd adds, deletes, or updates dial-up passwords for login shells. The dial-up password is prompted after a user's password has been authenticated, whenever the user logs in over a dial-up line. dpasswd prompts for the new password twice to make sure it was entered correctly. SHELL is the complete pathname of the login program (/bin/login). Using -a or neither option causes dpasswd to update the password if it exists or add the password if it doesn't exist. The -d option causes dpasswd to delete the password.

gpasswd

```
gpasswd GROUP
gpasswd { -a ¦ -d } USER GROUP
gpasswd { -R ¦ -r } GROUP
gpasswd [ -A USER_LIST ] [ -M USER_LIST ] GROUP
```

gpasswd is used to maintain group membership and password data. The -A and -M options are used by the system administrator to define group administrators and group members. Each USER_LIST is a comma-separated list of usernames. The OPTION command-line switches are defined according to the following table:

Option	Description
-a USER GROUP	Adds USER to GROUP.
-d USER GROUP	Deletes USER from GROUP.
-R GROUP	Disables access to GROUP.
-r GROUP	Removes the password for GROUP.

passwd

```
passwd [ -f ¦ -s ] [ NAME ]
passwd [ -g ] [ -r ¦ -R ] GROUP
passwd [ -x MAX ] [ -n MIN ] [ -w WARN ] [ -i INACT ] NAME
passwd { -l ¦ -u ¦ -d ¦ -S } NAME
```

passwd changes passwords for user and group accounts. A normal user can only change the password for his or her own account. Superusers can change passwords for any account. Group administrators can change the passwords for their groups. passwd also changes account information, such as the full name of the user, his or her login shell, or password expiration dates and intervals.

Option	Description
-f	Changes the account information for NAME or for invoking the user if NAME isn't specified.
-g	Changes the password for the group GROUP.
-i INACT	Disables the account for NAME after the password has been expired for INACT days.
-l	Disables the account for NAME by changing the password to a value that matches no possible encrypted value.
-n MIN	Changes the minimum number of days before the password of user NAME can be changed.
-R	Used with the -g option to restrict the group GROUP for all users.
-r	Used with the -g option to remove the password for the group GROUP. This allows group access to all members.
-S	Gives an account status for NAME. The status information consists of six parts. The first part indicates whether the user account is locked (L), has no password (NP), or has a usable password (P). The second part gives the date of the last password change. The next four parts are the minimum age, maximum age, warning period, and inactivity period for the password.

Option	Description
-s	Changes the login shell for *NAME* or for invoking the user if *NAME* isn't specified.
-u	Re-enables the account of *NAME* by changing the password back to its previous value.
-w *WARN*	Sets the number of days of warning that the user *NAME* will receive before his or her password will expire.
-x *MAX*	Sets the maximum number of days that the password for the user *NAME* remains valid.

User and Group Maintenance

This section describes commands that create, delete, and modify user and group accounts.

chage

```
chage [ -m MINDAYS ] [ -M MAXDAYS ] [ -d LASTDAY ] [ -I INACTIVE ]
➥[ -E EXPIREDATE ] [ -W WARNDAYS ] USER

chage -l USER
```

chage changes the number of days between password changes and the date of the last password change. The chage command is restricted to the root user except for the -l option, which can be used by an unprivileged user to determine when his or her password or account is due to expire. The other options are defined in the following table:

Option	Description
-d *LASTDAY*	The value of *LASTDAY* is the number of days since January 1, 1970 when the password was last changed. The date can also be expressed in the format *MM/DD/YY* or *MM/DD/YYYY*.
-E *EXPIREDATE*	Sets the date on which the user's account will no longer be accessible. *EXPIREDATE* is the number of days since January 1, 1970 on which the account is locked. The date can also be expressed in the format *MM/DD/YY* or *MM/DD/YYYY*.
-I *INACTIVE*	Sets the number of days of inactivity after a password has expired before the account is locked. *INACTIVE* is the number of days of inactivity. A value of **0** disables this feature.
-M *MAXDAYS*	The value of *MAXDAYS* is the maximum number of days during which a password is valid. When *MAXDAYS* plus *LASTDAY* is less than the current day, the user will be required to change the password before being able to use the account.
-m *MINDAYS*	The value of *MINDAYS* is the minimum number of days between password changes. A value of **0** for this field indicates that the user can change the password at any time.
-W *WARNDAYS*	*WARNDAYS* is the number of days of warning before a password change is required.

chfn

chfn [-f *FULL_NAME*] [-r *ROOM_NO*] [-w *WORK_PHONE*] [-h *HOME_PHONE*]
➥[-o *OTHER*] [*USER*]

chfn changes the user's full name, office number, office extension, and home phone number information for a user's account. This information is typically printed by finger and similar programs. A normal user can only change the fields for his or her own account, but the superuser can change the fields for any account. Also, only the superuser can use the -o option.

The only restriction placed on the contents of the fields is that no control characters can be present, nor any commas (,), colons (:), or equal signs (=). The *OTHER* field doesn't have this restriction, and is used to store accounting information used by other applications.

Without options, chfn operates interactively on the current user's account.

chsh

chsh

chsh [-s *LOGIN_SHELL*] [*USER*]

chsh changes the login shell for *USER* to *LOGIN_SHELL*. A normal user can only change the login shell for his or her own account. The superuser can change the login shell for any account. If *LOGIN_SHELL* isn't specified using the -s option, chsh prompts for the value of *LOGIN_SHELL*. The only restriction placed on *LOGIN_SHELL* is that the command name must be listed in /etc/shells unless the invoker is the superuser, in which case any value can be added. An account with a restricted login shell can't change his or her login shell.

groupadd

groupadd [-g *GID* [-o]] *GROUP*

The groupadd command creates a new group account using the values specified on the command line and the default values from the system. The new group will be entered into the system files as needed. The numerical value of the group's ID is specified by -g *GID*. This value must be unique unless the -o option is used, and must be non-negative. The default is to use the smallest ID value greater than 99 and greater than every other group. Values between 0 and 99 are typically reserved for system accounts.

groupdel

groupdel *GROUP*

The groupdel command modifies the system account files, deleting all entries that refer to *GROUP*. The named group must exist. The primary group of an existing user can't be removed without first removing the user.

groupmod

groupmod [-g GID [-o]] [-n GROUP_NAME] GROUP

The groupmod command modifies the system account files to reflect the changes that are specified on the command line.

Option	Description
-g GID	GID is the numerical value of the group's ID. This value must be unique unless the -o option is used, and must be non-negative. Values between 0 and 99 are typically reserved for system groups. Any files in which the old group ID is the file group ID must have the file group ID changed manually.
-n GROUP_NAME	Changes the name of the group from GROUP to GROUP_NAME.

newusers

newusers [NEW_USERS]

newusers reads a file of username and cleartext password pairs and uses this informa
tion to update a group of existing users or to create new users. Each line is in the
same format as the standard password file passwd, with the following exceptions:

- The password field will be encrypted and used as the new value of the encrypted password.

- The password age field will be ignored for shadow passwords if the user already exists.

- The group ID field can be the name of an existing group, in which case the named user will be added as a member. If a nonexistent numerical group is given, a new group will be created with this number.

- The directory field will be checked for existence as a directory and a new directory with the same name will be created if it doesn't already exist. The ownership of the directory will be set to that of the user being created or updated.

Authentication Data Maintenance

Authentication prior to login is based on two files: /etc/group and /etc/passwd.
This section describes these files and the commands used to maintain them.

/etc/group

The /etc/group file contains one line for each group account. Each line contains the
following fields separated by colon (:) characters:

- Group name.

- Optional encrypted group password.

- Numerical group ID.

- Comma-separated list of the names of all users who are members of the group.

For added security, some systems use shadow password files that are accessible only to the superuser and are used to store the passwords.

/etc/passwd

The /etc/passwd file contains one line for each user account. Each line contains the following fields separated by colon (:) characters:

- Login name.
- Optional encrypted password.
- Numerical user ID.
- Numerical group ID.
- Username or comment field.
- User home directory.
- User command interpreter.

/etc/shadow

The /etc/shadow file stores the user passwords on systems where password shadowing is used. It contains one line for each user account. Each line contains the following fields separated by colon (:) characters:

- Login name.
- Encrypted password.
- Days since January 1, 1970 that the password was last changed.
- Days before the password can be changed.
- Days after which the password must be changed.
- Days before the password is to expire that the user is warned.
- Days after the password expires that the account is disabled.
- Days since January 1, 1970 that the account is disabled.
- A reserved field.

grpck

grpck [-r] [*GROUP SHADOW*]

grpck check the integrity of group password files. All entries in /etc/group and /etc/gshadow are checked to see that the entry has the proper format and valid data in each field. The user is prompted to delete entries that are improperly formatted or that have other uncorrectable errors. The checks for correct number of fields and unique group name are fatal. If the entry has the wrong number of fields, the user will be prompted to delete the entire line. If the user doesn't answer affirmatively, all further checks are bypassed. An entry with a duplicated group name is prompted for deletion, but the remaining checks will still be made. All other errors are warnings and the user is encouraged to run the **groupmod** command to correct the error. The user

can select alternate files with the *GROUP* and *SHADOW* parameters. The -r flag causes all
questions regarding changes to be answered no without user intervention.

pwck

```
pwck [ -r ] [ PASSWD SHADOW ]
```

pwck verifies the integrity of user password files. All entries in /etc/passwd and
/etc/shadow are checked to see that the entry has the proper format and valid data
in each field. The user is prompted to delete entries that are improperly formatted or
that have other uncorrectable errors. The checks for correct number of fields and
unique username are fatal. If the entry has the wrong number of fields, the user will
be prompted to delete the entire line. If the user doesn't answer affirmatively, all
further checks are bypassed. An entry with a duplicated username is prompted for
deletion, but the remaining checks will still be made. All other errors are warnings
and the user is encouraged to run the usermod command to correct the error. The
user can select alternate files with the *PASSWD* and *SHADOW* parameters. The -r option
causes all questions regarding changes to be answered no without user intervention.

pwconv, pwunconv, grpconv, and grpunconv

```
pwconv
pwunconv
grpconv
grpunconv
```

These commands convert user and group password files to/from shadow format:

- pwconv creates shadow from passwd and an optionally existing shadow.
- pwunconv creates passwd from passwd and shadow and then removes shadow.
- grpconv creates gshadow from group and an optionally existing gshadow.
- grpunconv creates group from group and gshadow and then removes gshadow.

shadowconfig

```
shadowconfig { on ¦ off }
```

shadowconfig turns shadow passwords on and off.

useradd

```
useradd [ -c COMMENT ] [ -d HOME_DIR ] [ -e EXPIRE_DATE ] [ -f INACTIVE_TIME ]
➡[ -g INITIAL_GROUP ] [ -G GROUP_LIST ] [ -m [ -k SKELETON_DIR ] ]
➡[ -s SHELL ] [ -u UID [ -o ] ] LOGIN

useradd -D [ -g DEFAULT_GROUP ] [ -b DEFAULT_HOME ] [ -f DEFAULT_INACTIVE ]
➡[ -e DEFAULT_EXPIRE_DATE ] [ -s DEFAULT_SHELL ]
```

useradd is used to create new users or update default user information. When
invoked without the -D option, the useradd command creates a new user account
using the values specified on the command line and the default values from the
system. The new user account is entered into the system files as needed, the home
directory is created, and initial files copied, depending on the command-line options.

Command Options for Creating New Users

Option	Description
-c *COMMENT*	Places *COMMENT* in the comment field of the new user's record in the password file.
-d *HOME_DIR*	The new user will be created using *HOME_DIR* as the value for the user's login directory. The default is to append the *LOGIN* name to *DEFAULT_HOME* and use that as the login directory name.
-e *EXPIRE_DATE*	Date on which the user account will be disabled, specified in the format *MM/DD/YY* or *MM/DD/YYYY*.
-f *INACTIVE_DAYS*	Number of days after a password expires until the account is permanently disabled. A value of 0 disables the account as soon as the password has expired, and a value of -1 disables the feature. The default value is -1.
-g *INITIAL_GROUP*	Group name or number of the user's initial login group. The group name must exist. A group number must refer to an existing group. The default group number is 1.
-G *GROUP_LIST*	The new user is a member of *GROUP_LIST*, where *GROUP_LIST* is a comma-separated list of groups. The groups are subject to the same restrictions as the group given with the -g option. The default is for the user to belong only to the initial group.
-m	The user's home directory will be created if it doesn't exist. The files contained in *SKELETON_DIR* are copied to the home directory if the -k option is used; otherwise the files contained in /etc/skel are used. Any directories contained in *SKELETON_DIR* or /etc/skel are also created in the user's home directory. The -k option is valid only in conjunction with the -m option. The default is to not create the directory and not copy any files.
-s *SHELL*	Designates *SHELL* as the user's login shell. The default is to leave this field blank, which causes the system to select the default login shell.
-u *UID*	The numerical value of the user's ID. This value must be unique unless the -o option is used and must be non-negative. The default is to use the smallest ID value greater than 99 and greater than every other user. Values between 0 and 99 are typically reserved for system accounts.

Command Options for Changing Default Values

Option	Description
-b *DEFAULT_HOME*	Initial path prefix for a new user's home directory. The user's name will be affixed to the end of *DEFAULT_HOME* to create the new directory name if the -d option isn't used when creating a new account.
-e *DEFAULT_EXPIRE_DATE*	Date on which the user account is disabled.

Option	Description
-f *DEFAULT_INACTIVE*	Number of days between password expiration and disabling of the account.
-g *DEFAULT_GROUP*	Group name or ID for a new user's initial group. The named group must exist, and a numerical group ID must have an existing entry.
-s *DEFAULT_SHELL*	Designates *DEFAULT_SHELL* as the login shell for all future new user accounts.

userdel

userdel [-r] *LOGIN*

userdel removes all references to *LOGIN* from system account files. If the -r option is given, all files in the user's home directory are removed, along with the home directory.

usermod

```
usermod [-c COMMENT ] [ -d HOME_DIR [ -m ] ] [ -e EXPIRE_DATE ]
➥[ -f INACTIVE_TIME ] [ -g INITIAL_GROUP ] [ -G GROUP_LIST ]
➥[ -l LOGIN_NAME ] [ -s SHELL ] [ -u UID [ -o ] ] LOGIN
```

usermod modifies the system account files to reflect changes specified on the command line.

Option	Description
-c *COMMENT*	Places *COMMENT* in the comment field of the user *LOGIN*'s password file record.
-d *HOME_DIR*	The user's new login directory. If the -m option is given, the contents of the current home directory are moved to the new home directory, which is created if it doesn't already exist.
-e *EXPIRE_DATE*	Date on which the user account will be disabled, specified in the format *MM/DD/YY* or *MM/DD/YYYY*.
-f *INACTIVE_DAYS*	Number of days after a password expires until the account is permanently disabled. A value of **0** disables the account as soon as the password has expired, and a value of -1 disables the feature. The default value is -1.
-g *INITIAL_GROUP*	Group name or group number of the user's new initial login group. The group name must exist. A group number must refer to an existing group. The default group number is 1.
-G *GROUP_LIST*	*GROUP_LIST* is a comma-separated list of groups of which the user is also a member. The groups are subject to the same restrictions as the group given with the -g option. If the user is currently a member of a group that isn't listed, the user will be removed from the group.

continues >>

>>continued

Option	Description
-l *LOGIN_NAME*	The name of the user will be changed from *LOGIN* to *LOGIN_NAME*. Nothing else is changed. In particular, the user's home directory name should probably be changed manually to reflect the new login name.
-s *SHELL*	Designates *SHELL* as the user's new login shell. Setting this field to blank causes the system to select the default login shell.
-u *UID*	The numerical value of the user's ID. This value must be unique unless the -o option is used. The value must be non-negative. Values between 0 and 99 are typically reserved for system accounts. Any files that the user owns and that are located in the directory tree rooted at the user's home directory will have the file user ID changed automatically. Files outside the user's home directory must be altered manually.

vipw and vigr

```
vipw [ -s ]
vigr [ -s ]
```

vipw and vigr enable manual editing of the password and group files, respectively. The -s option causes the corresponding shadow files to be edited. The programs invoke the selected text editor and set appropriate locks to prevent file corruption. When looking for an editor, the programs first try the environment variable VISUAL, then the environment variable EDITOR, and finally the default editor vi.

See the earlier descriptions of /etc/passwd and /etc/group for descriptions of the contents of these files.

Quotas

Quotas are limits placed on the usage of disk space by user and group accounts. The commands described in this section are used to maintain quotas.

edquota

```
edquota [ -p PROTO_USER ] [ -ug ] NAME ...
edquota [ { -u ¦ -g } -t
```

edquota is a quota editor. One or more users or groups can be specified on the command line. A temporary file is created for each user or group with an ASCII representation of the current disk quotas for that user or group, and an editor is then invoked on the file. The quotas can then be modified, new quotas added, and so on. On leaving the editor, edquota reads the temporary file and modifies the binary quota files to reflect the changes made.

The editor invoked is vi unless the EDITOR environment variable specifies otherwise.

Option	Description
-u	Edits the quota for the user *NAME*. This is the default.
-g	Edits the quota for the group *NAME*.
-p	Duplicates the quotas of the specified prototypical user for each specified user. This is the normal mechanism used to initialize quotas for groups of users.
-t	Edits the soft time limits for each filesystem. If the time limits are zero, the default time limits in <linux/quota.h> are used. Time units of sec(onds), min(utes), hour(s), day(s), week(s), and month(s) are understood. Time limits are printed in the greatest possible time unit such that the value is greater than or equal to 1.

quota

```
quota [ -guv ¦ -q ]
quota [ -uv ¦ -q ] USER
quota [ -gv ¦ -q ] GROUP
```

quota displays users' disk usage and limits. By default only the user quotas are printed. Specifying both -g and -u displays both the user quotas and the group quotas (for the user).

Only the superuser can use the -u flag and the optional *USER* argument to view the limits of other users. Normal users can use the -g flag and optional *GROUP* argument to view only the limits of groups of which they're members.

The -q flag takes precedence over the -v flag.

quota reports the quotas of all the filesystems listed in /etc/fstab. For filesystems that are NFS-mounted, a call to the rpc.rquotad on the server machine is performed to get the information. If quota exits with a nonzero status, one or more filesystems are over quota.

Option	Description
-g	Prints group quotas for the group of which the user is a member.
-u	This option is equivalent to the default.
-v	Displays quotas on filesystems where no storage is allocated.
-q	Prints a message containing only information on filesystems where usage is over quota.

quotacheck

```
quotacheck [ -g ] [ -u ] [ -v ] -a
quotacheck [ -g ] [ -u ] [ -v ] FILESYS ...
```

quotacheck performs a filesystem scan for usage of files and directories used by either user or group. The output is the quota file for the corresponding filesystem. By default, the names for these files are as follows:

- User scan: quota.user.

- Group scan: quota.group.

The resulting file consist of a struct dqblk for each possible ID up to the highest existing user ID or group ID and contains the values for the disk file, block usage, and possibly excess time for these values (for definitions of struct dqblk, see <linux/quota.h>).

quotacheck should be run each time the system boots and mounts non-valid filesystems. This is most likely to happen after a system crash.

quotaon and quotaoff

```
quotaon [ -vug ] FILESYSTEM ...
quotaon [ -avug ]
quotaoff [ -vug ] FILESYSTEM ...
quotaoff [ -avug ]
```

quotaon announces to the system that disk quotas should be enabled on one or more filesystems. The filesystem quota files must be present in the root directory of the specified filesystem and be named quota.user for userquota or quota.group for groupquota.

quotaoff announces to the system that the filesystem(s) specified should have any disk quotas turned off.

Options for quotaon

Option	Description
-a	All filesystems in /etc/fstab marked read-write with quotas will have their quotas turned on. This is normally used at boot time to enable quotas.
-g	Manipulates group quotas.
-u	Manipulates user quotas. This is the default.
-v	Displays a message for each filesystem where quotas are turned on.

Options for quotaoff

Option	Description
-a	Forces all filesystems in /etc/fstab to have their quotas disabled.
-g	Manipulates group quotas.
-u	Manipulates user quotas. This is the default.
-v	Displays a message for each filesystem affected.

repquota

```
repquota [ -vug ] FILESYSTEM ...
repquota [ -avug ]
```

repquota prints a summary of the disk usage and quotas for each specified
FILESYSTEM. For each user, the current number of files and amount of space
(in kilobytes) is printed, along with any quotas created with edquota.

Option	Description
-a	Reports on all filesystems indicated in /etc/fstab to be read-write with quotas.
-g	Reports quotas for groups.
-u	Reports quotas for users. This is the default.
-v	Reports all quotas, even if there's no usage.

9

Startup and Shutdown

This chapter describes startup and shutdown processing.

Startup processing can be broken into two separate subprocesses:

- The bootup process involves loading the kernel image into RAM. The newly loaded kernel performs various hardware initializations before invoking the `init` process.

- The `init` process then enables terminal logins and starts daemon processes that provide additional services to both local and remote users.

System shutdown involves the termination of system activity in a manner that ensures the following:

- **Physical data integrity.** Linux, like other UNIX variants, caches disk data blocks in RAM as a means of enhancing performance. If memory-resident data blocks have been modified (these are often referred to as "dirty") and therefore no longer match the disk blocks that they represent, they need to be written out to the disk. This is accomplished by the `sync` system call.

- **Logical data integrity.** This is more difficult to achieve than physical data integrity. The best that can be done here is to notify users and processes that shutdown is in progress and any necessary cleanup processing needs to be done. This is accomplished by sending messages to logged-in users and by sending signals to processes.

Boot Management

Bootup involves the actual loading of the kernel image into RAM. This can be accomplished in many ways. For example, many systems have more than one operating system installed or allow the user to select different kernel images (production versus test kernels). Boot management deals with the exercise of these options.

This section focuses on the Linux loader (LILO), which is the boot loader most commonly used on Intel–based systems. For information pertaining to boot management on other architectures and using Linux with other operating systems, see Appendix C, "Web Resources."

lilo

lilo *OPTION* ...

Most Linux systems use the Linux Loader (LILO) for boot management. lilo installs the boot loader that will be activated the next time the system is booted.

Option	Description
-C *CONFIG_FILE*	Read the configuration from *CONFIG_FILE* instead of /etc/lilo.conf.
-c	Enable map file compaction. This will merge read requests from adjacent sectors and speed up booting.
-D *LABEL*	Use the kernel with label *LABEL* as the boot kernel, instead of the first one in the list.
-d *DELAY*	If several kernels are specified and the Shift key is pressed at boot time, the boot loader will allow the selection of the kernel with which to boot. After a timeout period of *DELAY* seconds, the first kernel in the list is booted.
-f *DISK_TAB*	Specifies the disk geometry parameter file *DISK_TAB*. The default is /etc/disktab.
-I *LABEL*	Print the pathname for the kernel file labeled with *LABEL*. The label of the currently running kernel can be found in /proc/cmdline, listed as BOOT_IMAGE=*LABEL*.
-i *BOOT_SECTOR*	Specifies the file *BOOT_SECTOR* to be used as the new boot sector instead of /boot/boot.b.
-l	Generate linear sector addresses instead of sector/head/cylinder addresses.
-m *MAP_FILE*	Use *MAP_FILE* instead of /boot/map for the map file.
-P { fix ¦ ignore }	Fix (or ignore) partition tables with linear and sector/head/cylinder addresses that don't correspond.
-q	List the currently mapped kernel files. lilo maintains a file (/boot/map by default) containing the name and location of the kernel(s) to boot.
-R *COMMAND_LINE*	Sets the default command for the boot loader the next time it executes. The boot loader will then erase this line; this is a once-only command. It's typically used in reboot scripts, just before calling shutdown -r.
-r *ROOT_DIRECTORY*	chroot to *ROOT_DIRECTORY* before doing anything else. This is used for repairing a setup from a boot floppy.
-S *SAVE_FILE*	Allow the save file *SAVE_FILE* to be overridden.

Option	Description
-s SAVE_FILE	Save the current boot sector to SAVE_FILE instead of the default /boot/boot.NNNN, where NNNN is the device number of the boot device. The boot sector will be restored from SAVE_FILE when used with -u.
-t	Test only; don't actually write a new boot sector of the map file. Used with the -v option to find out what lilo will do.
-U [DEVICE_NAME]	Same as -u except that the timestamp isn't checked.
-u [DEVICE_NAME]	Restore the backup copy of the specified boot sector. If DEVICE_NAME isn't specified, the value of the boot variable in the configuration file is used. If neither is available, the current root device is used. lilo validates the backup copy by checking a timestamp.
-v	Increase verbosity. Each -v given on the command line will make lilo more verbose.

The operation of lilo is largely driven by a configuration file. The default name for the configuration file is /etc/lilo.conf, but files by other names can be used as specified by lilo command options. The following sections describe the contents of these configuration files.

Global LILO Options

Option	Description
backup=BACKUP_FILE	Copy the original boot sector to BACKUP_FILE (which can also be a device such as /dev/null) instead of /boot/boot.NNNN, where NNNN is the device number of the boot device.
boot=BOOT_DEVICE	Sets the name of the device (usually a hard disk partition) that contains the boot sector. If this isn't specified, the currently mounted root device will be used.
compact	Merge read requests for adjacent sectors into a single read request. This drastically reduces load time and keeps the map smaller. Using compact is especially recommended when booting from a floppy disk.
default=NAME	Use NAME as the default boot image. If default is omitted, the image appearing first in the configuration file is used.
delay=TSECS	Wait TSECS tenths of a second before booting the first image. This is useful on systems that immediately boot from the hard disk after enabling the keyboard. The boot loader doesn't wait if delay is omitted or is set to zero.

continues >>

>>*continued*

Option	Description
`disk=DEVICE_NAME`	Defines nonstandard parameters for the specified disk. See the "Disk Geometry" section of the LILO user's manual for details.
`disktab=DISKTAB_FILE`	Specifies the name of the disk parameter table. The map installer looks for `/etc/disktab` if `disktab` is omitted. The use of disktabs is discouraged.
`fix-table`	Allows `lilo` to adjust 3D addresses in partition tables. Each partition entry contains a 3D (sector/head/cylinder) and a linear address of the first and the last sector of the partition. If a partition isn't track-aligned and if certain other operating systems such as MS–DOS or OS/2 are using the same disk, they may change the 3D address. `lilo` can store its boot sector only on partitions where both address types correspond. `lilo` readjusts incorrect 3D start addresses if `fix-table` is set.
`force-backup=BACKUP_FILE`	Like `backup`, but overwrites an old backup copy if it exists.
`ignore-table`	Tells `lilo` to ignore corrupt partition tables.
`install=BOOT_SECTOR`	Install the file `BOOT_SECTOR` as the new boot sector. If this option is omitted, `/boot/boot.b` is used.
`linear`	Generate linear sector addresses instead of sector/head/cylinder addresses. Linear addresses are translated at runtime and don't depend on disk geometry.
`lock`	Enable automatic recording of boot command lines as the defaults for the following boots. This way, lilo "locks" on a choice until it's manually overridden.
`map=MAP_FILE`	Specifies `MAP_FILE` as the map file. If this option is omitted, `/boot/map` will be used.
`message=MESSAGE_FILE`	Display the message contained in `MESSAGE_FILE` before the boot prompt. No message is displayed while waiting for input after printing `"LILO "`. A formfeed character in the file will clear the local screen. The size of the message file is limited to 65535 bytes. The map file has to be rebuilt if the message file is changed or moved.
`nowarn`	Disables warnings about possible problems.
`optional`	The per-image option `optional` (see the following section) applies to all images (an image is a bootable kernel image file).

Option	Description
password=*PASSWORD*	The per-image option password=... (see the following section) applies to all images (an image is a bootable kernel image file).
prompt	Forces entering the boot prompt without expecting any prior keypresses. Unattended reboots are impossible if prompt is set and timeout isn't.
restricted	The per-image option restricted (see the following section) applies to all images.
serial=*PARAMETERS*	Enables control from a serial line. The specified serial port is initialized and the boot loader is accepting input from it and from the PC's keyboard. Sending a break on the serial line corresponds to pressing a Shift key on the console to get the boot loader's attention. The *PARAMETERS* string has the following syntax:
	PORT[,*BPS*[*PARITY*[*BITS*]]]
	PORT is the number of the serial port. The lowest number is 0, which corresponds to the COM1 alias /dev/ttyS0.
	BPS is the baud rate. Supported baud rates are 110, 150, 300, 600, 1200, 2400, 4800, and 9600. The default is 2400 bps.
	PARITY is the parity used on the serial line. Valid values are n for no parity, e for even, and o for odd. Uppercase letters can also be used.
	BITS is the number of bits in a character. Only 7 and 8 bits are supported. The default is 8 if parity is none, 7 if parity is even or odd.
	If serial is set, the value of delay is automatically raised to 20.
timeout=*TSECS*	Sets the keyboard input timeout to *TSECS* tenths of a second. If keyboard input times out, the first image is automatically booted. Password input is aborted if the user is idle for too long. The default timeout is infinite.
verbose=*LEVEL*	Sets the level of detail of the information contained in progress reports. The maximum level is 5. If -v is given on the command line, the level is increased.

Per-Image LILO Options

A per-image section of the configuration file must start with either image=*PATHNAME*, where *PATHNAME* is the path to a Linux kernel, or other=*PATHNAME*, where *PATHNAME* is the device from which an arbitrary system will boot.

Other per-image options are described in the following table:

Option	Description
alias=*NAME*	An alternate name for the image.
label=*NAME*	Use *NAME* to identify the image at boot time.
loader=*CHAIN_LOADER*	Specifies the chain loader that should be used. By default, /boot/chain.b is used. The chain loader must be specified if booting from a device other than the first hard or floppy disk.
lock	See the lock description in the earlier section "Global LILO Options."
optional	Omit the image if it isn't available at map-creation time. This is useful for test kernels that aren't always present.
password=*PASSWORD*	Protect the image by password.
range=*START-END*	Range of sectors to use if image=*PATHNAME* indicates a device.
restricted	A password is only required to boot the image if parameters are specified on the command line.
table=*DEVICE*	Specifies the device that contains the partition table. The boot loader won't pass partition information to the booted operating system if this variable is omitted. Note that lilo must be rerun if a partition table map referenced with table is modified.
unsafe	Don't access the boot sector at map creation time. This disables some sanity checks, including a partition table check. If the boot sector is on a fixed-format floppy disk device, using unsafe avoids the need to put a readable disk into the drive when running the map installer. unsafe and table are mutually incompatible.

Kernel LILO Options

The following options can be used to pass parameters to a Linux kernel:

Option	Description
append=*STRING*	Appends the specified options to the parameter line passed to the kernel. This is typically used to specify parameters of hardware that can't be entirely auto-detected or for which probing may be dangerous.
literal=*STRING*	Like append, except that it removes all other options. Because critical options can be removed unintentionally with literal, this option can't be set in the global options section of the configuration file.
ramdisk=*SIZE*	Specifies the size of the optional RAM disk. A value of 0 indicates that no RAM disk will be created. If this variable is omitted, the RAM disk size configured into the boot image is used.
read-only	Mount the root filesystem as read-only. Typically, the system startup procedure re-mounts the root filesystem after it's checked with fsck. (For a description of fsck, see Chapter 12, "Filesystems.")

Option	Description
read-write	Mount the root filesystem as read-write.
root=*ROOT_DEVICE*	Mount *ROOT_DEVICE* as root. If the special name current is used, the root device is set to the device on which the root filesystem is currently mounted. If the root has been changed with the -r *ROOT_DIRECTORY* option of lilo, the device containing *ROOT_DIRECTORY* is used. If root is omitted, the root device setting contained in the kernel image is used.
vga=*MODE*	Set VGA text mode to *MODE* when booting. The following values are recognized (case is ignored): normal selects normal 80 × 25 text mode. extended selects 80 × 50 text mode. ask asks for user input at boot time. *NUMBER* uses the corresponding text mode. A list of available modes can be obtained by booting with vga=ask and pressing Enter.

The following is an example of a lilo.conf file that will boot either Linux or DOS where both reside on the same hard disk but in different partitions:

```
# LILO configuration file
#
# Start LILO global section
# Tell kernel where to find CDROM controller
append="sbpcd=0x630,LaserMate"
boot = /dev/hda
prompt
vga = normal     # force sane state
ramdisk = 0      # paranoia setting
# End LILO global section
# Linux bootable partition config begins
image = /vmlinuz
  root = /dev/hda2
  label = Linux
  read-only
# Linux bootable partition config ends
# DOS bootable partition config begins
other = /dev/hda1
  label = DOS
  table = /dev/hda
# DOS bootable partition config ends
```

Initialization and Runlevels

Initialization is handled by init. init is the first process to be run after the kernel is loaded and is the ultimate ancestor of all user processes. Its primary role is to create processes based on data stored in the file /etc/inittab. Typical entries create getty processes that prompt for login on serial ports with attached terminals. It's also responsible for the management of autonomous processes such as network service daemons.

A *runlevel* is a system state that allows only a selected group of processes to exist. The processes spawned by init for each runlevel are defined in the /etc/inittab file. Valid runlevels are the numbers 0 through 6, S, and s. Runlevels S and s are functionally identical. The runlevel can be changed by having a privileged user run telinit, which sends appropriate signals to init, telling it which runlevel to use.

Runlevels 0, 1, and 6 are reserved. Runlevel 0 halts the system, runlevel 6 reboots the system, and runlevel 1 gets the system down into single-user mode. Runlevel S isn't really meant to be used directly. It's normally used in the transition between bootup and the system's entry into multiuser mode. It's also used when transitioning from multiuser mode into single-user maintenance mode.

The inittab file describes which processes are started immediately after bootup and during normal operation. Each entry has the following format:

ID:RUNLEVELS:ACTION:PROCESS

Lines beginning with # are treated as comments and ignored by init.

ID is a unique sequence of from one to four characters that identifies an entry in inittab. *RUNLEVELS* lists the runlevel(s) for which the entry applies. *ACTION* describes which action(s) should be taken. *PROCESS* specifies the process(es) to be executed. If the *PROCESS* field starts with a plus (+) character, init won't do utmp and wtmp accounting for that process. This is needed for versions of getty that insist on doing their own utmp/wtmp maintenance.

The *RUNLEVELS* field can contain multiple characters, so that actions and processes for multiple runlevels can be specified.

The runlevels for ondemand entries can contain A, B, or C. The RUNLEVELS fields of sysinit, boot, and bootwait entries are ignored.

When the system runlevel is changed, any running processes that aren't specified for the new runlevel are killed, first with SIGTERM, and then with SIGKILL.

For more information on SIGTERM, SIGKILL, and signals in general, see the "Signals" section in Chapter 7, "Process Control."

The following table describes the valid values for the *ACTION* field:

Action	Description
boot	The process will be executed during system boot. The RUNLEVELS field is ignored.
bootwait	Same as boot except that init will wait for the process to terminate.
ctrlaltdel	The process will be executed when init receives the SIGINT signal. This means that someone on the system console has pressed the Ctrl+Alt+Del key combination.
initdefault	Specifies the runlevel that should be entered after system boot. If none exists, init will ask for a runlevel on the console. The PROCESS field is ignored.
kbrequest	The process will be executed when init receives a signal from the keyboard handler that a special key combination was pressed on the console keyboard.
off	This does nothing.

Action	Description
once	The process will be executed once when the specified runlevel is entered.
ondemand	The process will be executed whenever the specified ondemand runlevel is called. However, no runlevel change will occur (ondemand runlevels are A, B, and C).
powerfail	Same as powerwait except that init doesn't wait for the process to terminate.
powerfailnow	The process will be executed when init is told that the battery of the external UPS is almost empty and the power is failing (provided that the external UPS and the monitoring process are able to detect this condition).
powerokwait	The process will be executed as soon as init is informed that the power has been restored.
powerwait	The process will be executed when the power goes down. init is usually informed about this by a process talking to a UPS connected to the computer. init will wait for the process to finish before continuing.
respawn	The process will be restarted whenever it terminates.
sysinit	The process will be executed during system boot, before any boot or bootwait entries. The *RUNLEVELS* field is ignored.
wait	The process will be started once when the specified runlevel is entered, and init will wait for its termination.

getty

```
getty OPTION ... PORT BAUD_RATES [ TERM ]
getty OPTION ... BAUD_RATES PORT [ TERM ]
```

getty enables initiation of user terminal sessions by prompting for login on a specified TTY port and invoking the /bin/login command. It's normally invoked by init.

BAUD_RATES is a comma-separated list of one or more baud rates. Each time getty receives a BREAK character it advances through the list, which is treated as if it were circular. Baud rates should be specified in descending order, so that the null character can also be used for baud-rate switching.

PORT is a pathname relative to the /dev directory. If a hyphen (-) is specified, getty assumes that its standard input is already connected to a TTY port and that a connection to a remote user has already been established.

TERM is the value to be used for the TERM environment variable. This overrides whatever init may have set, and is inherited by login and the shell.

The following table describes command-line options for getty.

Option	Description
-f *ISSUE_FILE*	Display the contents of *ISSUE_FILE* instead of /etc/issue.
-h	Enables hardware (RTS/CTS) flow control.

continues >>

>>continued

Option	Description
-I *INIT_STRING*	Send *INIT_STRING* to the TTY or modem before sending anything else.
-i	Don't display the contents of the /etc/issue file.
-l *LOGIN_PROGRAM*	Run *LOGIN_PROGRAM* instead of /bin/login.
-m	Tries to extract the baud rate from the CONNECT status message produced by Hayes-compatible modems. getty assumes that the modem emits its status message at the same speed as specified with the first value in *BAUD_RATES* on the command line.
-n	Don't prompt the user for a login name. This is useful in conjunction with -l *LOGIN_PROGRAM* to execute a nonstandard login process. With the -n option, getty gets no input from the user who logs in, and won't be able to determine parity, character size, and newline processing of the connection. It defaults to space parity, 7-bit characters, and ASCII CR (13) end-of-line character.
-t *TIMEOUT*	Terminate if no username could be read within *TIMEOUT* seconds.
-L	Forces the line to be a local line with no need for carrier detect. This can be useful when you have a locally attached terminal where the serial line doesn't set the carrier detect signal.
-w	Wait for the user or the modem to send a carriage return or a linefeed character before sending the /etc/issue (or *ISSUE_FILE*) file and the login prompt. This is useful in connection with the -I option.

The issue file (/etc/issue or that specified by -f *ISSUE_FILE*) can contain character sequences that have special meanings. These sequences consist of \ immediately followed by one of these letters:

Character	Inserts...
b	Baud rate of the current line.
d	Current date.
s	Name of the operating system.
l	Name of the current TTY line.
m	Architecture identifier of the machine.
n	Hostname of the machine.
o	Domain name of the machine.
r	Release number of the operating system.
t	Current time.
u	Current number of users logged in.
U	String "1 user" or "*n* users" where *n* is the number of users currently logged in.
v	Version of the operating system.

On standalone workstations, `getty` is used to enable virtual console sessions. It can also be used to accept logins on terminals attached to serial ports. Terminals can be dumb terminals or other machines running terminal-emulation software (perhaps pre-i386 Intel–based or older PCs that are incapable of running Linux themselves). This could be an excellent way to save money by putting older (cheap) hardware to work.

For example, in the file `/etc/inittab`, this line:

```
S1:23:respawn:/sbin/getty -L 19200 ttyS1 vt102
```

enables a terminal or PC connected to ttyS1 (COM2 in MS-DOS) to run a session at 19200 baud. `vt102` is the terminal type. `getty` will set the `TERM` environment variable to this value. In this example, `getty` will run when entering runlevels 2 and 3 and will be automatically restarted every time it's killed.

For more information on using `getty` with character terminals, see the references listed in Appendix C.

telinit

```
telinit [ -t SECONDS ] ARGUMENT
```

`telinit` is linked to `init`. It takes a single character *ARGUMENT* and signals `init` to perform the appropriate action. The following arguments serve as directives to `telinit`:

Argument	Description
0 through 6	Switch to the specified runlevel.
a, b, or c	Process only those `/etc/inittab` entries with the corresponding runlevel.
Q or q	Reexamine the `/etc/inittab` file.
S or s	Switch to single-user mode.
U or u	Tells `init` to rerun itself but with the state preserved. The `/etc/inittab` file isn't reexamined. The current runlevel should be S, s, 1, 2, 3, 4, or 5; otherwise, the request will be silently ignored.

The `-t` *SECONDS* will cause `telinit` to tell `init` to wait *SECONDS* seconds between sending processes the `SIGTERM` and `SIGKILL` signals.

Shutdown

The commands in this section are used to shut down the system in a manner that ensures logical and physical data integrity. Rather than simply halting the processor, these commands send signals to processes that notify them that cleanup processing is to be accomplished if needed. They also send warning messages to terminal users and resynchronize disk caches with their associated disk blocks.

halt, poweroff, and reboot

```
halt OPTION ...
poweroff OPTION ...
reboot OPTION ...
```

halt notes that the system is being brought down in the file /var/log/wtmp and then tells the kernel to halt, reboot, or power off the system. poweroff and reboot are links to halt. If halt or reboot is called when the system is not in runlevel 0 or 6, shutdown will be invoked instead (with the flag -h or -r).

Option	Description
-d	Don't write the wtmp record. -n implies -d.
-f	Force halt or reboot. Don't call shutdown.
-i	Shut down all network interfaces just before halt or reboot.
-n	Don't sync. This option shouldn't normally be used since the sync is necessary to ensure the physical integrity of the disks that are mounted.
-p	When halting the system, do a power off. This is the default when halt is called as poweroff.
-w	Don't actually reboot or halt; just write the wtmp record in /var/log/wtmp.

shutdown

```
shutdown [ -t SECONDS ] [ OPTION ... ] TIME [ WARNING_MESSAGE ]
```

shutdown brings the system down in a safe and secure way. All users are notified that the system is going down and initiation of new sessions is blocked. All processes are first notified by the signal SIGTERM that the system is going down. This gives programs an opportunity to execute cleanup processing if they need to do so. shutdown does its job by signaling the init process to change the runlevel. Runlevel 0 is used to halt the system, runlevel 6 is used to reboot the system, and runlevel 1 is used to put the system into a state in which administrative tasks can be performed.

The TIME argument can have different formats. First, it can be an absolute time in the format HH:MM, in which HH is the hour (one or two digits) and MM is the minute of the hour (in two digits). Second, it can be in the format +M, in which M is the number of minutes to wait. The word now is an alias for +0.

Option	Description
-a	Use /etc/shutdown.allow.
-c	Cancels an already running shutdown.
-F	Force fsck on reboot.
-f	Skip fsck on reboot.
-h	Halt after shutdown.
-k	Only send warning messages and don't actually shut down the system.

Option	Description
-n	This option is deprecated. shutdown shuts down the system directly rather than signaling init to do it. The use of this option is discouraged, and its results are not always what you'd expect.
-r	Reboot after shutdown.
-t *SECONDS*	Tells init to wait *SECONDS* seconds between sending the processes for the warning and kill signal and before changing to another runlevel.
TIME	When to shut down.
WARNING_MESSAGE	Message to send to all users.

10

The Kernel and Its Interfaces

The *kernel* is responsible for managing hardware resources, which includes the CPU (or CPUs in a multiprocessor system), memory, and I/O devices. Kernels are contained in files that are loaded into memory when the system is booted and remain resident in memory until the system is rebooted.

Kernel modules are components of the kernel that can be loaded and unloaded as required. Modules are usually used to provide hardware or system-support services that are often not needed. They're loaded when these services are required and can be unloaded when the services are no longer needed.

This chapter describes the configuration, building, and installation of kernels and kernel modules. It also describes commands and special files that can be used to query a kernel's internal state.

Installing New Kernels

This section describes the configuration, building, and installation of kernels and kernel modules.

Configuring the Kernel

```
make config
make menuconfig
make xconfig
```

These commands, when issued from the root of the kernel source tree (typically but not necessarily /usr/src/linux), are used to configure the kernel. This step should be followed by a make dep, which sets up the file dependencies. These file dependencies are used by make to control the building of the kernel. For more information on make, see Chapter 4, "Programming."

When configuring the kernel, you should take several precautions:

- **Make sure that the right processor type is specified.** For example, a kernel compiled for a Pentium can't run on a 486 and will fail to boot.

- **Be careful with hardware support options.** Including support for nonexistent devices makes the kernel larger and can also cause other problems due to probing for devices that aren't physically installed.

- **Enable math emulation only if needed.** If floating-point math is supported by the hardware, a kernel with math emulation enabled will still run, although the floating-point routines will never be used. This will make the kernel slightly larger than necessary.

- **Don't enable "kernel hacking" options unless you're involved in kernel development.** These options make the kernel bigger, slower, and less stable.

Building the Kernel

Building a new kernel consists of one or more of the following steps:

- `make zImage`—Creates a compressed kernel image.

- `make zdisk`—Makes a boot disk if a disk is in drive A:.

- `make zlilo`—If the Linux loader (lilo) is set up, makes a new kernel, copies it to its boot location (commonly `/vmlinuz`), and runs the LILO installer to update the load map.

- `make bzImage`—Use this for kernels that are too large for `make zImage`.

Installing a New Kernel

If `make zlilo` was used to build the new kernel, the installation is already complete. Otherwise, the new kernel image should be copied from where it was built (usually `/usr/src/linux/arch/i386/boot/zImage`) to either a boot floppy or its location on the hard disk.

Installation on a boot floppy is already complete if `make zdisk` was done. Otherwise, this command will make a bootable floppy:

```
cp /usr/src/linux/arch/i386/boot/zImage /dev/fd0
```

If installation on hard disk is required, the new kernel needs to be copied to its boot location first; you can find this by looking at `/etc/lilo.conf`. Then `/sbin/lilo` must be run to update the loading map; otherwise, the system won't boot.

It's advisable to keep a backup copy of the old kernel in case there are problems with the new one. Also, `/etc/lilo.conf` should be edited so that the system will boot from the old one if the new one fails to boot.

Building and Installing Modules

If the `m` (module) switch was selected for any of the configuration options, the `make modules` command should be issued from the root of the kernel source tree after the kernel is built.

Next, issue the command `make modules_install` to copy the new modules into subdirectories under `/lib/modules/`*KERNEL_RELEASE*, where *KERNEL_RELEASE* is the version number of the current kernel.

Using Modules

This section describes the commands and utilities that use and manage modules.

depmod

```
depmod -a [VERSION]
depmod MODULE_NAME ...
```

depmod creates a dependency file that describes the dependencies between modules using makefile syntax. The dependency file can later be used by modprobe for loading the relevant modules automatically. The -a option creates a dependency file for all modules in /lib/VERSION, where VERSION is the kernel version. The second form creates a dependency file for the files named on the command line. The behavior of both depmod and modprobe is controlled by the configuration file /etc/conf.modules.

genksyms

```
genksyms [ -wq ] [ -dD ] [ -V ] -k VERSION [ -p STRING ] [ OUTPUT_DIRECTORY ]
```

genksyms reads preprocessed C source (the output from gcc -E) on standard input and generates a file containing version information. Depending on the output format indicated by the -k option, the output is written to a .ver file in the named OUTPUT_DIRECTORY or to the standard output.

genksyms normally looks for explicit symbol-table definitions in the source file. All definitions and declarations of typedef, struct, union, and enum are saved for later expansion. Every global symbol is also saved, together with pointers that will enable a full expansion later on.

When a symbol table is found in the source, the symbol is expanded to its full definition, where all structs, unions, enums, and typedefs are expanded down to their basic parts, recursively. This final string is then used as input to a CRC algorithm that will give an integer that changes as soon as the symbol's structure changes.

The version information in the kernel normally looks like this:

```
symbol-R12345678
```

where 12345678 is the hexadecimal representation of the CRC.

Option	Description
-D	Dumps expanded symbol definitions to stderr.
-d	Outputs debugging information. Repeating this increases the debug level. Debug level 1 generates moderate information about the actions being taken. Level 2 enables parser-recognition output. Level 3 enables lexical-analysis output.
-k	Specifies the version of the kernel for which to generate output. Omitting this option assumes a version below 2.1.0. Versions below 2.1.18 use checksum version 1 and produce their output in the directory given on the command line. Versions 2.1.18 and above use checksum version 2 and produce their output on standard output.

continues >>

>>continued

Option	Description
-p STRING	Prepends STRING to the CRCs generated for all symbols. This is intended for use in situations where the modules aren't compatible at a level below that described by the data types. This is primarily caused by inline function expansions in the module code itself.
-q	Quiet operation. Reverses the -w option.
-v	Prints genksyms version and exits.
-w	Enables warnings due to unrecognized syntax and declared but undefined structures. These warnings are normally suppressed.

insmod

```
insmod [ -fkmpsxXv ] [ -o MODULE_NAME ] OBJECT_FILE [ SYMBOL=VALUE ... ]
```

insmod installs a loadable module into the running kernel. insmod tries to link the module into the running kernel by resolving all symbols from the kernel's exported symbol table. If the object filename is given without extension, insmod searches for the module in some common default directories. The environment variable MODPATH can be used to override this default.

insmod can also initialize the values of variables identified by named symbols to specified values. In modules built for 2.0 series kernels, any integer or character pointer symbol can be treated as a parameter and modified. Beginning in the 2.1 series kernels, symbols are explicitly marked as parameters so that only specific values can be changed. Furthermore, type information is provided for checking the values provided at load time.

In the case of integers, all values can be in decimal, octal, or hexadecimal as in C: 17, 021, or 0x11. Array elements are specified sequences separated by commas. Elements can be skipped by omitting the value.

In 2.0 series modules, values that don't begin with a number are considered strings. Beginning in 2.1, the parameter's type information indicates whether to interpret the value as a string. If the value begins with double quotes ("), the string is interpreted as in C, escape sequences and all.

Option	Description
-f	Attempt to load the module even if the version of the running kernel and the version of the kernel for which the module was compiled don't match.
-k	Set the auto-clean flag on the module. This flag is used by kerneld to remove modules that haven't been used in some period of time (usually one minute).
-m	Output a load map, making it easier to debug the module in the event of a kernel panic.
-o MODULE_NAME	Explicitly name the module, rather than deriving the name from the base name of the source object file.
-p	Probe the module to see whether it can be loaded successfully. This includes locating the object file in the module path, checking version numbers, and resolving symbols.
-s	Output everything to syslog instead of the terminal.

Option	Description
SYMBOL=VALUE	Initialize the variable identified by the symbol SYMBOL to VALUE.
-v	Verbose operation.
-X or -x	Do or don't export all the module's external symbols, respectively. The default is for the symbols to be exported. This option is only effective if the module doesn't explicitly export its own controlled symbol table.

kdstat

```
kdstat
kdstat [debug¦nodebug]
kdstat [keep¦nokeep]
kdstat flush
kdstat delay=TIME
```

kdstat is used to view or change the state of the currently running kerneld. It can also be used to debug the kernel.

Option	Description
debug	Turns debugging mode on. When debugging mode is on, kerneld displays what it's doing on the console.
delay=TIME	Changes the time (in seconds) that kerneld waits before removing an unused module from the kernel.
flush	Flushes the IPC message queue used to communicate with kerneld.
keep	Turns on the keeping of modules. When keeping is off (the default), modules are unloaded when they haven't been used for a while.
nodebug	Turns off debugging mode.
nokeep	Turns off the keeping of modules.

kerneld

```
kerneld [ debug ] [ keep ] [ delay=SECONDS ] [ type=MESSAGE_NUMBER ]
```

In addition to removing modules that aren't in use, kerneld performs kernel actions from user space in response to the requests from the kernel via a dedicated IPC message queue.

Option	Description
debug	Enables debugging mode. This can also be turned on by kdstat.
delay=SECONDS	Changes the time for removal of unused modules.
keep	Ignore all requests for unloading modules.
type=MESSAGE_NUMBER	If MESSAGE_NUMBER is positive, only listen to messages with that type. The default is -255, which means that kerneld will listen for all messages where the type is less than or equal to 255.

kernelversion

```
kernelversion
```

kernelversion reports the major version of the currently running kernel.

ksyms

```
ksyms [ -a ] [ -h ] [ -m ]
```

ksyms displays information about exported kernel symbols.

Option	Description
-a	Displays all symbols. By default, symbols from the kernel proper are suppressed.
-h	Suppresses the column header.
-m	Displays module information. Includes each module's kernel load address and size in the listing.

lsmod

```
lsmod
```

lsmod shows information about all loaded modules. The format is identical to that in /proc/modules.

modinfo

```
modinfo [ OPTION ... ] MODULE_NAME
```

modinfo reports information extracted from the object file associated with the kernel module MODULE_NAME.

Option	Description
-a	Displays the module's author.
-d	Displays the module's description.
-fFORMAT_STRING or --formatFORMAT_STRING	Lets the user specify an arbitrary format string that can extract values from the ELF section in MODULE_NAME that contains the module information. Replacements consist of a percent sign (%) followed by a tag name in braces ({}).
-h or --help	Displays the usage message.
-p or --parameters	Displays the typed parameters that a module can support.
-V or --version	Displays the modinfo version.

modprobe

```
modprobe MODULE_FILE [symbol=VALUE ...]
modprobe -t TAG PATTERN
modprobe -a -t TAG PATTERN
modprobe -l [ -t TAG ] PATTERN
modprobe -r MODULE modprobe -c
```

modprobe can be used to load or unload one or more modules based on supplied module names, filename patterns, and dependency information supplied by depmod. It can also be used to list information related to module loading and configuration. The behavior of both depmod and modprobe is controlled by the configuration file /etc/conf.modules.

Option	Description
-a PATTERN	Adds the modules with the names matching PATTERN, along with all modules on which they depend.
-c	Prints all configuration information.
-l PATTERN	Lists all modules with a name matching PATTERN.
-r MODULE	Removes the module MODULE and all modules on which it depends.
-t TAG	Selects the modules in the subdirectory TAG.

rmmod

```
rmmod [ -as ] MODULE ...
```

rmmod unloads loadable modules from the running kernel.

Option	Description
-a	Removes all unused modules.
-s	Outputs everything to syslog instead of the terminal.

Device Files (MAKEDEV)

```
MAKEDEV [ -vcdnhIV ] NAME ...
```

MAKEDEV maintains the device file entries in the /dev directory. MAKEDEV uses names and device numbers contained in one or more of the following files:

- /etc/devinfo—Device information.

- /usr/local/etc/devinfo.local—Local device information.

- /etc/devinfo.local—Alternate location for local device information.

- /etc/makedev.cfg—File containing user and group ownerships and permissions for devices.

- /proc/devices—Virtual file containing the names and major device numbers of devices supported under the current configuration.

The following table describes MAKEDEV command-line options:

Option	Description
-v	Verbose mode. Describe each step that's executed.
-c	Create the device(s) specified by *NAME*.
-d	Delete the device(s) specified by *NAME*.
-n	Describe steps to be executed as in -v but don't actually execute them.
-h	Print the usage message.
-V	Print the version number.
-I	Create device files in the current working directory instead of /dev.

The *NAME*s are found in the devinfo files. The following are special values for *NAME*:

- update—Updates the entries in /dev to match those in /proc/devices. (See the next section for more information.)

- local—Creates system-specific device files. This option is obsolete and only prints a warning message. devinfo.local and makedev.cfg files are now used for this purpose.

When individual device files need to be created, the mknod command can be used. See Chapter 3, "File Utilities," for more information.

To find out more about supported devices and the special files through which they're accessed, read the file Documentation/devices.txt in the kernel source directory.

The /proc Filesystem

The /proc filesystem is a virtual filesystem that makes internal data maintained by the kernel available to user processes. The files under the /proc directory appear as files to user programs but function as portals into kernel data structures. Most of these files export data in ASCII format and, as a result, can be used by shell programs. For example, if a user wants to know the characteristics of the machine's CPU, the following command can be issued:

```
cat /proc/cpuinfo
```

This command displays information similar to the following:

```
processor      : 0
cpu            : 686
model          : 3
vendor_id      : GenuineIntel
stepping       : 4
fdiv_bug       : no
hlt_bug        : no
f00f_bug       : no
fpu            : yes
fpu_exception  : yes
cpuid          : yes
wp             : yes
flags          : fpu vme de pse tsc msr pae mce cx8 11 mtrr pge mca cmov mmx
bogomips       : 264.60
```

The /proc filesystem provides both global and process-specific data. Process-specific data is provided by files under the directory /proc/*PID*, where *PID* is the process ID of the process in question. The file /proc/self is a link that points to the directory for the current process.

Some files under /proc and its subdirectories are symbolic links pointing to filenames of the form [*DEV*]:*INODE*, where *DEV* is the device number and *INODE* is the inode number.

The structure of the /proc filesystem depends on the kernel version and the system's configuration. The following table describes the files available under a typical system.

File	Description
/proc/cmdlind	Parameters passed to the kernel when it was booted.
/proc/cpuinfo	Description of the CPU, including the vendor name, whether it has a floating-point unit, and so on.
/proc/devices	Major device numbers and their names.
/proc/dma	Direct Memory Access (DMA) channels and their device names.
/proc/filesystems	Filesystem types supported by the current configuration.
/proc/interrupts	For each interrupt request (IRQ) number, the number of interrupts that have been serviced and the name of the device.
/proc/ioports	I/O port addresses and the names of the associated devices.
/proc/kcore	Kernel memory image.
/proc/kmsg	Kernel message buffer.
/proc/ksyms	Names and addresses of kernel routine names and variables. Module names are included for those symbols defined by loadable modules.
/proc/loadavg	Load averages, number of running processes, total number processes on the system, and the PID of the last process created.
/proc/locks	Information on file locks currently held.
/proc/meminfo	Memory-usage statistics for RAM and swap space.
/proc/misc	Minor device numbers and names for miscellaneous devices (major number 10).
/proc/modules	For each loaded module, the name, the number of pages of memory the module uses, the number of processes using the module, and the modules that depend on it.
/proc/mounts	The volume mount table.
/proc/net/arp	Address Resolution Protocol (ARP) information. For each device using ARP, the IP address, hardware type, the hardware address, and so on.
/proc/net/dev	Performance statistics for each network interface device. Lists the number of packets sent and received, number of errors, and so on.
/proc/net/raw	Description of each raw socket in use. Lists remote and local addresses, queue lengths, and so on.
/proc/net/route	Routing table. For each route, lists destination and gateway addresses, maximum transfer unit, and so on.
/proc/net/rt_cache	Routing cache in the same format as /proc/net/route.

continues >>

>>continued

File	Description
/proc/net/snmp	Simple Network Management Protocol (SNMP) data.
/proc/net/sockstat	Socket descriptor usage. For each type of socket (TCP, UDP, and so on), shows the number in use and the number available.
/proc/net/tcp	Same as /proc/net/raw for TCP sockets.
/proc/net/udp	Same as for /proc/net/tcp for UDP sockets.
/proc/net/unix	Description of each UNIX local domain socket in use. Lists the filename, the inode where it resides, and so on.
/proc/pci	Descriptions of all currently installed PCI devices.
/proc/scsi/scsi	Descriptions of all currently installed SCSI devices.
/proc/stat	Kernel and system statistics: CPU time, disk reads and writes, page swaps, interrupts, context switches, and boot time.
/proc/uptime	Uptime and idle time in hundredths of a second.
/proc/version	Kernel version, the user who compiled it, the gcc version with which it was compiled, and the date and time it was compiled.

For each process on the system, a directory /proc/PID contains files describing the process in question. In addition, a file /proc/self exists that's a link pointing to the currently running process. The following table describes the files under /proc/PID.

File	Description
cwd	The link to the current working directory. The link target is of the form [DEV]:INODE, where DEV is the device on which the current working directory resides and INODE is the inode of the directory.
fd	A directory containing links to the open descriptor for the given process. They're named according their positions in the descriptor table (0 is for standard input, 1 is for standard output, and so on). Each link target is in the same format as that of cwd.
root	A link pointing to the root directory for the given process. The link target is in the same format as that of cwd.
cmdline	Command name and arguments, separated by null characters. This holds the complete command line for the process unless the process has been swapped out or is a zombie process.
environ	Environment variable name/value pairs, separated by null characters. Each name/value pair is of the form NAME=VALUE.
exe	A link to the process's executable. The link target is in the same format as that of cwd.
maps	A pipe containing virtual-address-to-disk-address mappings. For each address range, lists the page protection, the device and inode of the associated disk area, and the offset into the disk area. Zeroes for the inode and device indicate that no disk area is associated with the address range.
status	Formatted process information: executable name, process state (sleeping, running, and so on), PID and parent PID, user and group IDs, virtual memory usage, and signal-handling masks.

Kernel Message Logs

This section describes the facilities used for system and kernel logging and the trapping of kernel messages.

dmesg

```
dmesg [ -c ] [ -n LEVEL ]
```

dmesg is used to examine and control the kernel ring buffer. dmesg is used mainly to print boot-up messages.

Option	Description
-c	Clears the ring buffer contents after printing.
-n LEVEL	Sets the LEVEL at which the logging of messages is done to the console. For example, -n 1 prevents all messages (except panic messages) from appearing on the console. All levels of messages are still written to /proc/kmsg, so syslogd can still be used to control exactly where kernel messages appear. When the -n option is used, dmesg won't print or clear the kernel ring buffer.

syslogd

```
syslogd [ -d ] [ -f CONFIG_FILE ] [ -h ] [ -l HOSTLIST ] [ -m INTERVAL ] [ -n ]
➡[ -p SOCKET ] [ -r ] [ -s DOMAINLIST ] [ -v ]
```

Provides two system utilities that provide support for system logging and kernel message trapping. Support of both Internet and UNIX local domain sockets enables this utility package to support both local and remote logging.

The main configuration file /etc/syslog.conf (or an alternative file given with the -f option) is read at startup. Lines that begin with the hash mark (#) and empty lines are ignored. If an error occurs during parsing, the whole line is ignored.

Option	Description
-d	Turns on debug mode, which causes syslogd to remain in the foreground and log debug information to the terminal.
-f CONFIG_FILE	Specifies an alternative configuration file.
-h	Forwards any remote messages it receives to forwarding hosts that have been defined.
-l HOSTLIST	Specifies a hostname that should be logged only with its simple hostname and not the fully qualified domain name. Multiple hosts can be specified using the colon (:) separator.
-m INTERVAL	syslogd logs a mark timestamp regularly. The default interval between two -- MARK -- lines is 20 minutes. This setting can be changed with the -m option.
-n	Avoid auto-backgrounding. This is needed especially if syslogd is started and controlled by init.
-p SOCKET	Use SOCKET instead of /dev/log.

continues >>

>>continued

Option	Description
-r	Enables the facility to receive messages from the network using an Internet domain socket with the **syslog** service. The default is not to receive any messages from the network.
-s DOMAINLIST	Specifies a domain name that should be stripped off before logging. Multiple domains can be specified using the colon (:) separator. If multiple domains are specified, the first match is the one used.
-v	Print version and exit.

11
Network Administration

This chapter deals with administration of network transport and services. Commands, daemons, and configuration files are divided into several functional groups.

For more information regarding installation and setup of networks involving Linux servers and workstations, see the resources listed in Appendix C, "Web Resources."

Hardware/IP Address Mapping

Network hosts map hardware addresses to IP addresses and vice versa using the Address Resolution Protocol (ARP) and Reverse Address Resolution Protocol (RARP). The commands and configuration files in this section are used to set up ARP and RARP.

arp

```
arp [-vn] [-H TYPE] [-i IF] -a [HOSTNAME]
arp [-v] [-i IF] -d HOSTNAME [pub]
arp [-v] [-H TYPE] [-i IF] -s HOSTNAME HW_ADDR [temp]
arp [-v] [-H TYPE] [-i IF] -s HOSTNAME HW_ADDR [netmask NM] pub
arp [-v] [-H TYPE] [-i IF] -Ds HOSTNAME IFA [netmask NM] pub
arp [-vnD] [-H TYPE] [-i IF] -f FILENAME
```

arp is used to manipulate the kernel's ARP cache. It's mainly used for clearing address mapping entries and manually setting new ones. It can also produce formatted dumps of the ARP cache for diagnostic purposes. The following table describes the options that arp accepts. HOSTNAMEs can be either symbolic names or IP addresses in dotted decimal notation.

Option	Description
-a [HOSTNAME] or --display [HOSTNAME]	Shows entries for HOSTNAME. All entries will be displayed if HOSTNAME is omitted.
-D or --use-device	Used with the -s option. Uses the interface IFA's hardware address.

continues >>

>>continued

Option	Description
-d HOSTNAME or --delete HOSTNAME	Removes the entry for host HOSTNAME.
-f FILENAME or --file FILENAME	Like the -s option except that address information is read from the file FILENAME. The file /etc/ethers or another file of the same format can be used for this. See /etc/ethers for more information.
-H TYPE or --hw-type TYPE	Restricts operation to entries of hardware type TYPE. The default for TYPE is ether (IEEE 802.3 10Mbps Ethernet). Other possible values include arcnet (ARCnet), ax25 (AX.25), and netrom (NET/ROM).
-i IF or --device IF	Selects interface IF. When dumping the ARP cache, only entries matching interface IF will be printed. Setting a permanent or temporary ARP entry will use the specified device. If no device is given, the kernels guess the device from the routing table. For pub entries, the specified interface is the interface on which ARP requests will be answered.
-n or -numeric	Shows number addresses instead of trying to determine symbolic host, port, or usernames.
-s HOSTNAME HW_ADDR or --set HOSTNAME HW_ADDR	Manually creates an ARP address-mapping entry for host HOSTNAME with hardware address set to the HW_ADDR class. When adding proxy ARP entries (those with the publish flag set), a netmask can be specified to proxy ARP for entire subnets. If the temp flag isn't supplied, entries will be permanently stored into the ARP cache.
-v	Verbose operation.

rarp

```
rarp [-V] [--version] [-h] [--help]
rarp -a
rarp [-v] -d HOSTNAME ...
rarp [-v] [-t TYPE] -s HOSTNAME HW_ADDR
```

rarp is used to manage the kernel's RARP table. It's mainly used for setting and clearing address-mapping entries. For diagnostic purposes, it can also be used to produce a formatted dump of the RARP table.

The RARP protocol is typically used by diskless workstations that know their hardware addresses but don't know their IP addresses upon startup. They can send out a RARP request to find out their own IP addresses. In order to use RARP, the "Reverse ARP" networking option must be enabled in the kernel.

Option	Description
-a or --list	Lists entries in the RARP table.
-d *HOSTNAME* or --delete *HOSTNAME*	Removes the entries for *HOSTNAME*.
-s *HOSTNAME HW_ADDR* or --set *HOSTNAME HW*_ADDR	Creates a RARP address-mapping entry for host *HOSTNAME* with the hardware address set to the *HW_ADDR* class.
-V	Displays the version of rarp in use.
-v	Verbose operation.
-t *TYPE*	Restricts operation to entries of type *TYPE*. The default is ether (IEEE 802.3 10Mbps Ethernet). Other possible values for *TYPE* include ax25 (AX.25) and netrom (NET/ROM).

/etc/ethers

The /etc/ethers file is used to map 48-bit Ethernet station addresses to IP addresses and vice versa. Each line uses this form:

```
ETHERNET_ADDRESS IP_ADDRESS
```

where the separator is any number of spaces and/or tabs. Comments begin with #. The *ETHERNET_ADDRESS* is a list of six hexadecimal numbers ranging from 0 to ff and separated by colons (:). The *IP_ADDRESS* is either a dotted decimal IP address or a hostname that can be resolved by DNS. For example:

```
#Dotted decimal entry:
08:00:20:20:60:CB 205.146.27.34

#DNS resolvable entry:
08:00:21:20:AD:42 wilbur.leba.net
```

Domain Name to IP Address Mapping

Network software uses numeric IP addresses to route data, but symbolic hostnames are more convenient for users. Internet Domain Name Service (DNS) and resolver routines accomplish the mapping of symbolic domain names to IP addresses and vice versa.

named

```
named OPTION ... [ CONFIG_FILE ]
```

named is the Internet domain name server. Without any arguments, named will read the default configuration file /etc/named.conf, read any initial data, and listen for queries. A *CONFIG_FILE* argument given at the end of the command line will override any *CONFIG_FILE* specified by using the -b or -c flags (see the following table).

The operation of named is controlled mainly by its configuration file. For more information on configuring named, see the BIND documentation and other sources of information listed in Appendix C.

Option	Description
-b¦c *CONFIG_FILE*	Uses the alternate *CONFIG_FILE*. The default is /etc/named.conf.
-d *N*	Sets the debug level to *N*. Prints debug messages associated with the level.
-f	Run in the foreground; don't fork and don't run as a daemon. (The default is to run as a daemon.)
-p *PORT*	Sends queries on port *PORT* rather than the value specified for domain service in /etc/services.
-q	Traces all incoming queries if compiled with QRYLOG.
-r	Turns off recursion. Answers can come only from local (primary or secondary) zones. This can be used on root servers. The default is to use recursion.
-w *DIRECTORY*	Sets the working directory of the server.

/etc/hosts

The /etc/hosts file is used to map IP addresses to hostnames and vice versa. Each line contains an IP address, a hostname, and optional aliases for the hostnames. The fields are separated by spaces or tabs. Any characters following # are ignored and can be used as comments.

Example entries:

```
#It is customary to use "localhost" to refer to local machine
127.0.0.1      localhost
#
191.72.1.1     myhost  myhost.mydomain.net
```

/etc/host.conf

The file /etc/host.conf contains configuration information used by the resolver library. Each line is a keyword followed by arguments if applicable. Valid keywords are shown in the following table.

Keyword	Description
alert	If this option is set to on and the nospoof option is also set, the resolver will log a warning of the error via the syslog facility. The default value is off.
multi	Valid values are on and off. If set to on, the resolver library will return all valid addresses for a host that appears in the /etc/hosts file, instead of only the first address. This is off by default, as it may cause a substantial performance loss at sites with large host files.
nospoof	Valid values are on and off. If set to on, the resolver library will attempt to prevent hostname spoofing to enhance the security of rlogin and rsh. This is accomplished by validating each address lookup with a hostname lookup for the address that was found. If the two hostnames don't match, the query will fail.

Keyword	Description
order	Specifies the order in which host lookups are done. It should be followed by a comma-separated list of lookup methods. Valid methods are bind, hosts, and nis.
reorder	Valid values are on and off. If set to on, the resolver will attempt to reorder host addresses so that local addresses are listed first when a gethostbyname is performed. Reordering is done for all lookup methods. The default value is off.
trim	This keyword can be listed more than once. Each occurrence should be followed by a single domain name with the leading dot. When set, the resolver library will automatically trim the given domain name from the end of any hostname resolved via DNS. This is intended for use with local hosts and domains.

/etc/networks

The /etc/networks file is used to map IP network addresses to network names and vice versa. Each line contains a network name and a network address. The fields are separated by spaces or tabs. Comments start with # and blank lines are ignored.

Example entries:

```
#local network
localnet 127.0.0.0
myhost.mydomain.net 191.72.2.0
```

Diskless Client Support

The Internet Bootstrap Protocol (BOOTP) enables diskless workstations to boot themselves with the help of central servers.

bootparamd and rpc.bootparamd

rpc.bootparamd [-d] [-s] [-r *ROUTER*] [-f *FILE*]

bootparamd is a server that provides boot-related information to diskless clients. It gets the information it needs from /etc/bootparams by default.

Option	Description
-d	Displays debugging information.
-f *FILE*	Uses *FILE* instead of /etc/bootparams as the boot parameter file.
-r *ROUTER*	*ROUTER* is the hostname or IP address of the default router. The default is the machine running the server.
-s	Logs the debugging information to syslog.

bootpd and bootpgw

```
bootpd [ -v ] [ -i -s -t TIMEOUT -d LEVEL -c CHDIR_PATH ]
➥[ BOOTPTAB [ DUMPFILE ] ]

bootpgw [ -v ] [ -i -s -t TIMEOUT -d LEVEL ] SERVER
```

bootpd implements an Internet Bootstrap Protocol (BOOTP) server as defined in RFC951, RFC1532, and RFC1533. It's usually invoked by inetd but can be run in a standalone mode from a shell. Standalone mode is particularly useful when bootpd is used with a large configuration database, where the startup delay might otherwise prevent timely response to client requests. The configuration database is *BOOTPTAB*. If *BOOTPTAB* isn't supplied, /etc/bootptab is used. *DUMPFILE* is the file into which bootpd will dump its internal database when it receives a SIGUSR1 signal. This option is recognized only if it was compiled with the -DDEBUG flag.

bootpgw implements a simple BOOTP gateway that can be used to forward requests and responses between clients on one subnet and a BOOTP server (that is, bootpd) on another subnet. bootpgw can also run in standalone mode, but this isn't very useful since it has very little startup delay because it doesn't read a configuration file. *SERVER* is the name of the BOOTP server to which bootpgw will forward BOOTPREQUEST packets.

While either bootpd or bootpgw will forward BOOTREPLY packets, only bootpgw will forward BOOTREQUEST packets.

Option	Description
-c CHDIR_PATH	Sets the current directory used by bootpd while checking the existence and size of client boot files.
-d DEBUG_LEVEL	Sets the *DEBUG_LEVEL* variable that controls the number of debugging messages generated. For example, -d4 or -d 4 will set the debugging level to 4. For compatibility with older versions of bootpd, omitting the numeric parameter will simply increment the debug level by one.
-i	Forces inetd mode. This option is obsolete, but remains for compatibility with older versions of bootpd.
-s	Forces standalone mode. This option is obsolete, but remains for compatibility with older versions of bootpd.
-t TIMEOUT	Specifies the timeout value (in minutes) that a bootpd process will wait for a BOOTP packet before exiting. If no packets are received for *TIMEOUT* seconds, the program will exit. A *TIMEOUT* value of 0 (zero) means "run forever." In standalone mode, this option is forced to zero.
-v	Prints the version and exits.

bootpef

```
bootpef OPTION ... [ CLIENT_NAME ... ]
```

bootpef builds the Extension Path files described by RFC 1497 (tag 18). If any *CLIENT_NAME* arguments are specified, bootpef compiles the extension files for only those clients.

Option	Description
-c *CHDIR_PATH*	Sets the current directory used while creating extension files. This is useful when the extension filenames are specified as relative pathnames, and bootpef needs to use the same current directory as the TFTP server (typically /tftpboot).
-d *DEBUG_LEVEL*	Sets the *DEBUG_LEVEL* variable that controls the amount of debugging messages generated. For example, -d4 or -d 4 will set the debugging level to 4.
-f *CONFIG_FILE*	Sets the name of the configuration file that specifies the option data to be sent to each client. The default is /etc/bootptab.

bootptest

bootptest *OPTION* ... *SERVER_NAME* [*TEMPLATE_FILE*]

bootptest sends BOOTP requests to the host specified as *SERVER_NAME* at one-second intervals until a response is received or ten requests have gone unanswered. After a response is received, bootptest will wait one more second, listening for additional responses. A *TEMPLATE_FILE* can be specified, in which case bootptest uses the (binary) contents of this file to initialize the options area of the request packet.

Option	Description
-f *BOOTFILE*	Fills in the boot file field of the request with *BOOTFILE*. *BOOTFILE* is a file containing the binary image of an operating system image required to boot the client.
-h	Uses the hardware (Ethernet) address to identify the client. By default, the IP address is copied into the request, indicating that this client already knows its IP address.
-m *MAGIC_NUMBER*	Initializes the first word of the vendor options field with *MAGIC_NUMBER*.

Serial Line IP Networking

Serial Line IP (SLIP) and Point-to-Point Protocol (PPP) setup and configuration.

To use these protocols, TCP/IP networking must be enabled in the kernel, along with support for the PPP and/or SLIP network devices. Although serial line IP is typically used over modems, these protocols can be used over any serial point-to-point connection.

chat

chat [*OPTION* ...] [*SCRIPT*]

chat executes the dialogue between computer and modem that's required to establish the connection between the local Point-to-Point Protocol daemon (pppd) and pppd on the remote host.

SCRIPT defines the communications. It consists of one or more "expect–send" pairs of strings, separated by spaces, with an optional "subexpect–subsend" string pair, separated by a hyphen, as in the following example:

```
ogin:-BREAK-ogin: ppp ssword: mypassword
```

This line indicates that chat should expect the string ogin:. If it fails to receive a login prompt within the time interval allotted, it will send a break sequence to the remote and then expect the string ogin:. If the first ogin: is received, the break sequence isn't generated.

After it receives the login prompt, chat will send the string ppp and then expect the prompt ssword:. When it receives the prompt for the password, it will send the password mypassword.

For chat to work, TCP/IP networking must be enabled in the kernel, along with PPP network device support.

Option	Description
-e	Starts with the echo option turned on. When echoing is enabled, all output from the modem is echoed to standard error.
-f CHAT_FILE	Reads the chat script from CHAT_FILE.
-r REPORT_FILE	Sets the file for output of the report strings. If the REPORT keyword is used in the script, the resulting strings are written to this file. If this option isn't used and REPORT keywords are used, the standard error file is used for the report strings.
-S	Don't use syslog. (By default, error messages are sent to syslog.)
-s	Sends all log messages and error messages from -v to standard error.
-T PHONE_NUMBER	Substitutes PHONE_NUMBER for the \T metacharacter in a send string. This is usually a phone number.
-t TIMEOUT	Sets the timeout interval for expected strings to be received.
-U PHONE_NUMBER	Substitutes PHONE_NUMBER for the \U metacharacter in a send string. This is useful when dialing an ISDN terminal adapter that requires two numbers.
-v	Executes the script in verbose mode. Logs the execution state of the chat script. The default logging method is through syslog, although it can be altered with the -S and -s flags.
-V	Standard error verbose mode. Logs the execution state of the chat script through standard error.

dip, diplogin, and diplogini

```
dip [-v] [-m MTU] [-p PROTO] SCRIPTFILE
dip -t [-v]
dip -i [-a] [-v]
dip [-v] -k [-l TTY_LINE]
diplogin [USERNAME]
diplogini -v -k [-l tty_line]
```

`dip` handles dial-up IP connections used by SLIP and PPP. It can handle both incoming and outgoing connections and uses password authentication for incoming connections.

`diplogin` is equivalent to `dip -i`. `diplogini` is equivalent to `dip -i -a`. These are mainly used with versions of `login` that don't pass command-line parameters to the shell program.

SCRIPTFILE is a file containing commands used by `dip` to establish a connection. See Appendix C for sources of information on `dip` interactive mode commands and scripts.

Option	Description
-a	Prompts for username and password.
-i	Acts as a dial-in server.
-k	Kills the `dip` process that has locked the device specified by -l or the most recent invocation of `dip`.
-l *TTY_LINE*	Indicates the line to be killed using the -k option.
-m *MTU*	Sets the Maximum Transfer Unit (MTU). The default is 296.
-p *PROTO*	Sets the line protocol. *PROTO* must be SLIP, CSLIP, SLIP6, CSLIP6, PPP, or TERM.
-t	Runs in interactive test mode.
-v	Enables verbose mode.

The following is a sample **chat** script:

```
main:
  get $mtu 1006
  default
  port /dev/modem
  speed 57600
  reset
  if $errlvl != 0 goto error
  dial 5551212
  if $errlvl != 1 goto error

login:
#Wait for login prompt from remote host.
  wait ogin:
  if $errlvl != 0 goto error
#Send user ID with carriage return and wait for password prompt.
  send mistered\r
  wait ord:
  if $errlvl != 0 goto error
#Send password with carriage return
  send wilbur\r

#Remote and local IP addresses are supplied by remote host.
  get $rmtip remote
  if $errlvl != 0 goto error
  sleep 1
  get $locip remote
  if $errlvl != 0 goto error
```

continues >>

>>continued

```
#Make new connection default route and enter CSLIP (SLIP with compressed
#datagram headers) mode.
done:
  default
  mode CSLIP
  goto exit

error:
  print connection failed

exit:
```

pppconfig

pppconfig [--help] ¦ [--version]

pppconfig is an interactive menu-driven utility that can help automate the setup of dial-up PPP connections.

Option	Description
--help	Prints the help message and exits.
--version	Prints the version number and exits.

pppd

pppd [*TTY_NAME*] [*SPEED*] [*OPTIONS*]

pppd is the Point-to-Point Protocol (PPP) daemon. It's the preferred method for transmitting datagrams over serial point-to-point links. PPP is composed of three parts: a method for encapsulating datagrams over serial links, an extensible Link Control Protocol (LCP), and a family of Network Control Protocols (NCP) for establishing and configuring different network-layer protocols.

The encapsulation scheme is provided by driver code in the kernel. pppd provides the basic LCP, authentication support, and an NCP for establishing and configuring the Internet Protocol (IP)—called the IP Control Protocol, or IPCP.

pppd accepts a large number of command-line options. The most frequently used options are listed in the following table:

Option	Description
SPEED	Sets the baud rate to *SPEED* (in decimal).
TTY_NAME	Name of the serial device over which communication will take place. The /dev prefix will be added, if necessary. If no device name is given, or if the name of the terminal connected to the standard input is given, pppd will use that terminal, and will not fork to put itself in the background.

Option	Description
asyncmap MAP	Sets the async character map to MAP. This map describes which control characters can't be received successfully over the serial line. pppd will ask the peer to send these characters as a two-byte escape sequence. The argument is a 32-bit hex number with each bit representing a character to escape. Bit 0 (00000001) represents the character 0x00; bit 31 (80000000) represents the character 0x1f or ^_. If multiple asyncmap options are given, the values are combined with OR. If no asyncmap option is given, no async character map will be negotiated for the receive direction. The peer should then escape all control characters.
auth	Requires the peer to authenticate itself before allowing network packets to be sent or received.
call NAME	Reads options from the file /etc/ppp/peers/NAME. The name string can't begin with / or include .. as a pathname component.
connect SCRIPT	Uses the executable or shell command specified by SCRIPT to set up the serial line. This script would typically use the chat program to dial the modem and start the remote PPP session.
crtscts	Uses hardware flow control to control the flow of data on the serial port.
defaultroute	Adds a default route to the kernel routing table, using the peer as the gateway, when IPCP negotiation is successfully completed. This entry is removed when the PPP connection is broken.
disconnect SCRIPT	Runs the executable or shell command specified by SCRIPT after pppd has terminated the link.
escape CHARS	Specifies that certain characters should be escaped on transmission, regardless of whether the peer requests them to be escaped with its async control character map. CHARS is a list of hex numbers separated by commas.
file NAME	Reads options from the file NAME.
lock	Specifies that pppd should create a UUCP-style lock file for the serial device to ensure exclusive access to the device.
mru N	Sets the Maximum Receive Unit (MRU) value to N. pppd will ask the peer to send packets of no more than N bytes. The minimum MRU value is 128. The default MRU value is 1500.
mtu N	Sets the MTU (Maximum Transmit Unit) value to N. Unless the peer requests a smaller value via MRU negotiation, pppd will request that the kernel networking code send data packets of no more than N bytes through the PPP network interface.
passive	Enables the "passive" option in the LCP. If no reply is received from the peer when pppd attempts to initiate a connection, pppd will then just wait passively for a valid LCP packet from the peer instead of exiting, as it would without this option.

The following **bash** script is used to initiate a PPP connection. This is the first part of the pair of scripts. Although these scripts are simple, they're not secure because the codes are visible with the **ps** command.

```
#!/bin/sh
#
#
# These are the parameters. Change as needed.
TELEPHONE=555-1212        # The telephone number for the connection
ACCOUNT=mistered          # The account name for logon
PASSWORD=wilbur           # The password for this account
LOCAL_IP=0.0.0.0          # Local IP address if known. Dynamic = 0.0.0.0
REMOTE_IP=0.0.0.0         # Remote IP address if desired. Normally 0.0.0.0
NETMASK=255.255.255.0     # The proper netmask if needed
#
# Export them so that they will be available at 'ppp-on-dialer' time.
export TELEPHONE ACCOUNT PASSWORD
#
# This is the location of the script which dials the phone and logs
# in.  Please use the absolute file name as the $PATH variable is not
# used on the connect option.  (To do so on a 'root' account would be
# a security hole so don't ask.)
#
DIALER_SCRIPT=/etc/ppp/ppp-on-dialer
#
# Initiate the connection
#
# I put most of the common options on this command. Please, don't
# forget the 'lock' option or some programs such as mgetty will not
# work. The asyncmap and escape will permit the PPP link to work with
# a telnet or rlogin connection. You are welcome to make any changes
# as desired. Don't use the 'defaultroute' option if you currently
# have a default route to an ethernet gateway.
#
exec /usr/sbin/pppd debug lock modem crtscts /dev/ttyS0 38400 \
        asyncmap 20A0000 escape FF kdebug 0 $LOCAL_IP:$REMOTE_IP \
        noipdefault netmask $NETMASK defaultroute connect $DIALER_SCRIPT
```

This is part two of the PPP connection script. It will perform the connection protocol for the desired connection. It's referenced in the first part by the **DIALER_SCRIPT** variable.

```
#!/bin/sh
#
#
exec chat -v                                                    \
        TIMEOUT         3                                       \
        ABORT           '\nBUSY\r'                              \
        ABORT           '\nNO ANSWER\r'                         \
        ABORT           '\nRINGING\r\n\r\nRINGING\r'            \
        ''              \rAT                                    \
        'OK-+++\c-OK'   ATH0                                    \
        TIMEOUT         30                                      \
        OK              ATDT$TELEPHONE                          \
        CONNECT         ''                                      \
        ogin:--ogin:    $ACCOUNT                                \
        assword:        $PASSWORD
```

The following script can be used to shut down the PPP connection established by the preceding scripts.

```
#!/bin/sh
#####################################################################
#
# Determine the device to be terminated.
#
if [ "$1" = "" ]; then
      DEVICE=ppp0
else
    DEVICE=$1
fi


#####################################################################
#
# If the ppp0 pid file is present then the program is running. Stop it.
if [ -r /var/run/$DEVICE.pid ]; then
        kill -INT `cat /var/run/$DEVICE.pid`
#
# If the kill did not work then there is no process running for this
# pid. It may also mean that the lock file will be left. You may wish
# to delete the lock file at the same time.
        if [ ! "$?" = "0" ]; then
                rm -f /var/run/$DEVICE.pid
                echo "ERROR: Removed stale pid file"
                exit 1
        fi
#
# Success. Let pppd clean up its own junk.
        echo "PPP link to $DEVICE terminated."
        exit 0
fi
#
# The ppp process is not running for ppp0
echo "ERROR: PPP link is not active on $DEVICE"
exit 1
```

pppstats

pppstats OPTION ... [INTERFACE]

pppstats reports PPP related statistics at regular intervals for a selected PPP INTERFACE. If INTERFACE isn't given, ppp0 will be used.

Option	Description
-a	Displays absolute values rather than changes since the last report.
-c COUNT	Repeats the display COUNT times.
-r	Displays additional statistics summarizing the compression ratio achieved by the packet compression algorithm being used.
-v	Displays additional statistics related to the performance of the Van Jacobson TCP header compression algorithm.
-w SECONDS	Pauses SECONDS seconds between each display. The default interval is five seconds.
-z	Instead of the standard display, shows statistics indicating the performance of the packet compression algorithm in use.

slattach

slattach [-dehlLmnqv] [-c *COMMAND*] [-p *PROTO*] [-s *SPEED*] [*TTY*]

slattach will attach a serial device (typically modems) to a network interface. This enables the device to drive a point-to-point link to another computer.

Option	Description
-c *COMMAND*	Executes *COMMAND* when the line is hung up. This can be used to run scripts or reestablish connections when a link goes down.
-d	Enables debugging output. Useful when determining why a given setup doesn't work.
-e	Exits right after initializing the device, instead of waiting for the line to hang up.
-h	Exits when the carrier is lost. This works on both /dev/tty and /dev/cua devices by directly monitoring the carrier status every 15 seconds.
-L	Enables three-wire operation. The terminal is moved into CLOCAL mode, carrier watching is disabled.
-l	Creates a UUCP-style lockfile for the device in /var/lock.
-m	Don't initialize the line into 8-bits raw mode.
-n	Disables message access to the device. Equivalent to mesg n.
-p *PROTO*	Uses protocol *PROTO* on the line. The default is cslip (compressed SLIP). Other possible values are slip (normal SLIP), adaptive (adaptive CSLIP/SLIP), ppp (Point-to-Point Protocol) and kiss (a protocol used for communicating with AX.25 packet-radio terminal-node controllers).
-q	Quiet mode. No messages at all.
-s *SPEED*	Sets line speed to *SPEED*.
TTY	Attaches *TTY*. If not supplied, the current terminal line is used.
-v	Enables verbose mode.

Remote Procedure Calls

When managing the Remote Procedure Call (RPC) facility, it may be useful to note that some of the services (such as NFS) are based on RPC. Most of the filenames for the daemons that provide RPC–based services begin with rpc.

pmap_dump

pmap_dump

pmap_dump prints a list of all registered RPC programs that are running on the local host. The output can be used as input to pmap_set to restart the portmapper.

pmap_set

pmap_set

pmap_set is used to restart the RPC portmapper and restore its registry. It reads registry information from standard input in the format produced by pmap_dump.

portmap

```
portmap [-d] [-v]
```

portmap provides the mapping of TCP/IP and UDP/IP port numbers to RPC program numbers for use by RPC–based services. When clients of RPC programs request service, they first contact portmap to obtain the port number through which the service will communicate. portmap must be started before any RPC servers can be invoked.

Option	Description
-d	Debug mode. This prevents portmap from running as a daemon. Errors and debugging information are printed to standard error.
-v	Runs portmap in verbose mode.

rpcinfo

```
rpcinfo -p [HOST]
rpcinfo [-n PORTNUM] -u HOST PROGRAM [VERSION]
rpcinfo [-n PORTNUM] -t HOST PROGRAM [VERSION]
rpcinfo -b PROGRAM VERSION
rpcinfo -d PROGRAM VERSION
```

rpcinfo reports the status of the RPC server running on *HOST*. *PROGRAM* can be either a name (if included in /etc/rpc) or a number.

If *VERSION* is specified, rpcinfo attempts to call that version of the specified *PROGRAM*. Otherwise, rpcinfo attempts to find all the registered version numbers for the specified program by calling version 0 and attempting to call each registered version. *Note:* The version number is required for -b and -d options.

Option	Description
-b *PROGRAM VERSION*	Makes an RPC broadcast to procedure 0 of *PROGRAM* and *VERSION* using UDP, and reports all hosts that respond.
-d *PROGRAM VERSION*	Deletes registration for the version *VERSION* of *PROGRAM*.
-n *PORTNUM*	Uses *PORTNUM* as the port number for the -t and -u options, instead of the port number given by the portmapper.
-p *[HOST]*	Probes the portmapper on *HOST* and prints a list of all registered RPC programs. If *HOST* isn't provided, the local host is probed.
-t *HOST PROGRAM*	Makes an RPC call to version 0 of procedure *PROGRAM* on the specified *HOST* using TCP, and reports whether a response was received.
-u *HOST PROGRAM*	Makes an RPC call to version 0 of procedure *PROGRAM* on the specified *HOST* using UDP, and reports whether a response was received.

/etc/rpc

The /etc/rpc file is used to map RPC–based service names to their program numbers and vice versa. Each line contains the primary name for the service followed by the program number and any alias names that the service may have. Fields are separated by spaces and tabs. Comments begin with #.

Sample entry:

```
rstatd    100001  rstat rstat_svc rup perfmeter
```

General Network Services

Enabling, disabling, and managing network services.

inetd

```
inetd [-d] [-q QUEUELENGTH] [CONFIG_FILE]
```

inetd is normally run at boot time. It listens for connections on certain Internet sockets. When a connection is found on one of its sockets, it decides what service the socket corresponds to, and invokes a program to service the request. The basic function of inetd is to enable one daemon to invoke several others and reduce the load on the system. If given, inetd will read its configuration information from CONFIG_FILE. Otherwise it will use /etc/inetd.conf. See the next section for more information.

Option	Description
-d	Turns on debugging.
-q QUEUELENGTH	Sets the size of the socket listen queue to the specified value. The default is 128.

/etc/inetd.conf

The inetd daemon reads its configuration information from /etc/inetd.conf by default. Each line defines a service managed by inetd. The fields are separated by tabs or spaces. Comments begin with # and blank lines are ignored. Each field must contain a value. The record format is defined as follows:

```
SERVICE_NAME SOCKET_TYPE PROTOCOL { wait ¦ nowait[.MAX] } USER[.GROUP]
➥SERVER_PROGRAM SERVER_ARGS
```

To specify a Sun RPC–based service, the entry should contain these fields:

```
SERVICE_NAME/VERSION SOCKET_TYPE RPC/PROTOCOL { wait ¦ nowait[.MAX] }
➥USER[.GROUP] SERVER_PROGRAM SERVER_ARGS
```

SERVICE_NAME is the name of a valid service in the file /etc/services. When used to specify a Sun RPC–based service, this field is a valid RPC service name in the file /etc/rpc. The part to the right of the first slash (/) is the RPC version number. This can simply be a single numeric argument or a range of versions. A range is bounded by the low version to the high version (for example, rusers/1-3).

SOCKET_TYPE should be stream, dgram, raw, rdm, or seqpacket, depending on whether the socket is a stream, datagram, raw, reliably delivered message, or sequenced packet socket.

PROTOCOL must be a valid protocol as given in /etc/protocols. Examples might include tcp or udp. RPC–based services are specified with the rpc/tcp or rpc/udp service type.

wait is used for single-threaded servers that process all incoming datagrams on a socket and time out. nowait is for multithreaded servers that free the socket so that further messages can be received on it. *MAX* specifies the maximum number of server instances that can be spawned from inetd within an interval of 60 seconds. When omitted, *MAX* defaults to 40.

USER should contain the username of the user as whom the server should run. This allows for servers to be given less permission than root. An optional group name can be specified by appending a dot to the username followed by the group name. This allows for servers to run with a different primary group ID than specified in the password file.

SERVER_PROGRAM should contain the pathname of the program to be executed by inetd when a request is found on its socket. If inetd provides this service internally, this field should be internal.

SERVER_ARGS are the arguments supplied to *SERVER_PROGRAM*. If the service is provided internally, the word internal should be entered in this field.

/etc/protocols

The /etc/protocols file describes the various DARPA Internet protocols that are available from the TCP/IP subsystem. These numbers will occur in the protocol field of any IP header. This file should be used for reference only and shouldn't be modified, since changes would result in incorrect IP packets. Fields are delimited by spaces or tabs. Comments start with # and blank lines are ignored. Each entry uses the following format:

PROTOCOL NUMBER [ALIAS ...]

PROTOCOL is the name (ip, tcp, udp, etc.) for the protocol. *NUMBER* is the official number for the protocol as it would appear in IP headers. The *ALIAS*es are optional alias names for the protocol.

Sample entry:

```
tcp 6 TCP     # transmission control protocol
```

/etc/services

/etc/services provides mapping between text names of Internet services and their port numbers and protocol types. Fields are separated by spaces or tabs. Comments begin with # and blank lines are ignored.

Each entry is of this form:

```
SERVICE_NAME PORT/PROTOCOL [ ALIAS ... ]
```

SERVICE_NAME is the name by which the service is known and looked up. *PORT* is the decimal number of the port that will use the service. *PROTOCOL* is the type of protocol used. This value should match one of those found in /etc/protocols. Typical values include tcp and udp. The *ALIAS*es are other names for the same service.

Sample entries:

```
ftp   21/tcp
smtp  25/tcp mail
```

Diagnostic and Monitoring Tools

This section describes tools that can be used to investigate network problems and measure network performance.

fping

```
fping [ OPTION ... ] [ SYSTEM ... ]
```

fping uses Internet Control Message Protocol (ICMP) echo requests to determine whether one or more host *SYSTEM*s is reachable. The target hosts can be named on the command line or read from a file (including standard input). Unlike ping, the output of fping is suitable for automated processing by shell scripts. Exit status is 0 if all the hosts are reachable, 1 if some hosts were unreachable, 2 if any IP addresses aren't found, 3 for invalid command-line arguments, and 4 for a system call failure.

Option	Description
-A	Displays targets by IP address rather than DNS name.
-a	Shows systems that are alive.
-B N	In the default mode, fping sends several requests to a target before giving up, waiting longer for a reply on each successive request. This parameter is the value by which the wait time is multiplied on each successive request. It must be entered as a floating-point number. The default is 1.5.
-b N	Number of bytes in each packet of data to be sent. The minimum size (normally 12) allows room for the data that fping needs to do its work (sequence number, timestamp). The reported received data size includes the IP header (normally 20 bytes) and ICMP header (8 bytes), so the minimum total size is 40 bytes. The default is 56, as in ping.
-C N	Similar to -c except that the statistics are displayed in a format designed for automated response time analysis.
-c N	Number of request packets to send to each target. With this option, a line is displayed for each received response (this can be suppressed with -q or -Q). Statistics about responses for each target are displayed when all requests have been sent.
-d	Uses DNS to find hostnames for given IP addresses. This allows you to give fping a list of IP addresses as input and print hostnames in the output.
-e	Shows elapsed round-trip time for packets.

Option	Description
-f *FILE*	Reads the list of targets from the file *FILE*.
-h	Prints the usage message.
-i *N*	The minimum amount of time (in milliseconds) between sending ping packets to any target. The default is 25.
-l	Loops sending packets to each target indefinitely. Interruption with Ctrl+C will display response statistics for each target.
-m	Sends pings to each of a target host's multiple interfaces.
-n	Same as -d.
-p	In looping or counting modes (-l, -c, or -C), sets the time in milliseconds that fping waits between successive packets to an individual target. The default is 1000.
-Q *N*	Like -q, but shows summary results every *N* seconds.
-q	Quiet. Set exit status only and don't show per-target results.
-r *N*	Retry limit. This is the number of times an attempt at pinging a target will be made, not including the first try. The default is 3.
-s	Prints cumulative statistics on exit.
-t *N*	Initial target timeout in milliseconds. In the default mode, this is the amount of time that fping waits for a response to its first request. Successive timeouts are multiplied by the backoff factor. The default is 500.
-u	Shows targets that are unreachable.
-v	Prints fping version information.

netstat

```
netstat [-noca] [ADDRESS_FAMILIES]
netstat [-noca] [SOCKET_TYPES]
netstat -i [-a] [-c]
netstat -r [-c] [-n]
netstat -v
```

`netstat` displays network transport status information. The default operation with no options shows the active sockets of all configured address families. It can also print a formatted listing of the contents of the kernel routing table.

ADDRESS_FAMILIES can include one or more of --inet, --ipx, --netrom, --ddp, or --ax25, or -A followed by a list consisting of one or more of inet, ipx, netrom, ddp, or ax25, separated by commas.

For example,

```
netstat -A inet,ipx
```

or its equivalent,

```
netstat --inet --ipx
```

SOCKET_TYPES is one or more of { -t¦--tcp}, { -u¦--udp}, { -w¦--raw}, { -x¦--unix}, --ax25, --ipx, or --netrom.

For example,

netstat -u --tcp

or its equivalent,

netstat --udp -t

The following table describes the options used by netstat:

Option	Description
-a	Displays information about all sockets, even those that are listening only.
-c	Generates a listing of network status, one every second until interrupted.
-i	Shows network devices statistics.
-n	Disables the resolution of hostnames and service names when displaying remote and local addresses and ports. Shows hosts in dot notation (numbers).
-o	Displays timer states, expiration times, and backoff state.
-r	Displays the kernel routing table.
-v	Prints version information.

ping

ping *OPTION ... HOST*

ping uses the ICMP protocol's mandatory ECHO_REQUEST datagram to elicit an ICMP ECHO_RESPONSE from a host or gateway as designated by *HOST*.

If ping doesn't receive any reply packets at all, it will exit with code 1. On error, it exits with code 2. Otherwise, it exits with code 0. This makes it possible to use the exit code to see whether a host is alive.

Option	Description
-c *COUNT*	Stops after sending (and receiving) *COUNT* ECHO_RESPONSE packets.
-d	Sets the SO_DEBUG option on the socket being used.
-f	Floods ping. Outputs packets as fast as they come back or 100 times per second, whichever is greater. For every ECHO_REQUEST sent a period (.) is printed, while for every ECHO_REPLY received a backspace is printed. This provides a clear indication of how many packets are being dropped. This option should be used with caution, since it can put a great deal of stress on a network.
-i *WAIT*	Waits *WAIT* seconds between sending packets. The default is to wait for one second between packets. This option is incompatible with the -f option.
-l *PRELOAD*	Sends *PRELOAD* packets as fast as possible before falling into normal mode of operation. Only the superuser can use this option.

Option	Description
-n	Disables resolution of numeric addresses to symbolic names.
-p PATTERN	PATTERN is a pattern of bytes in hexadecimal format. Up to 16 bytes can be used to fill out the packets before sending them. This is useful for diagnosing data-dependent problems in a network. For example, -p ff will cause the sent packet to be filled with all 1s.
-R	Record route. Includes the RECORD_ROUTE option in the ECHO_REQUEST packet and displays the route buffer on returned packets. Note that the IP header is only large enough for nine such routes. Many hosts ignore or discard this option.
-r	Bypasses the normal routing tables and sends directly to a host on an attached network. If the host isn't on a directly attached network, an error is returned. This option can be used to ping a local host through an interface that has no route through it.
-s PACKETSIZE	Specifies the number of data bytes in each packet to be sent. The default is 56, which translates into 64 ICMP data bytes when combined with the 8 bytes of ICMP header data.
-v	Verbose output. Received ICMP packets other than ECHO_RESPONSE are listed.

traceroute

```
traceroute [ OPTION ... ] HOST [ PACKETSIZE ]
```

traceroute prints the route taken to a selected network HOST. The default probe datagram length is 38 but may be increased by specifying PACKETSIZE in bytes.

Option	Description
-l	Displays the "time to live" (ttl) value of the returned packet. This is useful for checking for asymmetric routing.
-m MAX_TTL	Sets the maximum time to live (maximum number of hops) used in outgoing probe packets. The default is 30 hops.
-n	Disables numeric-to-symbolic address resolution. Prints only the numeric address.
-p PORT	Sets the base UDP PORT number used in probes. The default is 33434.
-q NQUERIES	Sets the number of probes per ttl to NQUERIES. The default is 3.
-r	Bypasses the normal routing tables and sends directly to a host on an attached network. If the host isn't on a directly attached network, an error is returned. This option can be used to ping a local host through an interface that has no route through it.
-s SRC_ADDR	Uses the following IP address (which must be given as an IP number, not a hostname) as the source address in outgoing probe packets. On hosts with more than one IP address, this option can be used to force the source address to be something other than the IP address of the interface on which the probe packet is sent. If the IP address isn't one of this machine's interface addresses, an error is returned and nothing is sent.

continues >>

>>continued

Option	Description
-t *TOS*	Sets the "type-of-service" in probe packets to *TOS*. The default is **0** (zero). The value must be a decimal integer in the range **0** to **255**. This option can be used to see whether different type-of-service values result in different paths.
-v	Verbose output. Received ICMP packets other than TIME_EXCEEDED and UNREACHABLEs are listed.
-w	Sets the time (in seconds) to wait for a response to a probe. The default is **3** seconds.

Network Routing

Setup and configuration of network interface devices and kernel routing tables.

ifconfig

```
ifconfig [INTERFACE]
ifconfig INTERFACE [AFTYPE] OPTION ... ADDRESS ...
```

ifconfig is used to configure the kernel-resident network interfaces. It's used primarily at boot time to enable network transport. After that, it's usually needed only when debugging or tuning the system.

If no arguments are given, ifconfig displays the status of the currently active interfaces. If a single interface argument is given, it displays the status of the given interface only. With only the -a flag, it displays the status of all interfaces, even those that are down. Otherwise, it configures an interface.

The *AFTYPE* argument, if supplied, refers to a supported address family used for decoding and displaying all protocol addresses. Currently valid values for *AFTYPE* include inet (TCP/IP), ax25 (AMPR Packet Radio), ddp (Appletalk Phase 2), ipx (Novell IPX), and netrom (AMPR NET/ROM).

INTERFACE is the name of a network interface. This is usually a driver name followed by a unit number such as eth0 for the first Ethernet interface.

Valid arguments for *OPTION* are described in the following table:

Option	Description
-a	Displays the status of all interfaces, even those that are down.
ADDRESS	The IP address to be assigned to *INTERFACE*.
allmulti or -allmulti	Enables or disables "all-multicast" mode. If selected, all multicast packets on the network will be received by *INTERFACE*.
arp or -arp	Enables or disables the ARP protocol on *INTERFACE*.
[-]broadcast [*ADDRESS*]	If the *ADDRESS* argument is given, sets the protocol broadcast address for this interface. Otherwise, sets or clears the IFF_BROADCAST flag for the interface.
down	Deactivates *INTERFACE*.

Option	Description
-dstaddr *ADDRESS*	Sets the remote IP address for a point-to-point link. This keyword is obsolete and has been replaced by pointopoint.
hw *CLASS ADDRESS*	Sets the hardware address of this interface, if the device driver supports this operation. *CLASS* is the name of the hardware class. Hardware classes currently supported include ether (Ethernet), ax25 (AMPR AX.25), ARCnet, and netrom (AMPR NET/ROM). *ADDRESS* is the printable ASCII equivalent of the hardware address.
io_addr *ADDRESS*	Sets the start address in I/O space for the device.
irq *ADDRESS*	Sets the interrupt line used by this device.
media *TYPE*	Sets the physical port or medium type to be used by the device. Not all devices can change this setting, and those that can vary in what values they support. Typical values for *TYPE* are 10base2 (thin Ethernet), 10baseT (twisted-pair 10Mbps Ethernet), AUI (external transceiver) and so on. The special medium type of auto can be used to tell the driver to auto-sense the media.
mem_start *ADDRESS*	Sets the start address for shared memory used by this device.
metric *N*	Sets *INTERFACE* to metric. Presently, this argument isn't implemented but is accepted for compatibility.
mtu *N*	Sets the maximum transfer unit (MTU) for *INTERFACE*.
multicast	Sets the multicast flag on the interface. This normally isn't needed, since the drivers set the flag correctly themselves.
netmask *ADDRESS*	Sets the IP network mask for *INTERFACE*. This value defaults to the usual class A, B, or C network mask (as derived from the interface IP address), but it can be set to any value.
[-]pointopoint [*ADDRESS*]	Enables the point-to-point mode of an interface, meaning that it's a direct link between two machines with nobody else listening on it. If the *ADDRESS* argument is also given, sets the protocol address of the other side of the link. Otherwise, sets or clears the IFF_POINTOPOINT flag for the interface.
promisc or -promisc	Enables or disables "promiscuous" mode for *INTERFACE*. If selected, all packets on the network will be received by the interface.
txqueuelen *LENGTH*	Sets the length of the transmit queue for the device. It's useful to set this to small values for slower devices with a high latency (modem and ISDN links) to prevent fast bulk transfers from slowing down telnet sessions and other interactive traffic.
up	Activates *INTERFACE*. This is implied if an address is assigned to the interface.

ripquery

```
ripquery [-n] HOST
```

ripquery can request the listing of the kernel routing table from remote host *HOST*. The remote host must be running a RIP server in order to honor the request. The -n option can be used to suppress IP address-to-name resolution.

route

```
route [-CFvnee]
route [-v] [-A FAMILY] add OPTION ...
route [-v] [-A FAMILY] del OPTION ...
route [-V] [--version] [-h] [--help]
```

route is used to manage the kernel's routing table. It's used primarily to set up static routes to specific hosts or networks through an interface after they've been set up through ifconfig. Routes can be added with the **add** form and deleted with **del**.

Option	Description
-A *FAMILY*	*FAMILY* is the address family of the specified route. Valid values for *FAMILY* are inet, inet6, ddp, ipx, netrom, and ax25.
-C	Displays the kernel's route cache.
[dev]*IF*	Forces the route to be associated with device *IF*. The kernel will otherwise try to determine the device on its own (by checking already existing routes and device specifications, and where the route is added to). In most normal networks, you won't need this. If this is the last option on the command line, dev may be omitted.
-e	Uses netstat format for displaying the routing table. -ee will generate a very long line with all parameters from the routing table.
-F	Displays the kernel FIB routing table. The layout can be changed with -e and -ee.
-h	Displays the usage message.
-host *TARGET*	The other end of the link is a host with address *TARGET*.
irtt *I*	Sets the initial round-trip time for TCP connections over this route to *I* milliseconds (1-12000).
gw *GW*	IP packets for the target network or host will be routed through gateway *GW*. The specified gateway must be reachable first. Usually there must already be a static route to the gateway.
metric *M*	Sets the metric field in the routing table (used by routing daemons) to *M*. This option is currently not implemented.
mss *M*	Sets Maximum Segment Size (MSS) to *M* bytes. The default is 536.
-n	Disables address-to-hostname resolution. Prints the numeric address.
-net *TARGET*	The other end of the link is a network with address *TARGET*.
netmask *NM*	*NM* is the netmask of the route to be added.
reject	Installs a blocking route, which will force a route lookup to fail. This can be used to mask out networks before using the default route.

Option	Description
-V or --version	Displays version information.
-v	Verbose operation.
window W	Sets the TCP window size for connections over this route to W bytes.

routed

```
routed [-d] [-g] [-q] [-s]
```

routed is invoked at boot time to manage the network routing tables. It uses a variant of the Xerox NS Routing Information Protocol in maintaining up-to-date kernel routing table entries. It's currently used only for Internet routing within a cluster of networks.

Option	Description
-d	Enables debugging information to be logged.
-g	This flag is used on internetwork routers to offer a route to the "default" destination. This is typically used on a gateway to the Internet, or on a gateway that uses another routing protocol whose routes aren't reported to other local routers.
-q	This is the opposite of the -s option.
-s	Supplies routing information whether or not it's acting as an internetwork router. This is the default if multiple network interfaces are present, or if a point-to-point link is in use.

Network File System (NFS)

Sharing files with remote hosts using the Network File System (NFS) protocol.

mountd and rpc.mountd

```
mountd OPTION ...
```

mountd handles the mounting of local filesystems to remote directories through NFS. When receiving a mount request from an NFS client, it checks the request against the list of exported filesystems in /etc/exports. If the client is permitted to mount the filesystem, mountd creates a file handle for the requested directory and adds an entry to /etc/rmtab. On receipt of a umount request, it removes the client's entry from rmtab. mountd can also be started by inetd rather than at boot time. This can be enabled by adding the following lines to the configuration file for inetd:

```
mount/1-2 dgram rpc/udp wait root /usr/sbin/rpc.mountd rpc.mountd
mount/1-2 stream rpc/tcp wait root /usr/sbin/rpc.mountd rpc.mountd
```

Option	Description
`-d` or `--debug`	Logs each transaction verbosely to standard error. By default, log output is sent to `syslog` unless `mountd` runs in the foreground.
`-F` or `--foreground`	`mountd` won't detach from the terminal when given this option. If debugging is requested, output will be sent to standard error.
`-f FILE` or `--exports-file FILE`	Uses `FILE` instead of `/etc/exports`.
`-h` or `--help`	Provides a help summary.
`-n` or `--allow-non-root`	Allows incoming mount requests to be honored even if they don't originate from reserved IP ports.
`-P PORTNUM` or `--port PORTNUM`	Listens on port `PORTNUM`. By default, `mountd` will listen on the `mount/udp` port in `/etc/services`. If that's undefined, it will use some random port below 1024.
`-p` or `--promiscuous`	Serves any host on any network.
`-r` or `--re-export`	Allows imported NFS or SMB filesystems to be exported.
`-v` or `--version`	Reports the current version number.

nfsd and rpc.nfsd

`rpc.nfsd OPTION ... [ NUMCOPIES ]`

`nfsd` is an NFS service daemon that handles client filesystem requests. Unlike on some other systems, `nfsd` operates as a normal user-level process. The server also differs from other NFS server implementations in that it mounts an entire file hierarchy not limited by the boundaries of physical filesystems. The implementation allows the clients read-only or read-write access to the file hierarchy of the server machine.

`nfsd` is usually started at boot time. It can also be invoked from `inetd`. This can be enabled by adding the following two lines to `/etc/inetd.conf`:

```
nfs/2 dgram rpc/udp wait root /usr/sbin/rpc.nfsd rpc.nfsd
nfs/2 stream rpc/tcp wait root /usr/sbin/rpc.nfsd rpc.nfsd
```

`NUMCOPIES` enables the running of multiple instances of `nfsd` in parallel. If `NUMCOPIES` is greater than 1, `nfsd` will fork to `NUMCOPIES` - 1 times. Because the servers don't share a common file-handle cache, `nfsd` will disallow all write operations when invoked with this option.

`nfsd` also supports the WebNFS protocol. WebNFS is an extension to NFS that enables file retrieval by Web browsers. To support this, the `-R` or `--public-root` sets the directory to which all WebNFS transfers are relative. The public root directory must also be named in `/etc/exports`.

Option	Description
-d *FACILITY* or --debug *FACILITY*	Logs operations verbosely. The current legal values for *FACILITY* are call for RPC calls and arguments, fhcache for file handle cache operations, auth for authentication routines, and ugid for the UID mapping code. The debug message will be logged to syslog unless the daemon is run in the foreground.
-F or --foreground	With this option, nfsd won't detach from the terminal.
-f *FILE* or --exports-file *FILE*	Reads access permissions from *FILE* rather than /etc/exports.
-h or --help	Provides a short help summary.
-l or --log-transfers	For each file store or retrieve, a single line is written to the system log daemon containing the client's IP address, and the filename. The log level of these transfer records is daemon.info.
-n or --allow-non-root	Allows incoming NFS requests to be honored even if they don't originate from reserved IP ports. Some older NFS client implementations require this. Some newer NFS client implementations don't use reserved port checking. This check can be turned off for individual hosts by specifying the insecure export option in /etc/exports.
-P *PORTNUM* or --port *PORTNUM*	Makes nfsd listen on port *PORTNUM* instead of the default port 2049 or the nfs/udp port specified in /etc/services.
-p or --promiscuous	Puts the server into promiscuous mode, where it will serve any host on the network.
-R *DIRNAME* or --public-root *DIRNAME*	Makes *DIRNAME* the directory associated with the public file handle used by WebNFS.
-r or --re-export	Allows remotely mounted filesystems to be exported. This can be used to turn a machine into a multiplier for NFS or Novell servers. Caution should be used when re-exporting loopback NFS mounts because re-entering the mount point will result in deadlock between the NFS client and the NFS server. It can also result in re-exporting /proc, which can be a security risk.
-v or --version	Reports the version number.

showmount

```
showmount [ -adehv ] [ --all ] [ --directories ] [ --exports ] [ --help ]
➥[ --version ] [ HOST ]
```

showmount queries the mount daemon on *HOST* for information about the state of its NFS server. With no options, showmount lists the set of clients who are mounting from that host.

Option	Description
-a or --all	Lists both the client hostnames and mounted directories in *HOST:DIR* format.
-d or --directories	Lists only the directories mounted by some client.
-e or --exports	Shows the NFS server's export list.
-h or --help	Prints the usage summary.
--no-headers	Suppresses headings from the output.
-v or --version	Reports the current version number.

Network Information Services

This section describes the services that provide information to client programs such as Web browsers and finger clients. This also includes user and group authentication services used by other types of services.

apache

apache *OPTION* ...

apache is the Apache Web server. It serves Hypertext Markup Language (HTML) documents to Web browsers via the Hypertext Transfer Protocol (HTTP). It can be run as standalone or invoked through inetd.

Option	Description
-C *DIRECTIVE*	Processes the configuration *DIRECTIVE* before reading the configuration files.
-c *DIRECTIVE*	Same as -C.
-d *SERVERROOT*	Sets the initial value of ServerRoot to *SERVERROOT*. File references by Web browsers are relative to this value. This value can be overridden by the ServerRoot command in the configuration file.
-f *FILE*	Executes the commands in file *FILE* on startup. The name of this file is relative to ServerRoot if it doesn't start with /.
-h	Outputs a list of directives together with expected arguments and places where the directive is valid.
-l	Outputs a list of modules compiled into the server.
-S	Shows the settings from the configuration file.
-V	Prints the version and build parameters of apache and then exits.
-v	Prints the version number of apache and exits.

fingerd and in.fingerd

fingerd [-wul] [-pL *PATH*]

fingerd services requests from finger clients. See finger (Chapter 5, "Network Clients") for more information.

Option	Description
-L *PATH*	Same as -p.
-l	Logs information about requests that have been serviced.
-p *PATH*	Looks for the finger program in *PATH*.
-u	Requests of the form finger @*HOST* are rejected.
-w	Remote users will get an additional "Welcome to ..." banner that also shows some information (for example, uptime, operating system name and release) about the system on which fingerd is running.

identd and in.identd

identd [-i¦-w¦-b] *OPTION* ... [*KERNELFILE* [*KMEMFILE*]]

identd is a server that implements the TCP/IP proposed standard IDENT user identification protocol as specified in the RFC 1413 document. It operates by looking up specific TCP/IP connections and returning the username of the process owning the connection.

The -i flag, which is the default mode, should be used when starting the daemon from inetd with the nowait option in /etc/inetd.conf. Use of this mode will make inetd start one identd daemon for each connection request.

The -w flag should be used when starting the daemon from inetd with the wait option in /etc/inetd.conf. This is the preferred mode of operation since that will start a copy of identd at the first connection request, and then identd will handle subsequent requests without having to do the nlist lookup in the *KERNEL* file for every request as in the -i mode described earlier. The identd daemon will run forever until a bug makes it crash, or until a timeout occurs as specified by the -t flag.

The -b flag can be used to make the daemon run in standalone mode without assistance from inetd. This is the least preferred mode since a bug or any other fatal condition in the server will make it terminate and it will then have to be restarted manually. Other than that, it has the same advantage as the -w mode in that it parses the nlist only once.

KERNELFILE defaults to the currently running kernel file. *KMEMFILE* defaults to the memory space of the currently running kernel.

Option	Description
-a*ADDRESS*	Binds the socket to *ADDRESS* when using the -b option. *ADDRESS* must be an IP address and not a domain name. The default is INADDR_ANY, which normally means all local addresses.
-c*CHARSET*	According to the IDENT protocol, adds the optional character set designator to the reply generated. *CHARSET* should be a valid character set as described in the MIME RFC, in uppercase characters.
-d	Enables debugging code. This normally shouldn't be used, since it breaks the protocol and may reveal information that shouldn't be available to outsiders.

continues >>

>>*continued*

Option	Description
-e	Always returns UNKNOWN-ERROR in place of NO-USER or INVALID-PORT errors.
-g*GID*	Switches to group ID *GID* after binding to the TCP/IP port when using the -b option.
-l	Uses syslogd for logging.
-o	Don't reveal the operating system type to the client. Always return OTHER.
-m	Allows multiple requests to be processed per session. Each request is specified one per line and the responses will be returned one per line. The connection won't be closed until the connecting part closes its end of the line.
-N	Checks for a file .noident in each home directory for a user for which the daemon is about to return the username. If the file exists, returns HIDDEN-USER to the client rather than the actual user ID.
-n	Returns user numbers instead of usernames.
-p*PORT*	Binds to port *PORT* when using the -b mode of operation. *PORT* can be a name or a number. The default port is 113.
-t *SECONDS*	Sets the timeout to *SECONDS* seconds. Use with -w.
-u*UID*	Switches to user ID *UID* after binding to the TCP/IP port when using the -b option.
-V	Displays the version number and exits.

rpc.rusersd

rpc.rusersd

rpc.rusersd is the server for the rusers client program. It returns information about users currently logged onto the system. See rusers (Chapter 5) for more information.

rwhod

rwhod [-bpa]

rwhod is the server that maintains the database used by the rwho and ruptime client programs. It operates as both a producer and consumer of status information. As a producer of information, it periodically queries the state of the system and constructs status messages that are broadcast on a network. As a consumer of information, it listens for status messages from other rwhod servers, validates them, and records them in a collection of files located in the directory /var/spool/rwho. See the rwho and ruptime commands in Chapter 5 for more information.

Option	Description
-a	Uses all types of network interfaces. This is the default.
-b	Uses only broadcast interfaces such as Ethernet.
-p	Uses only point-to-point interfaces.

ugidd and rpc.ugidd

rpc.ugidd

ugidd handles RPC requests to map UID and GID numbers to string names. It's called by the nfsd server when the client and server don't share the same passwd file.

Network File Transfer

This section describes the services that enable the copying of files between network hosts.

ftpd and in.ftpd

ftpd [-dDhlMS] [-T MAXTIMEOUT [-t TIMEOUT] [-u MASK]

ftpd services requests from ftp clients. See ftp in Chapter 5 for more information.

Option	Description
-A	Permits only anonymous FTP connections or accounts listed in /etc/ftpchroot. Other connection attempts are refused.
-D	ftpd will detach and become a daemon, accepting connections on the FTP port and forking child processes to handle them. This has lower overhead than starting ftpd from inetd and is useful on busy servers to reduce load.
-d	Debugging information is written to the syslog using LOG_FTP.
-h	The server will use data ports in the high port range (normally 40000..44999) for passive connections.
-l	Each successful and failed FTP(1) session is logged using syslog with a facility of LOG_FTP. If this option is specified twice, the retrieve (get), store (put), append, delete, make directory, remove directory, and rename operations and their filename arguments are also logged.
-M	Enables multihomed mode. Instead of simply using the account's home directory (~), uses a directory matching the hostname to which the client is connected, and located inside ~. For example, if a host is known by multiple hostnames but the client connected to host.net, ftpd will use ~/host as its home directory.
-S	Logs all anonymous transfers to /var/log/ftpd if it exists.
-T MAXTIMEOUT	A client can request a different timeout period. The maximum period allowed can be set to MAXTIMEOUT seconds with the -T option. The default limit is two hours.
-t TIMEOUT	The inactivity timeout period is set to TIMEOUT seconds (the default is 15 minutes).
-u MASK	Changes the default umask from 027 to MASK.

tftpd and in.tftpd

`in.tftpd [-l] [-n] [DIRECTORY ...]`

`tftpd` is the server for Trivial File Transfer Protocol (`tftp`) clients. Since `tftp` doesn't require any authentication, it will only allow publicly readable files to be accessed. Files with names containing the string `/../` are inaccessible. If the `DIRECTORY` parameters are used, access can be restricted to files named with these prefixes. See `tftp` in Chapter 5 for more information.

Option	Description
-l	Logs all requests using `syslog`.
-n	Suppresses negative acknowledgement of requests for nonexistent relative filenames.

Remote Command Execution Service

This section describes the services that enable users to execute commands and establish sessions on remote hosts.

rexecd and in.rexecd

`in.rexecd`

`rexecd` is the server for the `rexec` client program. The server provides remote execution facilities with authentication based on usernames and passwords. For more information, see the `rexec` command in Chapter 5.

rlogind and in.rlogind

`in.rlogind [-ahlLn]`

`rlogind` is the server for the `rlogin` client program. The server provides a remote login facility with authentication based on privileged port numbers from trusted hosts. See `rlogin` (Chapter 5) for more information.

Option	Description
-a	Asks hostname for verification.
-h	Permits use of superuser `.rhosts` files.
-l	Prevents any authentication based on the user's `.rhosts` file. If the user is logging in as the superuser and the `-h` option is used, `.rhosts` processing is still enabled.
-L	Prevents any authentication based on `.rhosts` or `hosts.equiv` information.
-n	Disables transport-level keep-alive messages. The use of keep-alive messages allows sessions to be timed out if the client crashes or becomes unreachable.

rshd and in.rshd

`in.rshd [-ahlnL]`

`rshd` is the server for the `rcmd` library routine and for the `rsh` client program. The server provides remote execution facilities with authentication based on privileged port numbers from trusted hosts. See `rsh` in Chapter 5 for more details.

Option	Description
-a	Makes sure that the hostname and address of the client match. Otherwise, aborts the connection with the message `Host address mismatch`.
-h	Permits use of superuser `.rhosts` files.
-L	Logs all successful accesses to `syslog` as `auth.info` and all failed accesses to `auth.notice`.
-l	Prevents any authentication based on the user's `.rhosts` file. If the user is logging in as the superuser and the `-h` option is used, `.rhosts` processing is still enabled.
-n	Disables transport-level keep-alive messages. The use of keep-alive messages allows sessions to be timed out if the client crashes or becomes unreachable.

rwalld and rpc.rwalld

`rpc.rwalld`

`rwalld` is the server for the `rwall` client program. It will send a message to users currently logged onto the system. See `rwall` in Chapter 5 for more information.

talkd, in.talkd, and in.ntalkd

`in.talkd`

`talkd` is the server for the `talk` client program. See the `talk` command in Chapter 5 for more information.

telnetd and in.telnetd

`in.telnetd OPTION ...`

`telnetd` is the server for the `telnet` clients. See the `telnet` command in Chapter 5 for more information.

Option	Description
-debug *PORT*	Runs `telnetd` in interactive mode and accepts connections on port *PORT*.
-D *DEBUGMODE*	Debugging modes. Valid values for *DEBUGMODE* are as follows:
	`options` prints information about the negotiation of `telnet` options.
	`report` prints the options information plus some additional information about what processing is going on.
	`netdata` displays the data stream received by `telnetd`.

continues >>

>>continued

Option	Description
	`ptydata` displays data written to the pty (pseudo terminal).
	`exercise` is not implemented yet.
`-h`	Disables the printing of host-specific information before login has been completed.
`-L LOGINPRG`	Use `LOGINPRG` as the login program instead of `/bin/login`.
`-n`	Disable TCP keep-alives. Normally `telnetd` enables the TCP keep-alive mechanism to probe connections that have been idle for some period of time to determine whether the client is still there, so that idle connections from machines that have crashed or can no longer be reached may be cleaned up.

Mail Transfer Service

This section describes mail transfer service.

sendmail and smail

`smail [ OPTION ... ] ADDRESS ...`

`sendmail` is a mail transport agent. Many installations use BSD `sendmail` but others use `smail` instead. Although `smail` is different internally, it's designed to be a plug-in replacement for `sendmail` and is preferred by many people who are concerned with security and ease of use. In any case, the command-line options given here should be valid for both `smail` and `sendmail`. When `smail` is installed, `sendmail` is typically a link to `smail`.

For more information on `sendmail` and `smail`, see the references in Appendix C.

Option	Description
`-bc`	Displays the copyright notice and exits.
`-bd`	Runs as daemon. Listens for connection requests on a socket bound in the Internet domain.
`-bm`	Delivers mail to the recipient `ADDRESS`es.
`-bp`	Lists information about messages currently in the input spool directories. This is the default mode of operation if `smail` is invoked as `mailq`.
`-bi`	Initializes the aliases file. This is the default option when invoked as `newaliases`.
`-bP`	Takes addresses given on the command line as configuration-file variable names and writes the corresponding values to standard output.
`bt`	Enters address test mode. Addresses are read on standard input and host routing and resolving results are printed on standard output. This is useful for debugging configuration files.
`-bv`	Verify addresses including routing and resolving results, but don't deliver. Also show which addresses can't be resolved and the reasons why.
`-C FILENAME`	Sets the configuration filename if the default is not to be used.

Option	Description
`-d` *N*	Sets the debugging level to *N*.
`-F` *FULLNAME*	Explicitly sets the full name of the sender for incoming mail.
`-f` *NAME*	Explicitly sets the sender address for incoming mail.
`-h` *N*	Sets the hop count to *N*. Mail will be bounced after *N* hops.
`-n`	Don't perform alias processing.
`-oO` *VALUE*	Sets the value of processing option *O* to *VALUE*.
`-q[`*INTERVAL*`]`	Specifies how often the input spool queue should be processed. *INTERVAL* is a sequence of numbers followed by a unit suffix. A unit suffix can be `s` for seconds, `m` for minutes, `h` for hours, `d` for days, `w` for weeks, and `y` for years. For example, `-q2h30m` means to check the queue every 2½ hours.

12
Filesystems

The term *filesystems* refers to collections of files stored on disk volumes. This chapter describes the management of filesystems. The volume format most often used on Linux systems is the *Second Extended File System*, otherwise known as *ext2fs*. For more information on ext2fs, see the references in Appendix C, "Web Resources."

The Linux Filesystem Hierarchy Standard

The Linux Filesystem Hierarchy Standard is based on the *Filesystem Hierarchy Standard* (*FHS*). The FHS consists of a set of requirements and guidelines for file and directory placement under UNIX-like operating systems. It should be noted that the FHS is a guideline only, and the level of conformance may vary from one distribution to another. For more information, consult Appendix C.

The Root Filesystem

Directory	Description
/bin	Essential user command binaries used by all users.
/boot	Static files for the boot loader.
/dev	Device files.
/etc	Host-specific system configuration.
/etc/X11	Configuration for the X Window system.
/etc/opt	Configuration files for /opt.
/home	User home directories (optional).
/lib	Essential shared libraries and kernel modules.
/mnt	Mount point for temporarily mounted filesystems.
/opt	Add-on application software packages.
/proc	Kernel and process information virtual filesystem.
/root	Home directory for root user (optional).
/sbin	System binaries.
/tmp	Temporary files.

The /usr Filesystem

Directory	Description
/usr/X11R6	The X Window system (X11, Release 6).
/usr/bin	Most user commands.
/usr/include	Directory for standard include files.
/usr/lib	Libraries for programming and packages.
/usr/local	Local programs and utilities.
/usr/sbin	Nonessential standard system binaries.
/usr/share	Architecture-independent data.
/usr/share/dict	Word lists.
/usr/share/man	Manual pages.
/usr/share/misc	Miscellaneous architecture-independent data.
/usr/src	Source code.

The /var Filesystem

Directory	Description
/var/account	Process accounting logs (if supported).
/var/cache	Application data caches.
/var/cache/fonts	Locally generated fonts.
/var/cache/man	Locally formatted manual pages (optional).
/var/crash	System crash dumps (if supported).
/var/games	Variable data for games.
/var/lock	Lock files.
/var/log	Log files and directories.
/var/mail	User mailbox files.
/var/opt	Variable data for /opt.
/var/run	Runtime variable files.
/var/spool	Application spool data and directories.
/var/spool/cron	Data for cron and at jobs.
/var/spool/lpd	Line-printer daemon print queues.
/var/spool/rwho	Files for rwhod.
/var/state	Variable state data.
/var/APPLICATION	Variable state data for APPLICATION.
/var/tmp	Temporary files preserved between system reboots.
/var/yp	Network Information Service (NIS) database files.

Creating Filesystems

This section describes commands used to create filesystems.

mke2fs

mke2fs [OPTION ...] DEVICE [BLOCKS_COUNT]

mke2fs is used to create a Linux second extended filesystem on the device specified by the block special device file *DEVICE* (usually a disk partition). *BLOCKS_COUNT* is the number of blocks on the device. If *BLOCKS_COUNT* is omitted, mke2fs automatically determines the filesystem size.

Option	Description
-c	Check the device for bad blocks before creating the filesystem.
-f FRAGMENT_SIZE	Specifies the size of fragments in bytes.
-i BYTES_PER_INODE	mke2fs creates an inode for every BYTES_PER_INODE bytes of disk space. This value defaults to 4096. BYTES_PER_INODE must be at least 1024.
-l FILENAME	Read the bad blocks list from FILENAME.
-m RESERVED_BLOCKS_PERCENTAGE	Specifies the percentage of blocks reserved for the superuser. The default value is 5%.
-o CREATOR_OS	Manually overrides the default value of the "creator OS" field of the filesystem. Normally the creator field is set by default to the native operating system of the mke2fs executable.
-q	Quiet execution.
-v	Verbose execution.
-F	Forces mke2fs to run even if the specified device isn't a block special device.
-L VOLUME_LABLE	Sets the volume label for the filesystem.
-M LAST_MOUNTED_DIRECTORY	Sets the last mounted directory for the filesystem. This might be useful for the sake of utilities that key off the last mounted directory to determine where the filesytem should be mounted.
-r REVISION	Sets the filesystem revision for the new filesystem.
-R RAID_OPTIONS	Sets RAID-related options for the filesystem. RAID options are comma-separated, and can take an argument using the equal (=) sign.
-S	Write superblock and group descriptors only. This is useful if all the superblocks and backup superblocks are corrupted and a last-ditch recovery method is desired. It causes mke2fs to reinitialize the superblock and group descriptors, while not touching the inode table and the block and inode bitmaps. The e2fsck program should be run immediately after this option is used, and there's no guarantee that any data will be salvageable.

mkfs

mkfs [-V] [-t FSTYPE] [FS_OPTIONS] FILESYS [BLOCKS]

mkfs is used to build a Linux filesystem on a device—usually a hard disk partition. FILESYS is either the device name (for example, /dev/hda1 or /dev/sdb2) or the mount point (for example, /, /usr, or /home) for the filesystem. BLOCKS is the number of blocks to be used for the filesystem.

mkfs returns exit code 0 on success and 1 on failure.

mkfs is actually a front end for the various filesystem builders (mkfs.FSTYPE). The filesystem-specific builder is searched for in /sbin/fs first, then in /sbin, and finally in the directories listed in the PATH environment variable.

Option	Description
-V	Produces verbose output, including all filesystem-specific commands that are executed. Specifying this option more than once inhibits execution of any filesystem-specific commands.
-t FSTYPE	Specifies the type of filesystem to be built. If not specified, the type is deduced by searching for FILESYS in /etc/fstab and using the corresponding entry. If the type can't be deduced, the default filesystem type (currently minix) is used.
FS_OPTIONS	Filesystem-specific options to be passed to the real filesystem builder. Although not guaranteed, the following options are supported by most filesystem builders:
	-c checks the device for bad blocks before building the filesystem.
	-1 FILENAME reads the bad blocks from FILENAME.
	-v produces verbose output.

Accessing Filesystems

This section describes commands used to enable and disable access to filesystems.

losetup

losetup [-e ENCRYPTION] [-o OFFSET] LOOP_DEVICE FILE
losetup [-d] LOOP_DEVICE

losetup is used to associate loop devices with regular files or block devices, to detach loop devices, and to query the status of a loop device. If only the LOOP_DEVICE argument is given, the status of the corresponding loop device is shown.

Option	Description
-d	Detaches the file or device associated with the specified loop device.
-e ENCRYPTION	Enables data encryption. The following keywords are recognized:
	NONE—Use no encryption (the default).
	XOR—Use simple XOR encryption.

Option	Description
	DES—Use DES encryption. DES encryption is available only if the optional DES encryption package has been added to the kernel. DES encryption uses an additional start value that's used to protect passwords against dictionary attacks.
-o OFFSET	The data start is moved OFFSET bytes into the specified file or device.

mount

```
mount [ -hV ]
mount -a [ -fFnrsvw ] [ -t VFSTYPE ]
mount [ -fnrsvw ] [ -o OPTIONS { DEVICE ¦ DIR }
mount [ -fnrsvw ] [ -t VFSTYPE ] [ -o OPTIONS ] DEVICE DIR
```

All files accessible in a UNIX system are arranged in a tree rooted at /. These files can be spread over several devices. The mount command serves to attach the filesystem found on some device to the file tree. Most devices are indicated by a filename of a block special device such as /dev/sda1, but there are other possibilities. For example, in the case of an NFS mount, the device may look like ftp.digital.com:/archive.

The file /etc/fstab may contain lines describing which devices are usually mounted where, using which options. This file is used in three ways:

- The command mount -a [-t TYPE] (usually given in a boot script) causes all filesystems mentioned in fstab (of the proper type) to be mounted as indicated, except for those containing the noauto keyword. Adding the -F option makes mount fork, so that the filesystems are mounted simultaneously.

- When mounting a filesystem mentioned in fstab, giving only the device or only the mount point is sufficient.

- Normally, only the superuser can mount filesystems. However, when fstab contains the user option on a line, anybody can mount the corresponding system.

The programs mount and umount maintain a list of currently mounted filesystems in the file /etc/mtab. If no arguments are given to mount, this list is printed.

The full set of options by an invocation of mount is determined by first extracting the options for the filesystem from the fstab table, applying any options specified by the -o argument, and finally applying the -r or -w option, when present.

Option	Description
-a	Mounts all filesystems of the given types mentioned in fstab.
-F	Forks off a new invocation of mount for each device. This will do the mounts on different devices or different NFS servers in parallel.

continues >>

>>continued

Option	Description
-f	Causes everything to be done except for the actual `mount` system call. This option is useful in conjunction with the -v flag to determine what the `mount` command is trying to do. It can also be used to add entries for devices that were mounted earlier with the -n option.
-h	Prints a help message.
-n	Mounts without writing in /etc/mtab.
-o *OPTIONS*	Options are specified with the -o flag followed by a comma-separated string of options. Some of these options are useful only when they appear in the /etc/fstab file. The following options apply to any filesystem that's being mounted: async—All I/O to the filesystem should be done asynchronously. atime—Update inode access time for each access. This is the default. auto—Can be mounted with the -a option. defaults—Use default options: rw, suid, dev, exec, auto, nouser, and async. dev—Interpret character or block special devices on the filesystem. exec—Permit execution of binaries. noatime—Don't update inode access times on this filesystem. noauto—Can only be mounted explicitly (that is, the -a option won't cause this filesystem to be mounted). nodev—Don't interpret character or block special devices on the filesystem. noexec—Don't allow execution of any binaries on the mounted filesystem. nosuid—Don't allow set-user-identifier or set-group-identifier bits to take effect. nouser—Forbid an ordinary user to mount the filesystem. This is the default. remount—Attempt to remount an already-mounted filesystem. ro—Mount the filesystem read-only. rw—Mount the filesystem read-write. suid—Allow set-user-identifier or set-group-identifier bits to take effect. sync—All I/O to the filesystem should be done synchronously. user—Allow an ordinary user to mount the filesystem. This implies the options noexec, nosuid, and nodev (unless overridden by subsequent options, as in the option line user,exec,dev,suid).

Option	Description
-r	Mount the filesystem read-only. Equivalent to -o ro.
-s	Tolerate sloppy mount options rather than failing. This will ignore mount options not supported by a filesystem type. Not all filesystems support this option.
-t VFSTYPE	VFSTYPE is the filesystem type. The filesystem types currently supported are listed in linux/fs/filesystems.c. Support for other filesystems is also available. For more information, see the references in Appendix C.
-w	Mount the filesystem read-write. (This is the default.) Equivalent to -o rw.
-V	Output version.
-v	Verbose mode.

umount

```
umount [ -hV ]
umount -a [ -nrv ] [ -t VFSTYPES ]
umount [ -nrv ] { DEVICE ¦ DIRECTORY ... }
```

umount detaches the given filesystem(s) from the file hierarchy. A filesystem is specified either by giving the directory where it has been mounted, or by giving the special device on which it lives.

The umount command will free the loop device (if any) associated with the mount, in case it finds the option loop=... in /etc/mtab. Any pending loop devices can be freed using losetup -d.

Option	Description
-a	All filesystems described in /etc/mtab are unmounted.
-h	Print help messages and exit.
-n	Unmount without updating /etc/mtab.
-r	In case unmounting fails, try to remount read-only.
-t VFSTYPES	Indicates that the actions should be taken only for the filesystems indicated by VFSTYPES. VFSTYPES is a comma-separated list of filesystem types. The list of filesystem types can be prefixed with no to specify the filesystem types on which no action should be taken.
-V	Print version and exit.
-v	Verbose mode.

Checking and Tuning Filesystems

This section describes commands used for tuning filesystems and diagnosing filesystem problems.

badblocks

badblocks [OPTION ...] DEVICE BLOCKS_COUNT [START_BLOCK]

badblocks is used to search for bad blocks on a device (usually a disk partition). DEVICE is the special file corresponding to the device. BLOCKS_COUNT is the number of blocks on the device.

Option	Description
-b BLOCK_SIZE	Specifies the size of blocks in bytes.
-o OUTPUT_FILE	Writes the list of bad blocks to the specified file. Without this option, badblocks displays the list on its standard output.
-v	Verbose mode.
-w	Use write-mode test. With this option, badblocks scans for bad blocks by writing some patterns on every block of the device, reading every block, and comparing the contents. This option shouldn't be used on a device containing an existing filesystem because it erases data.

debugfs

debugfs [OPTION ...] [DEVICE]

debugfs is a filesystem debugger. It can be used to examine and change the state of an ext2 filesystem. DEVICE is the special file corresponding to the device containing the ext2 filesystem. The following table describes the command-line options.

Option	Description
-f CMD_FILE	Read commands from CMD_FILE and execute them. When finished executing the commands, exit.
-R REQUEST	Execute the single command REQUEST and then exit.
-w	Opens the filesystem in read-write mode. Read-only mode is the default.

debugfs is an interactive debugger. It understands a number of commands:

Command	Description
cat FILESPEC	Dumps the contents of the inode FILESPEC to standard output.
cd FILESPEC	Changes the current working directory to FILESPEC.
chroot FILESPEC	Changes the root directory to be the directory FILESPEC.
close	Closes the currently open filesystem.
clri FILE	Clears the contents of the inode FILE.

Command	Description
dump [-p] FILESPEC OUT_FILE	Dumps the contents of the inode FILESPEC to the output file OUT_FILE. If the -p option is given, sets the owner, group, and permissions information on OUT_FILE to match FILESPEC.
expand_dir FILESPEC	Expands the directory FILESPEC.
find_free_block [GOAL]	Finds the first free block, starting from GOAL, and allocates it.
find_free_inode [DIR [MODE]]	Finds a free inode and allocates it. If present, DIR specifies the inode number of the directory in which the inode is to be located. The second optional argument MODE specifies the permissions of the new inode.
freeb BLOCK	Marks the block number BLOCK as not allocated.
freei FILESPEC	Frees the inode specified by FILESPEC.
help	Prints a list of commands understood by debugfs.
icheck BLOCK ...	Prints a listing of the inodes that use the BLOCK(s) specified on the command line.
initialize DEVICE BLOCKSIZE	Sets up superblock and block descriptors for an ext2 filesystem on DEVICE with size BLOCKSIZE.
kill_file FILESPEC	Deallocates the inode FILESPEC and its blocks.
ln FILESPEC DEST_FILE	Creates a link named DEST_FILE that's a link to FILESPEC.
ls [-l] FILESPEC	Prints a listing of the files in the directory FILESPEC.
modify_inode FILESPEC	Modifies the contents of the inode structure in the inode for FILESPEC.
mkdir FILESPEC	Makes a directory.
mknod FILESPEC [p ¦ [[c ¦ b] MAJOR MINOR]]	Creates a named pipe, a character special device, or a block special device. If a character or block device is to be made, the MAJOR and MINOR device numbers must be specified.
ncheck INODE_NUM ...	Prints a listing of pathnames to the requested inodes.
open [-w] DEVICE	Opens a filesystem for editing.
pwd	Prints the current working directory.
quit	Quits debugfs.
rm PATHNAME	Unlinks PATHNAME. If this causes the inode pointed to by PATHNAME to have no other references, deallocates the file.

continues >>

>>continued

Command	Description
setb *BLOCK*	Marks the block number *BLOCK* as allocated.
seti *FILESPEC*	Marks the inode *FILESPEC* as in use in the inode bitmap.
show_super_stats	Lists the contents of the superblock.
stat *FILESPEC*	Displays the contents of the structure or the inode for *FILESPEC*.
testb *BLOCK*	Determines whether the block *BLOCK* is allocated in the block bitmap.
testi *FILESPEC*	Determines whether the inode for *FILESPEC* is allocated in the inode bitmap.
unlink *PATHNAME*	Removes the link specified by *PATHNAME* to an inode.
write *SOURCE_FILE OUT_FILE*	Creates a file in the filesystem named *OUT_FILE* and copies the contents of *SOURCE_FILE* into the destination file.

dumpe2fs

dumpe2fs [-b] [-V] *DEVICE*

dumpe2fs prints the superblock and blocks group information for the filesystem present on *DEVICE*.

Option	Description
-b	Print the blocks that are reserved as bad in the filesystem.
-V	Print the dumpe2fs version number and exit.

e2fsck

e2fsck [*OPTION* ...] *DEVICE*

e2fsck is used to check the second extended filesystem on *DEVICE*.

The exit code returned by e2fsck is the sum of the following conditions:

0	No errors.
1	Filesystem errors corrected.
2	Filesystem errors corrected; the system should be rebooted if the filesystem was mounted.
4	Filesystem errors left uncorrected.
8	Operational error.
16	Usage or syntax error.
128	Shared library error.

Option	Description
-a	Equivalent to -p. Provided for backward compatibility only; -p is the preferred option.
-b *SUPERBLOCK*	Instead of using the normal superblock, use the alternative superblock specified by *SUPERBLOCK*.
-B *BLOCKSIZE*	Normally, e2fsck will search for the superblock at various block sizes in an attempt to find the appropriate block size. This search can be fooled in some cases. This option forces e2fsck to try locating the superblock only at a particular block size. If the superblock isn't found, e2fsck terminates with a fatal error.
-c	Causes e2fsck to run the badblocks program to find any blocks that are bad on the filesystem, and then marks them as bad by adding them to the bad block inode.
-d	Prints debugging output.
-f	Forces checking even if the filesystem seems clean.
-F	Flushes the filesystem device's buffer caches before beginning.
-l *FILENAME*	Adds the blocks listed in the file specified by *FILENAME* to the list of bad blocks.
-L *FILENAME*	Sets the bad blocks list to be the list of blocks specified by *FILENAME*.
-n	Opens the filesystem as read-only and assumes an answer of "no" to all questions. This allows e2fsck to be used noninteractively.
-p	Automatically repairs ("preens") the filesystem without any questions.
-r	Not used. Provided for backward compatibility.
-s	Byte-swaps the filesystem so that it's using the normalized, standard byte order.
-S	Byte-swaps the filesystem regardless of its current byte order.
-t	Prints timing statistics for e2fsck. If this option is used twice, additional timing statistics are printed on a pass-by-pass basis.
-v	Verbose mode.
-V	Prints e2fsck version information and exits.
-y	Assumes an answer of "yes" to all questions.

fsck

fsck [*OPTION* ...] *FILESYS* ...

fsck is used to check and optionally repair a Linux filesystem. Each *FILESYS* is either the device name or the mount point for the filesystem.

The exit code returned by **fsck** is the sum of the following conditions:

0   No errors.

1   Filesystem errors are corrected.

2   The system should be rebooted.

4   Filesystem error left uncorrected.

8   Operational error.

16   Usage or syntax error.

128 Shared library error.

fsck is actually a front end for the various filesystem checkers (**fsck.***FSTYPE*) available under Linux. The filesystem-specific checker is searched in **/sbin** first, then in **/etc/fs** and **/etc**, and finally in the directories listed in the **PATH** environment variable.

Option	Description
-A	Walk through the /etc/fstab file and try to check all filesystems in one run.
-R	When checking all filesystems with the -A flag, skip the root filesystem.
-T	Don't show the title on startup.
-N	Don't execute. Just show what would be done.
-P	When the -A flag is set, check the root filesystem in parallel with the other filesystems.
-s	Serialize fsck operations.
-V	Produce verbose output, including all filesystem-specific commands that are executed.
-t FSTYPE	Specifies the type of filesystem to be checked. When the -A flag is specified, only filesystems that match FSTYPE are checked. If FSTYPE is prefixed with no, only filesystems that aren't of type FSTYPE are checked.

Filesystem-Specific Options

Any options that aren't understood by **fsck** or that follow the - - option are treated as filesystem-specific options to be passed to the filesystem-specific checker.

Currently, standardized filesystem-specific options are somewhat in flux. Although not guaranteed, the following options are supported by most filesystem checkers:

Option	Description
-a	Automatically repair the filesystem without any questions.
-r	Interactively repair the filesystem (ask for confirmations).

mklost+found

mklost+found

mklost+found is used to create a **lost+found** directory in the current working directory on a Linux second extended filesystem. It preallocates disk blocks to the directory to make it usable by **e2fsck**.

tune2fs

tune2fs [*OPTION* ...] *DEVICE*

tune2fs adjusts tunable filesystem parameters on a Linux second extended filesystem. It should never be used on a filesystem that's mounted read–write.

Option	Description
-c *MAX_MOUNT_COUNTS*	Adjusts the maximal mounts count between two filesystem checks.
-e *ERRORS_BEHAVIOR*	Changes the behavior of the kernel code when errors are detected. *ERRORS_BEHAVIOR* is one of the following: continue Continue normal execution. remount-ro Remount the filesystem read-only. panic Cause a kernel panic.
-g *GROUP*	Sets the user group that can benefit from the reserved blocks. *GROUP* can be a numerical GID or a group name.
-i *INTERVAL_BETWEEN_CHECKS*[d ¦ m ¦ w]	Adjusts the maximal time between two filesystem checks. No postfix or d result in days, m in months, and w in weeks. A value of 0 (zero) disables the time-dependent checking.
-l	Lists the contents of the filesystem superblock.
-m *RESERVED_BLOCKS_PERCENTAGE*	Adjusts the reserved blocks percentage.
-r *RESERVED_BLOCKS_COUNT*	Adjusts the reserved blocks count.
-s *SPARSE_SUPER_FLAG*	Sets and resets the *SPARSE_SUPERBLOCK_FLAG* flag. The *SPARSE_SUPERBLOCK_FLAG* feature saves space on very large filesystems. **Warning:** Don't use this option unless you know what you're doing.
-u *USER*	Sets the user who can use reserved blocks. *USER* can be a numerical UID or a username.
-L *VOLUME_LABEL*	Sets the volume label for the filesystem.
-M *LAST_MOUNTED_DIRECTORY*	Sets the last-mounted directory for the filesystem.

continues >>

>>continued

Option	Description
-U *UUID*	Sets the UUID of the filesystem. A sample UUID would be something like "`bce7e5d0-37fc-11d3-9f6a-dd38c3a503ad`", `null` (sets the UUID to the null UUID), or `random` (generates a new random UUID).

Reporting Space Usage

This section describes commands that control disk space usage and availability.

df

```
df [ OPTION ... ] [ FILE ... ]
```

df reports the amount of used and available disk space on filesystems. With no arguments, df reports used and available space on all currently mounted filesystems. Otherwise, df reports on the filesystems associated with each *FILE*.

If a filesystem is mounted to *FILE*, df shows space usage for that filesystem. Otherwise, df shows space usage for the filesystem containing that file.

Disk space is shown in 1024–byte blocks by default, unless the environment variable POSIXLY_CORRECT is set, in which case 512–byte blocks are used (unless the -k option is given).

Option	Description
-a or --all	Includes in the listing filesystems that have a size of 0 blocks, which are omitted by default.
-h or --human-readable	Appends a size letter to each size, such as M for megabytes.
-i or --inodes	Lists inode usage information instead of block usage.
-k or --kilobytes	Reports sizes in 1024–byte blocks (kilobytes). This over-rides the environment variable POSIXLY_CORRECT.
-m or --megabytes	Reports sizes in megabytes (1024–kilobyte blocks).
--no-sync	Don't invoke the sync system call before getting any usage data. This is the default.
-P or --portability	Use the POSIX output format. This will generate one line of output for each filesystem but will also cause misaligned columns when mount devices are more than 20 characters in length.

Option	Description
--sync	Invoke the sync system call before getting any usage data.
-t FSTYPE or --type=FSTYPE	Limits the listing to filesystems of type FSTYPE. Multiple filesystem types can be specified by giving multiple -t options.
-T or --print-type	Prints each filesystem's type. The types printed are the same ones you can include or exclude with -t and -x.
-x FSTYPE or --exclude-type=FSTYPE	Excludes filesystems of FSTYPE from listing. Multiple filesystem types can be eliminated by giving multiple -x options.
-v	Ignored but included for compatibility with System V versions of df.

du

```
du [ OPTION ... ] [ FILE ... ]
```

du reports the amount of disk space used by each *FILE*. Each *FILE* can be a file or directory.

With no arguments, du reports the disk space for the current directory. The output is in 1024–byte units by default, unless the environment variable POSIXLY_CORRECT is set, in which case 512–byte blocks are used (unless -k is specified).

Option	Description
-a or --all	Shows counts for all files, not just directories.
-b or --bytes	Shows counts in bytes instead of kilobytes.
-c or --total	Prints a total of all arguments after all arguments have been processed.
-D or --dereference-args	De-references *FILE* arguments that are symbolic links.
-h or --human-readable	Appends a size letter (such as M for megabytes) to each size.
-k or --kilobytes	Reports sizes in kilobytes. This overrides the environment variable POSIXLY_CORRECT.
-l or --count-links	Counts the size of all files, even if they have appeared already.
-L or --dereference	De-references symbolic links.
-m or --megabytes	Reports sizes in megabytes (1024–kilobyte blocks).
-s or --summarize	Displays only a total for each argument.
-S or --separate-dirs	Reports the size of each directory separately, without including the sizes of subdirectories.
-x or --one-file-system	Skips directories that are on different filesystems from the ones on which the arguments are being processed.

Managing Swap Space

This section describes commands used to format, enable, and disable swap space.

mkswap

```
mkswap [ -c ] SPECIALFILE [ SIZE_IN_BLOCKS ]
```

mkswap sets up a Linux swap area on a device or in a file. The *SPECIALFILE* is usually one of these forms:

- /dev/hda[*N*]

- /dev/hdb[*N*]

- /dev/sda[*N*]

- /dev/sdb[*N*]

where *N* is a number from 1 to 8. *SPECIALFILE* can also be a regular disk file. The *SIZE-IN-BLOCKS* parameter is the desired size of the filesystem, in blocks. This information is determined automatically by mkswap if it's omitted. Block counts are rounded down so that the total size is an integer multiple of the machine's page size. Only block counts in the range MINCOUNT..MAXCOUNT are allowed. If the block count exceeds the MAXCOUNT, it's truncated to that value and a warning message is issued.

The MINCOUNT and MAXCOUNT values for a swap area are as follows:

```
MINCOUNT = 10 * PAGE_SIZE / 1024
MAXCOUNT = (PAGE_SIZE - 10) * 8 * PAGE_SIZE / 1024
```

To set up a regular disk file for swapping, create that file before running mkswap. A sequence of commands similar to the following is reasonable for this purpose:

```
dd if=/dev/zero of=swapfile bs=1024 count=8192
mkswap swapfile 8192
sync
swapon swapfile
```

The -c option is used to check the device for bad blocks before creating the filesystem. If any are found, the count is printed. This option is meant to be used for swap partitions only, and shouldn't be used for regular files. To make sure that regular files don't contain bad blocks, the partition that contains the regular file should have been created with mkfs -c.

swapoff and swapon

```
swapon [ -h -V ]
swapon -a [ -v ]
swapon [ -v ] [ -p PRIORITY ] SPECIALFILE ...
swapon [ -s ]
swapoff [ -h -V ]
swapoff -a
swapoff SPECIALFILE ...
```

swapon enables devices and files for paging and swapping. swapoff disables them.

Option	Description
-a	Enables or disables all devices marked as sw in /etc/fstab.
-h	Provides help.
-p *PRIORITY*	Sets swap priority to *PRIORITY*. Swap pages are allocated from areas in priority order, highest priority first. For areas with different priorities, a higher-priority area is exhausted before using a lower-priority area. If two or more areas have the same priority, and it's the highest priority available, pages are allocated on a round-robin basis between them.
SPECIALFILE	*SPECIALFILE* is a file or block device that has been prepared using mkswap.
-s	Displays swap usage summary by device.
-V	Displays the version.
-v	Verbose operation.

Archival and Backup

This section describes commands used for backing up and archiving data.

dump

```
dump [ OPTION ... ] FILESYSTEM
dump [ OPTION ... ] DIRECTORY
dump [ -W ¦ -w ]
```

dump examines files in a filesystem or directory and determines which ones need to be backed up. These files are copied to the given disk, tape, or other storage medium for archival storage. A dump that's larger than the output medium is broken into multiple volumes. On most media, the size is determined by writing until an end-of-media indication is returned. On media that can't reliably return an end-of-media indication (such as some cartridge tape drives), each volume is of a fixed size; the actual size is determined by the tape size and density and/or block count options (described shortly). By default, the same output filename is used for each volume after prompting the operator to change media.

dump requires operator intervention on these conditions: end of tape, end of dump, tape write error, tape open error, or disk read error (if there are more than a threshold of 32). In addition to alerting all operators implied by the -n key, dump interacts with the operator on dump's control terminal at times when dump can no longer proceed, or if something is grossly wrong. All questions dump poses must be answered by typing yes or no as appropriate.

dump exits with 0 status on success. Startup errors are indicated with an exit code of 1; abnormal termination is indicated with an exit code of 3.

Option	Description
-N	N is a dump level that's an integer from 0 to 9. Level 0, full backup, guarantees that the entire filesystem is copied (but see also the -h option). A level number above 0, incremental backup, tells dump to copy all files new or modified since the last dump of the same or lower level. The default level is 9.
-B RECORDS	The number of dump records per volume. Overrides the calculation of tape size based on length and density.
-b BLOCKSIZE	The number of kilobytes per dump record.
-c	Modifies the calculation of the default density and tape size to be more appropriate for cartridge tapes.
-d DENSITY	Sets tape density to DENSITY. The default is 1600BPI.
-f FILE	Writes backup to FILE, which may be a special device file such as /dev/rmt12 (a tape drive), /dev/rsd1c (a disk drive), an ordinary file, or – (the standard output). Multiple filenames can be given as a single argument, separated by commas. Each file will be used for one dump volume in the order listed. If the dump requires more volumes than the number of names given, the last filename is used for all remaining volumes after prompting for media changes. If the name of the file is of the form host:file or user@host:file, dump writes to the named file on the remote host.
-h LEVEL	Honors the user nodump flag only for dumps at or above the given level. The default honor level is 1, so that incremental backups omit such files but full backups retain them.
-n	Whenever dump requires operator attention, notifies all operators in the group operator by means similar to a wall.
-s FEET	Attempts to calculate the amount of tape needed at a particular density. If this amount is exceeded, dump prompts for a new tape. The default tape length is 2300 feet.
-T DATE	Uses the specified DATE as the starting time for the dump instead of the time determined from looking in /var/lib/dumpdates. The format of DATE is the same as that of ctime. The -T option is mutually exclusive from the -u option.
-u	Updates the file /var/lib/dumpdates after a successful dump. The file's format is human-readable and consists of one free-format record per line: filesystem name, increment level, and ctime format dump date. There can be only one entry per filesystem at each level. The file can be edited manually to change the dates.
-W	dump tells the operator which filesystems need to be dumped. This information is obtained from the files /var/lib/dumpdates and /etc/fstab. The -W option causes dump to print out for each filesystem in /var/lib/dumpdates the most recent dump date and level, and highlights those filesystems that should be dumped. If the -W option is set, all other options are ignored, and dump exits immediately.
-w	Like -W but prints only those filesystems that need to be dumped.

restore

restore [OPTION ...] [[FILE ...]

restore performs the inverse function of dump. A full backup of a filesystem can be restored and subsequent incremental backups layered on top of it. Single files and directory subtrees can be restored from full or partial backups.

Exactly one of the following mode flags is required:

Mode	Description
-C	Allows comparison of files from a dump. restore reads the backup and compares its contents with files present on the disk. It first changes its working directory to the root of the filesystem that was dumped and then compares the tape with the files in its new current directory.
-h	Suppresses hierarchical directory traversals.
-i	Allows interactive restoration of files from a dump. After reading the directory information from the dump, restore provides a shell-like interface that allows the user to move around the directory tree, selecting files to be extracted. The available commands are as follows (for those commands that require an argument, the default is the current directory):
	add [ARG] The current directory or specified argument is added to the list of files to be extracted. If a directory is specified, it and all its descendents are added to the extraction list.
	cd ARG Changes the current working directory to ARG.
	delete [ARG] Deletes ARG from the list of files to be extracted.
	help Prints a summary of available commands.
	ls [ARG] Lists files in the current directory or ARG.
	pwd Prints the pathname of the current working directory.
	quit Exits restore immediately.
	setmodes All the directories that have been added to the extraction list have their owner, modes, and times set. Nothing is extracted from the dump.
	verbose Toggles the -v flag.
-R	Requests a particular tape of a multi-volume set on which to restart a full restore (see the -r flag).
-r	Rebuilds a filesystem.
-t	The names of the specified files are listed if they occur on the backup. If no FILE argument is given, the root directory is listed, which results in the entire contents of the backup being listed, unless the -h flag has been specified.
-v	Verbose operation.
-x	The named files are read from the given media. If a named file matches a directory whose contents are on the backup and the -h flag isn't specified, the directory is extracted recursively. The owner, modification time, and mode are restored (if possible). If no FILE argument is given, the root directory is extracted, which results in the entire contents of the backup being extracted, unless the -h flag has been specified.

The following additional options can be specified:

Option	Description
-b *BLOCKSIZE*	The number of kilobytes per dump record.
-c	Only allows reading the dump in the old format (prior to 4.4).
-D *FILESYSTEM*	Allows the user to specify the filesystem name when using restore with the -C option to check the backup.
-f *FILE*	Reads the backup from *FILE*, which can be a device file, an ordinary file, or - (standard input). If the name of the file is of the form *host:file* or *user@host:file*, restore reads from the named file on the remote host.
-h	Extracts the actual directory rather than the files that it references. This prevents hierarchical restoration of complete subtrees from the dump.
-m	Extracts by inode numbers rather than by filename.
-N	Prints only filenames. Files aren't restored.

tar

tar *OPTION* ... [*NAME* ...]

tar is used to store files in an archive, to extract them from an archive, and to accomplish other types of archive manipulations. The primary argument to tar, the "operation," specifies which action to take. The other arguments to tar are either "options," which change the way tar performs an operation, or filenames or archive members, which specify the files or members on which tar is to act. Arguments can be given in any order, although the main operation is usually given first.

Each *NAME* is interpreted as an archive member name when the main command is --compare (--diff, -d), --delete, --extract (--get, -x), --list (-t), or --update (-u). When naming archive members, the exact name of the archive member must be given, as it's printed by --list (-t). For --append (-r) and --create (-c), the *NAME* arguments specify the names of either files or directory hierarchies to place in the archive. These files or hierarchies should already exist in the filesystem prior to the execution of the tar command.

tar interprets relative filenames as being relative to the working directory. tar makes all filenames relative (by removing leading slashes when archiving or restoring files), unless otherwise specified by using the --absolute-names (-P) option.

If a directory is given as either a filename or member name, tar acts recursively on all the files and directories beneath that directory. For example, the name / identifies all the files in the filesystem to tar.

Operations

The following table summarizes tar operations.

Operation	Description
--append or -r	Appends files to the end of the archive.
--catenate or -A	Same as --concatenate.
--compare or -d	Compares archive members with their counterparts in the filesystem and reports differences in file size, mode, owner, modification date, and contents.

Operation	Description
--concatenate or -A	Appends other tar archives to the end of the archive.
--create or -c	Creates a new archive.
--delete	Deletes members from the archive. Not to be used with archives stored on tapes.
--diff or -d	Same as --compare.
--extract or -x	Extracts members from the archive into the filesystem.
--get or -x	Same as --extract.
--list or -t	Lists the members in an archive.
--update or -u	Adds files to the end of the archive, but only if they're newer than their counterparts already in the archive or if they don't already exist in the archive.

Options

The following table describes tar options.

Option	Description
--absolute-names or -P	When creating an archive, tar strips an initial / from member names by default. This option disables that behavior.
--after-date=DATE	Same as --newer=DATE.
--atime-preserve	Preserves the access time field in a file's inode when dumping it.
--backup[=BACKUP_TYPE]	With this option, rather than deleting files from the filesystem, tar backs them up using simple or numbered backups, depending on BACKUP_TYPE. BACKUP_TYPE is one of the following: t or numbered—Always makes numbered backups. nil or existing—Makes numbered backups of files that already have them, simple backups of the others. never or simple—Always makes simple backups.
--block-number or -R	Prints error messages for read errors with the block number in the archive file.
--blocking-factor=BLOCKING or -b BLOCKING	Sets the blocking factor to BLOCKING blocks. Each block is 512 bytes in length.
--checkpoint	Prints periodic checkpoint messages as the archive is read.
--compress or --uncompress or -Z	Uses the compress program to save space when reading or writing the archive.

continues >>

>>continued

Option	Description
`--confirmation`	Same as `--interactive`.
`--dereference` or `-h`	Follows symbolic links when archiving, instead of archiving the links.
`--directory=DIR` or `-C DIR`	Changes the working directory to *DIR* before doing anything else.
`--exclude=PATTERN`	Skips files that match *PATTERN*. See Appendix A, "Regular Expressions," for information on specifying *PATTERN*.
`--exclude-from=FILE` or `-X FILE`	Same as `--exclude`, except that patterns are contained in *FILE*.
`--file=ARCHIVE` or `-f ARCHIVE`	Uses *ARCHIVE* as the archive file.
`--files-from=FILE` or `-T FILE`	Uses the contents of *FILE* as a list of archive members or files on which to operate, in addition to those specified on the command line.
`--force-local`	Interprets the filename given to `--file` as a local file, even if it looks like the name of a remote tape drive.
`--group=GROUP`	Files added to the archive will have a group ID of *GROUP* rather than the group from the source file. *GROUP* is first decoded as a group symbolic name, but if this interpretation fails it's assumed to be a decimal numeric group ID.
`--gunzip` or `--gzip` or `--ungzip` or `-z`	Reads or writes archives through gzip. This allows `tar` to operate directly (and transparently) on several kinds of compressed archives.
`--help`	Prints a short description of operations and options.
`--ignore-failed-read`	Exits successfully if unreadable files are encountered.
`--ignore-umask`	See `--preserve-permissions`.
`--ignore-zeros` or `-i`	Ignores zeroed blocks in the archive. These would otherwise indicate EOF.
`--incremental` or `-G`	Informs `tar` that it's working with an old GNU-format incremental backup archive. Intended primarily for backward compatibility only.
`--info-script=SCRIPT_FILE` or `--new-volume-script=SCRIPT_FILE` or `F SCRIPT_FILE`	When performing multiple-tape backups, *SCRIPT_FILE* is run at the end of each tape.
`--interactive` or `--confirmation` or `-w`	Asks the user for confirmation before performing potentially destructive operations such as overwriting files.

Option	Description
`--keep-old-files` or `-k`	When extracting files, doesn't overwrite existing files.
`--label=`*NAME* or `-V` *NAME*	When creating an archive, writes *NAME* as a name record in the archive. When extracting or listing archives, only operates on archives that have a label matching the pattern specified in *NAME*.
`--listed-incremental=`*SNAPSHOT_FILE* or `-g` *SNAPSHOT_FILE*	During a `--create` operation, specifies that the archive being created is a new GNU-format incremental backup, using *SNAPSHOT_FILE* to determine which files to back up.
`--mode=`*PERMISSIONS*	When adding files to an archive, sets archive member access permissions to *PERMISSIONS* rather than the permissions from the files. The format of *PERMISSIONS* is the same as that used by chmod. See the section on chmod in Chapter 3, "File Utilities," for more information.
`--multi-volume` or `-M`	Indicates to tar that it's working with a multiple-volume archive.
`--new-volume-script`	See `-info-script`.
`--newer=`*DATE* or `--after-date=`*DATE* or `-N` *DATE*	When creating an archive, only adds files that have changed since *DATE*. See Appendix B, "Date Input Formats," for information on how to specify *DATE*.
`--newer-mtime`	In conjunction with `--newer`, only adds files whose contents have changed (as opposed to just `--newer`, which also backs up files for which any status information has changed).
`--no-recursion`	Doesn't operate on subdirectories unless a directory is explicitly named as an argument.
`--null`	When using the `--files-from` option, expects filenames terminated with NUL so that filenames containing newline characters can be processed.
`--numeric-owner`	Uses numeric user and group IDs rather than names when creating an archive.
`--old-archive`	See `--portability`.

continues >>

>>continued

Option	Description
--one-file-system or -l	When creating an archive, doesn't process directories that reside on different filesystems from the current directory.
--owner=USER	Uses USER as the owner of members when creating archives, instead of the user associated with the source file. USER is first decoded as a user symbolic name, but if this interpretation fails it's assumed to be a decimal numeric user ID.
--portability or --old-archive or -o	Creates an archive that's compatible with UNIX V7 tar.
--posix	Creates a POSIX-compliant tar archive.
--preserve	Synonymous with specifying both --preserve-permissions and --same-order.
--preserve-order	See --same-order.
--preserve-permissions or --same-permissions or -p	When extracting, sets file permissions to those assigned to the corresponding archive members.
--read-full-records or -B	Re-blocks input. This option is intended to be used when reading from pipes on systems with buggy implementations.
--record-size=SIZE	Uses SIZE bytes per record when accessing the archive.
--recursive-unlink	Similar to --unlink-first. Removes existing directory hierarchies before extracting directories of the same name from the archive.
--remove-files	Removes the source files from the filesystem after appending it to an archive.
--rsh-command=CMD	Uses CMD to communicate with remote devices.
--same-order or --preserve-order or -s	Indicates to tar that the list of file arguments has already been sorted to match the order of files in the archive. This option is intended for use on machines with small amounts of memory.
--same-owner	When extracting, attempts to preserve the owner specified in the archive.
--same-permissions	See --preserve-permissions.

Option	Description
`--show-omitted-dirs`	Mentions directories that are being skipped when operating on an archive.
`--sparse` or `-S`	Invokes a GNU extension when adding files to an archive that handles sparse files efficiently.
`--starting-file=NAME` or `-K NAME`	When extracting, skips files until NAME is found.
`--suffix=SUFFIX`	Use SUFFIX when backing up files instead of the default ~.
`--tape-length=NUM` or `-L NUM`	Sets the length of tapes to $NUM \times 1024$ bytes.
`--to-stdout` or `-O`	Extracts files to standard output rather than to the filesystem.
`--totals`	Displays the total number of bytes written after creating an archive.
`--touch` or `-m`	Sets the modification time of extracted files to the extraction time, rather than the modification time stored in the archive.
`--uncompress`	See `--compress`.
`--ungzip`	See `--gzip`.
`--unlink-first` or `-U`	Removes the corresponding file from the filesystem before extracting it from the archive.
`--use-compress-program=PROG`	Accesses the archive through PROG, which is presumed to be a compression program of some sort.
`--verbose` or `-v`	Verbose operation. This option can be specified multiple times for some operations to increase the amount of information displayed.
`--verify` or `-W`	Verifies that the archive was correctly written when creating an archive.
`--version`	Prints the version number, copyright message, and some credits, and exits.
`--volno-file=FILE`	Used in conjunction with `--multi-volume`. Keeps track of which volume of a multi-volume archive is working in FILE.

For example, the following command stores the files in the directory `dir` into the archive named `dir.tar`:

```
tar --create --file=dir.tar dir
```

The same can be accomplished using a shorter form:

```
tar -cf dir.tar dir
```

Software packages are often stored in compressed (`gzipped`) `tar` archives. A command similar to the following is typically used to uncompress (`gunzip`) and extract an archive named `package.tar.gz`:

```
tar -xvzf package.tar.gz
```

13

Security

This chapter describes some commonly used security mechanisms. Many more are available. For more information on system security, consult the references listed in Appendix C, "Web Resources."

Root Password Protection

The su command allows one user to temporarily become another user. If it's necessary for the user to become the superuser, the user must know the password for root. The sudo command is provided as an alternative to giving ordinary users the root password.

The sudo command allows non-privileged users to perform a limited number of privileged functions. It eliminates the need to give the root password to anyone but the system administrator. This section describes how to limit the tasks that can be performed by users of sudo.

/etc/sudoers

The /etc/sudoers file controls which users can run which programs as root using sudo. It's composed of an optional host alias section, an optional command alias section, and the user specification section. The format of this file is defined by a powerful command language. For a complete definition, see the sudoers(5) manual page.

Following is a simple example in which a user needs root capability to run /usr/bin/build and all the commands in /usr/bin that begin with dpkg:

```
# Cmnd alias specification
Cmnd_Alias DPKG=/usr/bin/dpkg*
Cmnd_Alias BUILD=/usr/bin/build
# User privilege specification
epetron ALL=DPKG
epetron ALL=BUILD
```

In this example, the user epetron is allowed to execute /usr/bin/build (defined by the BUILD alias) and any files with names starting with dpkg in the /usr/bin directory (defined by the DPKG alias). The keyword ALL means that epetron can execute these files from any host.

Restricting Batch Access

Restricting the running of scheduled and/or non-interactive jobs.

/etc/at.access and /etc/at.deny

The /etc/at.access and /etc/at.deny files determine which users can submit batch jobs via at or batch. Each file contains a list of usernames, one name per line. Whitespace is not permitted. If the file /etc/at.allow exists, only users mentioned in it are allowed to use at. If /etc/at.allow doesn't exist, /etc/at.deny is checked. If neither exists, only root has access to the at command. If /etc/at.deny is empty, all users have access to the at command.

Restricting Login Privileges

Restricting logins, trusted access (no passwords required), and the designation of login shells.

/etc/login.access

/etc/login.access is an access control table that determines which users are allowed to log in from which origins. Origins can be specified as serial line (TTY) devices and/or network hosts.

Each line of the file has the following form:

PERMISSION:USERS:ORIGINS

PERMISSION is either + (access granted) or - (access denied). USERS is a list of login names, group names, or ALL (always matches). ORIGINS is a list of one or more TTY names, hostnames, domain names (beginning with a period), host addresses, network addresses (ending with a period), ALL (always matches) or LOCAL (matches any string that doesn't contain a period). The EXCEPT operator can be used to exclude sets of users and login origins. Lines beginning with # are treated as comments.

The group file is searched only when a name doesn't match that of the logged-in user. Only groups are matched in which users are explicitly listed. A user's primary group ID value is not considered.

Examples:

```
# Disallow console logins to all but a few accounts.
#
-:ALL EXCEPT wheel shutdown sync:console
#
# Disallow non-local logins to privileged accounts (group wheel).
#
-:wheel:ALL EXCEPT LOCAL .win.tue.nl
```

checkrhosts

checkrhosts checks the .rhosts files for each user for any potential security problems. It shows which .rhosts files are insecure and gives a short description of the reasons why they're insecure and how the problems can be corrected.

.rhosts

The $HOME/.rhosts file grants or denies trusted access (no passwords required) via the r-commands (rlogin, rsh, rcp, and so on). Entries take the following form:

HOSTNAME [USERNAME]

The entry grants trusted r-command access for the user with login name *USERNAME* from remote host *HOSTNAME*. If *USERNAME* isn't specified, the user must have the same login name on the remote host as on the local host. It's advisable to always use the fully-qualified domain name and not the short hostname for *HOSTNAME*.

Netgroups can be specified by preceding the netgroup with the at (@) sign.

The .rhosts file must have permissions 600 (readable and writable only by the owner).

/etc/hosts.equiv

/etc/hosts.equiv grants or denies trusted (no passwords required) access via r-commands (rlogin, rsh, rcp, and so on). Each entry is in this format:

[+ ¦ -] [HOSTNAME] [USERNAME]

HOSTNAME is the name of a host that's logically equivalent to the local host. Users logged into that host are allowed to access like-named user accounts on the local host without supplying a password. *HOSTNAME* can be optionally preceded by the plus (+) sign. If the plus sign is used alone, it allows any host to access the system. Access can be denied by using the minus (-) sign. Users from that host must always supply a password. It's advisable to always use the fully-qualified domain name for *HOSTNAME*.

USERNAME grants a specific user access to all user accounts except root without supplying a password. The user is *not* restricted to like-named accounts. *USERNAME* can be optionally preceded by the + sign. Access can be explicitly denied to a specific user by preceding the username with the - sign. This says that the user is not trusted, no matter what other entries exist for that host.

Netgroups can be specified by preceding the netgroup with the @ sign.

/etc/netgroup

/etc/netgroup defines network-wide groups. Each line of the netgroup file defines a group and has this form:

GROUPNAME MEMBER ...

where *GROUPNAME* is the name of the group and *MEMBER* takes the following form:

(HOSTNAME, USERNAME, DOMAINNAME)

Any of the three fields can be empty. An empty field signifies a "wildcard"—for example, the group universal (,,) to which everyone belongs.

The groups defined in netgroup are referenced in various network-access control schemes.

`/etc/securetty`

`/etc/securetty` contains the device names of TTY lines (one per line without a leading `/dev/`) on which root is allowed to log in.

`/etc/shells`

The `chsh` (change shell) command allows users to change their login shell. `/etc/shells` contains the full pathnames (one per line) of valid login shells. It's used by the `chsh` command to validate a user's choice of login shell.

Restricting NFS File Sharing

Controlling the sharing of filesystems and subdirectories.

`/etc/exports`

`/etc/exports` is the access control list for filesystems that can be exported to NFS clients. It's used by both the NFS mount daemon `mountd` and the NFS file server `nfsd`.

Each line contains a mount point and a list of machine or netgroup names allowed to mount the filesystem at that point. An optional list of mount parameters can follow each machine name. Blank lines are ignored and comments start with the `#` character. Long entries can be continued across multiple lines by using the backslash (\) character.

For example:

```
#
#Allow read/write access to "/usr" to all hosts in
#"local.domain" and read/write access to everybody in the netgroup
#"trusted":
/usr *.local.domain(ro) @trusted(rw)
```

For a complete description of hostname formats, access options, and user ID mapping options, see the `exports(5)` manual page.

Restricting Network File Transfers

Restricting access to files through network file transfers.

`/etc/ftpchroot`

This file contains a list of usernames, one per line. If a user's name is in this file, the session's root will be changed to the user's login directory by `chroot` as for an `anonymous` or `ftp` account. This is intended as a compromise between a fully anonymous account and a fully privileged account.

/etc/ftpusers

This file contains a list of usernames, one per line. If a user's name appears in this file, no ftp session can be established as that user.

The TCP Wrapping Facility

Controlling access to network services based on the username and/or the host requesting the service.

tcpd

```
tcpd FILENAME [ ARG ... ]
```

tcpd is an access-control facility for Internet services such as telnet, ftp, finger, and others that have a one-to-one mapping to executable files. It's invoked by inetd when a service is requested by a remote client. Instead of the server being run directly by inetd, tcpd is run instead. The fully-qualified pathname for the server and the server's arguments are passed to tcpd as arguments. For example, the following is a typical entry that might appear in inetd.conf:

```
telnet  stream  tcp  nowait  root  /usr/sbin/tcpd  /usr/sbin/in.telnetd
```

tcpd will allow or disallow the requesting host's access, depending on directives listed in /etc/hosts.allow and/or /etc/hosts.deny.

tcpdchk

```
tcpdchk [-a] [-d] [-i INETD_CONF] [-v]
```

tcpdchk examines the system's TCP wrapper configuration and reports all potential and real problems it can find. It examines the /etc/hosts.allow, /etc/hosts.deny, and /etc/inetd.conf files and reports problems such as nonexistent pathnames, invalid service designations, services that shouldn't be wrapped, and so on. Where possible, it suggests fixes for problems.

Option	Description
-a	Report access control rules that permit access without an explicit ALLOW keyword.
-d	Examine hosts.allow and hosts.deny files in the current directory instead of the default files.
-i INETD_CONF	Check the inetd configuration in INETD_CONF instead of the one in /etc/inetd.conf.
-v	Display the contents of each access-control rule.

tcpdmatch

```
tcpdmatch [-d] [-i INETD_CONF] DAEMON CLIENT
tcpdmatch [-d] [-i INETD_CONF] DAEMON[@SERVER] [USER@]CLIENT
```

tcpdmatch predicts how the TCP wrapper will handle a specific request for service.

Option	Description
CLIENT	CLIENT is a hostname, network address, or one of the unknown or paranoid wildcard patterns.
DAEMON	DAEMON is the process name. This is typically the last component of the daemon's executable pathname.
-d	Examine hosts.allow and hosts.deny files in the current directory instead of the default files.
-i INETD_CONF	Check inetd configuration in INETD_CONF instead of the one in /etc/inetd.conf.
SERVER	A hostname, network address, or one of the unknown or paranoid wildcard patterns. The default server name is unknown.
USER	A client user identifier. Typically, a login name or a numeric user ID. The default username is unknown.

/etc/hosts.allow and /etc/hosts.deny

/etc/hosts.allow and /etc/hosts.deny are host access-control files. They contain statements written in a simple access-control language that's based on client (hostname/address, username), and server (process name, hostname/address) patterns. Access is granted when a server/client pair matches an entry in the /etc/hosts.allow file. Otherwise, access will be denied when a server/client pair matches an entry in the /etc/hosts.deny file. If neither of these conditions is true, access will be granted. If either file doesn't exist, it's treated as an empty file. Access control can be turned off by eliminating the files.

Long lines can be continued with the backslash (\) character. Blank lines and lines that begin with # are ignored. Statements use this form:

DAEMON_LIST : CLIENT_LIST [: SHELL_COMMAND]

DAEMON_LIST is a list of one or more process names. Wildcards can also be used. CLIENT_LIST is a list of one or more hostnames, host addresses, and wildcard patterns that will be matched against the client's hostname or address. SHELL_COMMAND, if included, is a shell command to be run using /bin/sh with standard input, output, and error connected to /dev/null.

Following are some examples:

```
ALL: LOCAL @some_netgroup
ALL: .foobar.edu EXCEPT terminalserver.foobar.edu
```

If /etc/hosts.allow contained these lines, access to all services would be granted from all hosts in the local domain (no . in the hostname), from members of the some_netgroup netgroup, and from all hosts in .foobar.edu except terminalserver.foobar.edu.

The complete descriptions of wildcard patterns, argument passing for SHELL_COMMAND, and other parts of the access-control language are described in the hosts_access(5) manual page. Extensions to the access-control language are described in the hosts_options(5) manual page. The extensions are available if the access-control library was compiled with -DPROCESS_OPTIONS.

IP Firewall Administration

The IP firewall and accounting facilities in the kernel provide mechanisms for IP accounting, for building firewalls based on packet-level filtering, for building firewalls using transparent proxy servers (by redirecting packets to local sockets), and for masquerading forwarded packets. The administration of these functions is maintained in the kernel as four separate lists, each containing zero or more rules. Each rule contains specific information about source and destination addresses, protocols, port numbers, and some other characteristics. A packet matches with a rule when the characteristics of the rule match those of the IP packet. These are the four categories of rules:

- **Accounting.** The accounting rules are used for all IP packets that are sent or received via one of the local network interfaces. Every packet is compared with all rules in this list, and every match causes an increment of the packet and byte counters associated with that rule.

- **Input firewall.** These rules regulate the acceptance of incoming IP packets. All packets coming in through one of the local network interfaces are checked against the input firewall rules. The first rule that matches with a packet determines the policy to use and also causes the rule's packet and byte counters to be incremented. When no matching rule is found, the default policy for the input firewall is used.

- **Output firewall.** These rules define the permissions for sending IP packets. All packets that are ready to be sent through one of the local network interfaces are checked against the output firewall rules. The first rule that matches with a packet determines the policy to use and also causes the rule's packet and byte counters to be incremented. When no matching rule is found, the default policy for the output firewall is used.

- **Forwarding firewall.** These rules define the permissions for forwarding IP packets. All packets sent by a remote host having another remote host as destination are checked against the forwarding firewall rules. The first rule that matches with a packet determines the policy to use and also causes the rule's packet and byte counters to be incremented. When no matching rule is found, the default policy for the forwarding firewall is used.

Each of the firewall rules contains a policy specifying what action has to be taken when a packet matches with the rule. Three policies are possible:

- `accept` lets the packet pass the firewall.

- `reject` refuses the packet and sends an ICMP host unreachable message back to the sender as notification.

- `deny` ignores the packet without sending any notification.

For all three types of firewalls there also exists a default policy, which applies to all packets for which none of the rules match.

Version 2.0 and higher kernels provide `ipfadm` firewall support. Version 2.2 provides an update to `ipfadm` called `ipchains`.

ipchains-restore

```
ipchains-restore [ -f ] [ -v ]
```

`ipchains-restore` restores firewall chains from standard input.

Option	Description
-f	Clear chains without asking.
-v	Print the rules.

ipchains-save

```
ipchains-save [CHAIN] [ -v ]
```

`ipchains-save` prints firewall chains to standard output. If *CHAIN* is given, only the named chain will print. -v causes all rules to print.

ipchains

```
ipchains -[ADC] CHAIN RULE_SPECIFICATION [OPTION ... ]
ipchains -[RI] CHAIN RULENUM RULE_SPECIFICATION [OPTION ... ]
ipchains -D CHAIN RULENUM [OPTION ... ]
ipchains -[LFZNX] [CHAIN] [OPTION ... ]
ipchains -P CHAIN TARGET [OPTION ... ]
ipchains -M [ -L ¦ -S ] [OPTION ... ]
```

`ipchains` is used to set up, maintain, and inspect the IP firewall rules in the Linux kernel. A firewall rule specifies criteria for a packet and a target. If the packet doesn't match the rule, the next rule in the chain is examined. If it does match, then the next rule is specified by the value of the target, which can be the name of a user-defined chain or one of the special values ACCEPT, DENY, REJECT, MASQ, REDIR, or RETURN. ACCEPT means to let the packet through. DENY means to drop the packet on the floor. REJECT means the same as drop, but is more polite and easier to debug, since an ICMP message is sent back to the sender indicating that the packet was dropped. DENY and ACCEPT are the same for ICMP packets.

MASQ is only legal for the forwarding and user-defined chains and can be used only when the kernel is compiled with CONFIG_IP_MASQUERADE defined. With this option, packets will be masqueraded as if they originated from the local host. Furthermore, reverse packets will be recognized as such and demasqueraded automatically, bypassing the forwarding chain.

REDIR is only legal for the input and user-defined chains and can be used only when the Linux kernel is compiled with CONFIG_IP_TRANSPARENT_PROXY defined. With this option, packets will be redirected to a local socket, even if they were sent to a remote host. If the specified redirection port is 0, which is the default value, the destination port of a packet will be used as the redirection port. When this target is used, an optional extra argument (the port number) can be supplied.

If the end of a user-defined chain is reached or a rule with the target RETURN matches, the next rule in the previous (calling) chain is examined. If the end of a built-in chain is reached, or a rule in a built-in chain with target RETURN matches, the target specified by the chain policy determines the fate of the packet.

The options recognized by **ipchains** are divided into three types: commands that indicate specific actions to perform, parameters that make up rule specifications, and additional options.

The following table describes the command options accepted by **ipchains**.

Option	Description
-A	Appends one or more rules to the end of the selected chain. When the source and/or destination names resolve to more than one address, a rule will be added for each possible address combination.
-C	Checks the given packet against the selected chain. The same arguments used to specify firewall rules are used to construct the packet to be tested. In particular, the -s (source), -d (destination), -p (protocol), and -i (interface) flags are compulsory.
-D	Deletes one or more rules from the selected chain. There are two versions of this command: The rule can be specified as a number in the chain (starting at 1 for the first rule) or a rule to match.
-F	Flushes the selected chain. This is equivalent to deleting all the rules one at a time.
-h	Help. Gives a brief description of command syntax.
-I	Inserts one or more rules in the selected chain as the given rule number. If the rule number is 1, for example, the rule(s) are inserted at the head of the chain.
-L	Lists all rules in the selected chain. If no chain is selected, all chains are listed. It's legal to specify the -Z (zero) option as well, in which case no chain may be specified. The exact output is affected by the other arguments given.
-M	Allows viewing of the currently masqueraded connections (in conjunction with the -L option) or to set the kernel masquerading parameters (with the -S option).
-N NAME	Creates a new user-defined chain with the name *NAME*. A chain with this name must not already exist.
-P	Sets the policy for the chain to the given target. Only non–user-defined chains can have policies, and neither built-in nor user-defined chains can be policy targets.
-R	Replaces a rule in the selected chain. If the source and/or destination names resolve to multiple addresses, the command will fail. Rules are numbered starting at 1.
-S TCP TCPFIN UDP	Changes the timeout values used for masquerading. This command always takes three parameters, representing the timeout values (in seconds) for TCP sessions, TCP sessions after receiving a FIN packet, and UDP packets, respectively. A timeout value of 0 means that the current timeout value of the corresponding entry is preserved. This option is allowed only in combination with the -M flag.
-X	Deletes the specified user-defined chain. There must be no references to the chain. If references exist, the referring rules must be deleted before the chain can be deleted. If no argument is given, this option attempts to delete every non–built-in chain.

continues >>

>>continued

Option	Description
-Z	Zeroes the packet and byte counters in all chains. It's legal to specify the -L (list) option as well, to see the counters immediately before they're cleared. If this is done, no chain can be specified (they'll all be displayed and cleared).

The following `ipchains` command arguments are used for rule specifications.

Option	Description
-d [!]*ADDRESS*[/*MASK*] [!] [*PORT* ...]	Destination specification. *ADDRESS* can be a hostname, a network name, or a plain IP address. *MASK* can be either a network mask or a plain number, specifying the number of 1's at the left side of the network mask. The ! character inverts the address specification. The source can include a port specification or ICMP type. This can be a service name, a port number, a numeric ICMP type, or one of the ICMP-type names shown by the command `ipchains -h icmp`. An inclusive range can also be specified, using the format *PORT*:*PORT*. If the first port is omitted, 0 is assumed. If the last is omitted, 65535 is assumed. Ports can only be specified in combination with the tcp, udp, or icmp protocol. The ! character inverts the port specification.
[!] -f	The rule refers only to second and further fragments of fragmented packets. The ! character inverts the specification.
-i [!]*NAME*	*NAME* of the interface through which the packet is received or will be sent. *NAME* is the empty string if this flag is omitted. The ! character inverts the sense of the specification. If the interface name ends in +, any interface that begins with this name matches.
-j *TARGET*	Specifies the target of the rule. *TARGET* is what to do if the packet matches. The target can be a user-defined chain (not the one this rule is in) or one of the special targets that decide the fate of the packet immediately.
-p [!]*PROTOCOL*	The *PROTOCOL* of the rule or of the packet to check. The specified protocol can be tcp, udp, icmp, all, or a numeric value that represents one of these protocols or a different protocol. The ! character inverts the test. A 0 for *PROTOCOL* is equivalent to all. all is taken as the default if this option is omitted.
-s [!] *ADDRESS*[/*MASK*] [!] [*PORT* ...]	Source specification. See the -d flag earlier in this table for a detailed description of the syntax.

The following table describes the remaining options accepted by `ipchains`.

Option	Description
-b	Bidirectional mode. The rule will match IP packets in both directions.
-l	Turns on kernel logging of matching packets. Information will be printed via `printk`.

Option	Description
-m *MARKVALUE*	Marks matching packets. Packets can be marked with a 32-bit unsigned value. If *MARKVALUE* begins with + or -, the value is added to or subtracted from the current marked value.
-n	Numeric output. IP addresses and port numbers are printed in numeric format.
-o[*MAXSIZE*]	Copies matching packets to the user space device. *MAXSIZE* limits the number of bytes to be copied.
-t *ANDMASK XORMASK*	When a packet matches a rule, its **Type of Service** (TOS) field is first bitwise AND'ed with *ANDMASK* and the result is bitwise XOR'ed with *XORMASK*. Masks should be specified as hexadecimal 8-bit values.
-v	Verbose output. This option makes the list command show the interface address, the rule options (if any), and the TOS masks. The packet and byte counters are also listed, with the suffixes K, M, or G for 1000, 1,000,000, and 1,000,000,000 multipliers, respectively. (See the -x flag to change this setting.) When used in combination with -M, information related to delta sequence numbers is also listed. For appending, insertion, deletion, and replacement, this causes detailed information on the rule or rules to be printed.
-x	Expands numbers. Displays exact values of packet and byte counters instead of rounded kilobyte (K), megabyte (M), or gigabyte (G) numbers. Used with the -L command.
[!] -y	Matches only TCP packets with the SYN bit set and the ACK and FIN bits cleared. Inverts if ! is given.

ipfwadm

```
ipfwadm { -A ¦ -I ¦ -O ¦ -F } COMMAND_PARAMETERS [OPTION ... ]
ipfwadm -M [ -l ¦ -s ] [OPTION ... ]
```

`ipfwadm` is used to set up, maintain, and inspect the IP firewall and account rules in the kernel. The first argument indicates the category of rules to which the given command applies:

- The -A [*DIRECTION*] form applies to IP accounting rules. *DIRECTION* can be in, out, or both. The default direction is both.

- The -I form applies to IP input firewall rules.

- The -O form applies to IP output firewall rules.

- The -F form applies to IP forwarding rules.

- -M applies to IP masquerading administration.

The following table describes the *COMMAND_PARAMETERS* arguments.

Option	Description
-a [POLICY]	Appends one or more rules to the end of the selected list. For the account chain, POLICY should not be specified. For firewall chains, POLICY is required. POLICY can be accept, deny, reject, or masquerade. When the source and/or destination names resolve to more than one address, a rule is added for each possible address combination.
-c	Checks whether this IP packet would be accepted, denied, or rejected by the selected type of firewall.
-d [POLICY]	Deletes one or more entries from the selected list of rules. The semantics are the same as with the -a and -i commands. Only the first matching rule in the list is deleted.
-h	Help. Gives a brief description of the command syntax.
-i [POLICY]	Inserts one or more rules at the beginning of the selected list. See the -a command earlier in this table for details.
-f	Flushes the selected list of rules.
-l	Lists all the rules in the selected list.
-p POLICY	Changes the default policy for the selected type of firewall. The given policy has to be accept, deny, reject, or masquerade. The default policy is used when no matching rule is found.
-s TCP TCPFIN UDP	Changes the timeout values used for masquerading. This command always takes three parameters representing the timeout values (in seconds) for TCP sessions, TCP sessions after receiving a FIN packet, and UDP packets, respectively. A timeout value of 0 means that the current timeout value of the corresponding entry is preserved.
-z	Resets the packet and byte counters of all the rules in the selected list.

The following arguments can be used with the append, insert, delete, or check commands.

Option	Description
-P PROTOCOL	The PROTOCOL of the rule or of the packet to check. PROTOCOL can be tcp, udp, icmp, or all. all cannot be used in conjunction with the check command.
-D ADDRESS[/MASK] [PORT ...]	Destination specification. ADDRESS can be a hostname, a network name, or a plain IP address. MASK can be a network mask or a plain number indicating the number of 1's at the left side of the mask. The PORT parameters, if specified, can be service names or port numbers.

Option	Description
-S ADDRESS[/MASK] [PORT ...]	Source specification. The semantics are identical to those of -D except that -S also allows ICMP types for PORT.
-V ADDRESS	Optional address of an interface via which a packet is received or will be sent. ADDRESS can be either a hostname or a plain IP address. When a hostname is specified, it should resolve to exactly one IP address. When this option is omitted, the address 0.0.0.0 is assumed, which has a special meaning and will match with any interface address. For the check command, this option is mandatory.
-W NAME	Optional NAME of an interface through which a packet is received or will be sent. If omitted, the empty string is assumed, which matches any interface name. For the check command, this is mandatory.

The following table describes the remaining options accepted by ipfwadm.

Option	Description
-b	Bidirectional mode. The rule matches with IP packets in both directions.
-c	Extended output. Shows interface addresses, rule options, packet and byte counters, TOS masks, and delta sequence numbers. Only valid with the list command.
-k	Matches only TCP packets with the ACK bit set. Valid only with the append, insert, and delete commands.
-m	Masquerade packets accepted for forwarding. When this option is set, packets accepted by this rule will be masqueraded as if they originated from the local host. Reverse packets will be recognized as such and demasqueraded automatically, bypassing the forwarding firewall. This option is only valid in forwarding firewall rules with policy accept (or when specifying accept as the default policy) and can only be used when the kernel is compiled with CONFIG_IP_MASQUERADE defined.
-n	Numeric output. IP addresses and port numbers are printed in numeric format.
-o	Turns on kernel logging of matching packets using printk. Valid only when the kernel is compiled with CONFIG_IP_FIREWALL_ VERBOSE defined.

continues >>

>>continued

Option	Description
`-r [PORT]`	Redirects packets to the local socket. When this option is set, packets accepted by this rule are redirected to a local socket even if they were destined for a remote host. If the specified redirection port is `0`, which is the default value, the destination port of the packet is used as the redirection port. This option is valid only in input firewall rules with policy `accept` and can only be used when the Linux kernel is compiled with `CONFIG_IP_TRANSPARENT_PROXY` defined.
`-t ANDMASK XORMASK`	When a packet matches a rule, its `Type of Service` (`TOS`) field is first bitwise AND'ed with `ANDMASK` and the result is bitwise XOR'ed with `XORMASK`. Masks should be specified as hexadecimal 8-bit values.
`-v`	Verbose output. Prints detailed information of the rule or packet to be added, deleted, or checked.
`-x`	Expands numbers. Displays the exact value of packet and byte counters instead of rounded kilobyte (K), megabyte (M), or gigabyte (G) numbers.
`-y`	Matches only TCP packets with the SYN bit set and the ACK bit cleared.

ipfwadm-wrapper

```
ipfwadm-wrapper { -A ¦ -I ¦ -O ¦ -F } COMMAND_PARAMETERS [OPTION ... ]
ipfwadm-wrapper -M [ -l ¦ -s ] [OPTION ... ]
```

`ipfwadm-wrapper` emulates `ipfwadm`. It's used with `ipchains` to maintain rules created under `ipfwadm`. The command options are identical to those of `ipfwadm`.

Appendixes

A
Regular Expressions

A *regular expression* is a pattern that describes a set of strings. Like arithmetic expressions, regular expressions can consist of multiple subexpressions and operators. This appendix describes the syntax and semantics of regular expressions.

Most characters, including all letters and digits, are regular expressions in and of themselves. There are some characters that have special meanings. These special characters are known as *metacharacters*. Metacharacters can also match themselves if they are preceded by the backslash (\) character.

A list of characters enclosed by brackets ([ ]) matches any character in the list. If the first character of the list is a caret (^), it matches any character *not* in the list. A range of ASCII characters can be specified by an expression of the form *FIRST_CHAR*-*LAST_CHAR*. For example, [a-z] will match any lowercase character and [0-9] will match any digit. The following symbolic class names can be used:

[:alnum:]	[:print:]
[:alpha:]	[:punct:]
[:cntrl:]	[:space:]
[:digit:]	[:upper:]
[:graph:]	[:xdigit:]
[:lower:]	

The brackets in the class names must appear in addition to the brackets delimiting the list. For example, [[:alnum:]] is equivalent to [0-9a-z]. Most of the metacharacters lose their meaning within the brackets. A closing bracket ( ]) can be an element of a list if it appears first. A caret (^) can be part of a list if it's *not* first. A hyphen (-) can be part of the list if it's last.

Two regular expressions can be concatenated. The resulting regular expression matches any string formed by concatenating two substrings that respectively match the concatenated subexpressions.

Two regular expressions can be joined by the infix operator (¦). The resulting regular expression matches the subexpression on either side of the vertical bar.

Repetition takes precedence over concatenation, which in turn takes precedence over alternation. A whole subexpression can be enclosed in parentheses to override these precedence rules.

The following table describes the meanings of some character sequences when used in regular expressions:

Expression	Meaning
.	Matches any single character.
\w	Equivalent to [[:alnum:]].
\W	Equivalent to [^[:alnum:]].
^	Matches the empty string at the beginning of a line.
$	Matches the empty string at the end of a line.
\<	Matches the empty string at the beginning of a word.
\>	Matches the empty string at the end of a word.
\b	Matches the empty string at the edge of a word.
\B	Matches the empty string if it's *not* at the edge of a word.
?	Matches the preceding item at most once.
*	Matches the preceding item zero or more times.
+	Matches the preceding item at least once.
{N}	Matches the preceding item N times.
{N,}	Matches the preceding item at least N times.
{,N}	Matches the preceding item at most N times.
{N,M}	Matches the preceding item at least N times but not more than M times.
\N	If N is a single digit, matches the substring previously matched by the Nth parenthesized subexpression.

Example

The following shell command can be used to list information on files with names beginning with an alphabetic character and ending with .zip or .gz:

```
ls -l | grep -E '\<[:alpha:].*\.(gz|zip)\>'
```

The ls -l command is used to generate a file listing containing one line for each file with dates, permissions, and so on. The output from ls is piped into grep. The -E option enables full regular expression processing within grep. The \<[:alpha:] subexpression makes sure that the filename begins with a letter. .* allows any other characters to be included between the initial letter character and the extension. The literal period in the extension is given in the regular expression by the \. subexpression. The (gz|zip)\> subexpression says that the filename must end with either gz or zip. \> makes sure that the gz or zip occurs at the end of the filename and prevents files with names like a.zipa or b.gzb from being matched.

B

Date Input Formats

Many commands accepts dates as command-line options. This appendix describes the formats accepted by these commands.

The general format for dates is a string with multiple components separated by whitespace. In cases where no ambiguity is introduced, the whitespace can be eliminated. The items included in date strings consist of the following:

- Calendar date.

- Time of day.

- Time zone.

- Day of week.

- Relative items.

- Pure numbers.

Calendar Dates

For numeric months, the ISO 8601 format *YEAR-MONTH-DAY* is allowed, where *YEAR* is any positive number, *MONTH* is a number from 01 to 12, and *DAY* is a number from 01 to 31. A leading zero must be present if a number is less than 10. If *YEAR* is less than 100, then 1900 is added to it to force a date in this century. *YEAR* can also be given as a full four-digit date to specify years beyond 1999. The construct *MONTH/DAY/YEAR*, popular in the United States, is accepted, as is *MONTH/DAY*, omitting the year.

Literal months can be spelled out in full: January, February, and so on. They can also be abbreviated to the first three letters, possibly followed by an abbreviating period or dot (.). It's also possible to write Sept instead of September.

When months are written literally, the calendar date may be given as any of the following:

- *DAY MONTH YEAR*

- *DAY MONTH*

- *MONTH DAY YEAR*

- *DAY-MONTH-YEAR*

- *MONTH DAY*

Time of Day

The time of day can be given as *HOUR:MINUTE:SECOND*, where *HOUR* is a number from 0 to 23, *MINUTE* is a number from 0 to 59, and *SECOND* is a number from 0 to 59. *SECOND* can be omitted, in which case it defaults to 0.

The time can be followed by am, a.m, pm, or p.m. When these are used, the *HOUR* is restricted to values from 1 to 12.

The time can be followed by a time zone correction expressed as *SHHMM*, where *S* is + (plus) or - (minus), *HH* is the number of zone hours, and *MM* is the number of zone minutes. When a time zone correction is given this way, it forces interpretation of the time in UTC, overriding any previous specification for the time zone or the local time zone. The *MINUTE* part of the time of day cannot be elided when a time zone correction is used. This is the only way to specify a time zone correction by fractional parts of an hour.

Either am/pm or a time zone correction can be used, but not both.

Time Zone

The time zone part of a date string is the standard abbreviation for an international time zone. Included periods are ignored. Military designations use single letters.

The following table lists the non-DST (Daylight Savings Time) time zones, indexed by their zone hour values.

Zone Hour	Abbreviation(s)
+000	GMT for Greenwich Mean Time, UT or UTC for Universal Coordinated Time, WET for Western European, and Z for militaries.
+100	WAT for West Africa, A for militaries.
+200	Mid Atlantic, AT for Azores, B for militaries.
+300	Greenland, C for militaries.
+400	AST for Atlantic Standard, D for militaries.
+500	EST for Eastern Standard, E for militaries.
+600	CST for Central Standard, F for militaries.
+700	MST for Mountain Standard, G for militaries.
+800	PST for Pacific Standard, H for militaries.

Zone Hour	Abbreviation(s)
+900	YST for Yukon Standard, I for militaries.
+1000	AHST for Alaska-Hawaii Standard, CAT for Central Alaska, HST for Hawaii Standard, K for militaries.
+1100	NT for Nome, L for militaries.
+1200	IDLW for International Date Line West, M for militaries.
-100	CET for Central European, FWT for French Winter, MET for Middle European, MEWT for Middle European Winter, SWT for Swedish Winter, N for militaries.
-200	EET for Eastern European, Russia Zone 1, O for militaries.
-300	BT for Baghdad, Russia Zone 2, P for militaries.
-400	ZP4 for Russia Zone 3, Q for militaries.
-500	ZP5 for Russia Zone 4, R for militaries.
-600	ZP6 for Russia Zone 5, S for militaries.
-700	WAST for West Australian Standard, CCT for China Coast, Russia Zone 6, T for militaries.
-800	CCT for China Coast, Russia Zone 7, JST (Japan Standard), U for militaries.
-900	EAST for East Australian Standard, Russia Zone 8, V for militaries.
-1000	Russia Zone 9, W for militaries.
-1100	Russia Zone 10, X for militaries.
-1200	IDLE for International Date Line East, NZST for New Zealand Standard, NZT for New Zealand, Russia Zone 11, Y for militaries.

The following table lists the DST time zones indexed by their zone hour values. If the string DST follows a non-DST time zone, the corresponding DST time zone can be specified.

Zone Hour	Abbreviation(s)
0	BST for British Summer.
+400	ADT for Atlantic Daylight.
+500	EDT for Eastern Daylight.
+600	CDT for Central Daylight.
+700	MDT for Mountain Daylight.
+800	PDT for Pacific Daylight.
+900	YDT for Yukon Daylight.
+1000	HDT for Hawaii Daylight.
-100	MEST for Middle European Summer, MESZ for Middle European Summer, SST for Swedish Summer, and FST for French Summer.
-700	WADT for West Australian Daylight.
-1000	EADT for Eastern Australian Daylight.
-1200	NZDT for New Zealand Daylight.

Day of Week

Naming a day of the week will forward the date if necessary to reach that day of the week in the future. The day of the week can be spelled out in full or abbreviated by using the first three letters, optionally followed by a period. The special abbreviations `tues` for `tuesday`, `wednes` for `wednesday`, and `thur` or `thurs` for `thursday` are also allowed.

A number can precede a day of week item to move forward supplementary weeks. It's best used in expressions such as `third monday`. In this context, `last` *DAY* or `next` *DAY* is also acceptable, moving one week before or after the day that *DAY* by itself would represent.

A comma following a day of week item is ignored.

Relative Items

Relative items such as `2 days` or `1 year ago` adjust a date forward or backward. If more than one relative item is given, the values accumulate.

The unit of time displacement can be selected by the string `year` or `month` for moving by whole years or months. These are fuzzy units, as years and months are not all of equal duration. More precise units are `fortnight` (which is worth 14 days), `week` (worth 7 days), `day` (worth 24 hours), `hour` (worth 60 minutes), `minute` or `min` (worth 60 seconds), and `second` or `sec` (worth one second). The `s` suffix on these units is accepted and ignored.

The unit of time can be preceded by a multiplier, given as an optionally signed number. Unsigned numbers are taken as positively signed. No number at all implies 1 for a multiplier. Following a relative item with the string `ago` is equivalent to preceding the unit by a multiplicator with value `-1`.

The string `tomorrow` is worth one day into the future (equivalent to `day`). The string `yesterday` is worth one day into the past (equivalent to `day ago`).

The strings `now` and `today` are relative items corresponding to zero-valued time displacement. These strings come from the fact that a zero-valued time displacement represents the current time when not otherwise changed by previous items. The string `this` also has the meaning of a zero-valued time displacement, but is preferred in date strings like `this thursday`.

When a relative item makes the resulting date cross the boundary between DST and non-DST (or vice versa), the hour is adjusted according to the local time.

Pure Numbers

The exact interpretation of pure decimal numbers is dependent on the context within the date string:

- If the decimal number is of the form *YYYYMMDD* and no other calendar date item appears before it in the date string, *YYYY* is read as the year, *MM* as the month number, and *DD* as the day of the month for the specified calendar date.

■ If the decimal number is of the form *HHMM* and no other time of day item
   appears before it in the date string, *HH* is read as the hour of the day and *MM* as the
   minute of the hour for the specified time of day. *MM* can also be omitted.

■ If both a calendar date and a time of day appear to the left of a number in the
   date string, but no relative item, the number overrides the year.

C
Web Resources

This appendix contains a selection of URLs for reference and further reading. Many of these are part of the Linux Documentation Project (LDP) which is mirrored in many places throughout the world. The master page is located at `http://metalab.unc.edu/mdw/`. The list of mirrors is located at `http://metalab.unc.edu/mdw/mirrors.html`. Users should use the closest mirror. The LDP links in the tables below are prefixed with *LDP_MIRROR*, which indicates the URL of the mirror being used.

Note: All addresses are `http://` unless otherwise noted. Each address should be typed as a single line.

Distributions

Resource Name	Location
Caldera Open Linux	`www.caldera.com`
Linux Mandrake	`www.linux-mandrake.com`
Redhat Software	`www.redhat.com`
Debian Distribution	`www.debian.org`
Slackware	`ftp://ftp.cdrom.com/pub/linux/slackware`
S.u.S.E.	`www.suse.com`
Trans-Ameritech Linuxware	`www.trans-am.com/linux.htm#LinuxwareSuite`
WGS Linux Pro	`www.wgs.com`

General Information

Resource Name	Location
The Linux Documentation Project	*LDP_MIRROR*`/linux.html`
Linux Gazette	`www.linuxgazette.com`
Linux International	`www.li.org`
The Linux Journal	`www.linuxjournal.com`
Linux Today	`linuxtoday.com`

Networking

Resource Name	Location
The Linux Electronic Mail HOWTO	*LDP_MIRROR*/HOWTO/Mail-HOWTO.html
The Linux Networking HOWTO	*LDP_MIRROR*/HOWTO/NET3-4-HOWTO.html
The Linux Networking Overview HOWTO	*LDP_MIRROR*/HOWTO/Networking-Overview-HOWTO.html
Linux PPP HOWTO	*LDP_MIRROR*/HOWTO/PPP-HOWTO.html
The Linux Network Administrator's Guide	*LDP_MIRROR*/LDP/nag/nag.html
DNS Howto	*LDP_MIRROR*/HOWTO/DNS-HOWTO.html

Non-Intel Platforms

Resource Name	Location
Alpha Linux	www.alphalinux.org
Li/Next	www.black.linux-m68k.org
Linux/m68k	www.linux-m68k.org
Linux/m68k for Macintosh	www.mac.linux-m68k.org
Linux/sun3 Homepage	www.netppl.fi/~pp/sun3
Linux for 680x0 based VME boards	www.sleepie.demon.co.uk/linuxvme/index.html
Linux for PowerPC Systems	www.linuxppc.org
Linux on the Fujitsu AP1000+	cap.anu.edu.au/cap/projects/linux
Linux VAX	www.mssl.ucl.ac.uk/~atp/linux-vax/index.html
Monolithic Linux on the PCI Power Macintoshes	www.cs.wisc.edu/~tesch/linux_info
Alpha Miniloader Howto	*LDP_MIRROR*/HOWTO/MILO-HOWTO.html
ARM Linux	www.arm.uk.linux.org/~rmk/armlinux.html
Brief Introduction to Alpha Systems and Processors	*LDP_MIRROR*/HOWTO/Alpha-HOWTO.html
iMac Linux	www.imaclinux.net/
The Linux/MIPS FAQ	lena.fnet.fr
Linux/MIPS Howto	*LDP_MIRROR*/HOWTO/MIPS-HOWTO.html
Linux on the IBM ESA/390 Mainframe Architecture	linas.org/linux/i370.html
The Puffin Group's PA-RISC/Linux Development Project	www.thepuffingroup.com/parisc

Embedded and Hand-Held Systems

Resource Name	Location
Calcaria Linux7k	www.calcaria.net
The Embeddable Linux Kernel Subset (ELKS)	www.elks.ecs.soton.ac.uk/cgi-bin/ELKS
Linux/Microcontroller Home Page	www.uclinux.org
uClinux/ColdFire Project	www.moretonbay.com/coldfire/linux-coldfire.html
VMELinux	www.vmelinux.com

Security

Resource Name	Location
Firewalling and Proxy Server HOWTO	LDP_MIRROR/HOWTO/Firewall-HOWTO.html
Linux IPCHAINS-HOWTO	LDP_MIRROR/HOWTO/IPCHAINS-HOWTO.html
Linux Security HOWTO	LDP_MIRROR/HOWTO/Security-HOWTO.html

Programming and Building Software Packages

Resource Name	Location
Building and Installing Software Packages for Linux	LDP_MIRROR/HOWTO/Software-Building-HOWTO.html
The Linux Programmer's Guide	LDP_MIRROR/LDP/lpg/index.html
Software Release Practice HOWTO	LDP_MIRROR/HOWTO/Software-Release-Practice-HOWTO.html

Applications

Resource Name	Location
Application Marketplace	www.redhat.com/appindex
Linux Applications and Utilities Page	www.xnet.com/~blatura/linapps.shtml
SAL (Scientific Applications on Linux)	sal.kachinatech.com/index.shtml

Kernel Resources

Resource Name	Location
The Linux Kernel	LDP_MIRROR/LDP/tlk/tlk.html
Linux 2.0.35 Kernel Source Tour	www.tamacom.com/tour/linux/index.html
Linux Kernel Man Pages	www.muppetlabs.com/linux/man9
Linux Kernel Module Programming Guide	LDP_MIRROR/LDP/lkmpg/mpg.html
Linux Source Navigator	metalab.unc.edu/linux-source

Filesystems

Resource Name	Location
Filesystem Hierarchy Standard	www.pathname.com/fhs/2.0/fhs-toc.html
ext2fs Home Page	web.mit.edu/tytso/www/linux/ext2.html
Linux Development Projects	LDP_MIRROR/devel.html#kernel

Linux with Other Operating Systems

Resource Name	Location
From DOS/Windows to Linux HOWTO	LDP_MIRROR/HOWTO/DOS-Win-to-Linux-HOWTO.html
Linux-DOS-Win95-OS2 mini-HOWTO	LDP_MIRROR/HOWTO/mini/Linux+DOS+Win95+OS2.html
The Linux+FreeBSD mini-HOWTO	LDP_MIRROR/HOWTO/mini/Linux+FreeBSD.html
NT OS Loader + Linux mini-HOWTO	LDP_MIRROR/HOWTO/mini/Linux+NT-Loader.html
Linux+Win95 mini-HOWTO	LDP_MIRROR/HOWTO/mini/Linux+Win95.html
The Loadlin+Win95 mini-HOWTO	LDP_MIRROR/HOWTO/mini/Loadlin+Win95.html

Index

Symbols/Numbers

\ (backslash)
  character sequences, 188
  line-continuation character, bash, 133
  metacharacters, 283
  quoting, bash, 133

[ ] (brackets), 283

% command (bash), 151

/ configuration files
  /etc/at.access, 268
  /etc/at.deny, 268
  /etc/ethers, 207
  /etc/exports, 270
  /etc/fstab, 177
  /etc/ftpchroot, 270
  /etc/ftpusers, 271
  /etc/group, 169
  /etc/host.conf, 208-209
  /etc/hosts, 208
  /etc/hosts.allow, 272
  /etc/hosts.deny, 272
  /etc/hosts.equiv, 269
  /etc/inetd.conf, 220-221
  /etc/issue, suppressing content
    display, 188
  /etc/lilo.conf, 181
  /etc/login.access, 268
  /etc/netgroup, 269
  /etc/networks, 209
  /etc/passwd, 170
  /etc/protocols, 221
  /etc/rpc, 220
  /etc/securetty, 270
  /etc/services, 221-222
  /etc/shadow, 170
  /etc/shells, 270
  /etc/sudoers, 267

/proc filesystem, 200
  process-specific data, displaying, 201
  structure, 201-202

/usr filesystem, 242

/var filesystem, 242

3D addresses (partition tables),
  adjusting, 182

48-bit addresses (Ethernet), mapping
  to IP addresses, 207

A

accept policy (IP firewalls), 273

access control, Internet
  services, 271
  displaying rules, 271
  filesystems, 270
  user access, 268

accessing filesystems, 244-247

accounting rules, IP firewall
  administration, 273

accounts
  group
    creating, 168
    passwords, changing or removing, 166
  quotas
    displaying, 175
    editing, 174
    enabling on filesystems, 176
    maintaining, 174-177
  user
    creating, 171-172
    expiration date, specifying, 173
    fields, changing, 168
    login shell, changing, 168, 172
    name, displaying status, 166
    numerical value, 172
    passwords, 166
    status, displaying, 166
    trusted access, 269
    user ID, changing, 174

ACTION field (inittab file), values,
  186-187

actions, specifying for gawk
  command, 45

activating
  debugging mode (kdstat
    command), 197
  promiscuous mode (interfaces), 227
  see also enabling

adding
  dial-up passwords, 165
  line numbers to standard output,
    26-27

E

H

U

Books for Networking Professionals

New Riders

Windows NT Titles

Windows NT TCP/IP
By Karanjit Siyan
1st Edition
480 pages, $29.99
ISBN: 1-56205-887-8

If you're still looking for good documentation on Microsoft TCP/IP, then look no further—this is your book. *Windows NT TCP/IP* cuts through the complexities and provides the most informative and complete reference book on Windows-based TCP/IP. Concepts essential to TCP/IP administration are explained thoroughly, then related to the practical use of Microsoft TCP/IP in a real-world networking environment. The book begins by covering TCP/IP architecture, advanced installation, and configuration issues, then moves on to routing with TCP/IP, DHCP Management, and WINS/DNS Name Resolution.

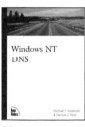

Windows NT DNS
By Michael Masterson, Herman L. Knief, Scott Vinick, and Eric Roul
1st Edition
340 pages, $29.99
ISBN: 1-56205-943-2

Have you ever opened a Windows NT book looking for detailed information about DNS only to discover that it doesn't even begin to scratch the surface? DNS is probably one of the most complicated subjects for NT administrators, and there are few books on the market that really address it in detail. This book answers your most complex DNS questions, focusing on the implementation of the Domain Name Service within Windows NT, treating it thoroughly from the viewpoint of an experienced Windows NT professional. Many detailed, real-world examples illustrate further the understanding of the material throughout. The book covers the details of how DNS functions within NT, then explores specific interactions with critical network components. Finally, proven procedures to design and set up DNS are demonstrated. You'll also find coverage of related topics, such as maintenance, security, and troubleshooting.

Windows NT Registry
By Sandra Osborne
1st Edition
564 pages, $29.99
ISBN: 1-56205-941-6

The NT Registry can be a very powerful tool for those capable of using it wisely. Unfortunately, there is very little information regarding the NT Registry, due to Microsoft's insistence that their source code be kept secret. If you're looking to optimize your use of the Registry, you're usually forced to search the Web for bits of information. This book is your resource. It covers critical issues and settings used for configuring network protocols, including NWLink, PTP, TCP/IP, and DHCP. This book approaches the material from a unique point of view, discussing the problems related to a particular component, and then discussing settings, which are the actual changes necessary for implementing robust solutions. There is also a comprehensive reference of Registry settings and commands, making this the perfect addition to your technical bookshelf.

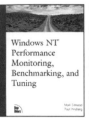

Windows NT Performance

By Mark Edmead and Paul Hinsberg

1st Edition

288 pages, $29.99

ISBN: 1-56205-942-4

Performance monitoring is a little like preventive medicine for the administrator: No one enjoys a checkup, but it's a good thing to do on a regular basis. This book helps you focus on the critical aspects of improving the performance of your NT system, showing you how to monitor the system, implement benchmarking, and tune your network. The book is organized by resource components, which makes it easy to use as a reference tool.

Windows NT Terminal Server

By Ted Harwood

1st Edition

416 pages, $29.99

ISBN: 1-56205-944-0

It's no surprise that most administration headaches revolve around integration with other networks and clients. This book addresses these types of real-world issues on a case-by-case basis, giving tools and advice for solving each problem. The author also offers the real nuts and bolts of thin client administration on multiple systems, covering such relevant issues as installation, configuration, network connection, management, and application distribution.

Windows NT Security

By Richard Puckett

1st Edition Fall 1999

600 pages, $29.99

ISBN: 1-56205-945-9

Swiss cheese. That's what some people say Windows NT security is like. And they may be right, because they only know what the NT documentation says about implementing security. Who has the time to research alternatives; play around with the features, service packs, hot fixes, and add-on tools; and figure out what makes NT rock solid? Well, Richard Puckett does. He's been researching Windows NT security for the University of Virginia for a while now, and he's got pretty good news. He's going to show you how to make NT secure in your environment, and we mean really secure.

Windows NT Network Management

By Anil Desai

1st Edition

400 pages, $34.99

ISBN: 1-56205-946-7

Administering a Windows NT network is kind of like trying to herd cats—an impossible task characterized by constant motion, exhausting labor, and lots of hairballs. Author Anil Desai knows all about it—he's a Consulting Engineer for Sprint Paranet, and specializes in Windows NT implementation, integration, and management. So we asked him to put together a concise manual of best practices, a book of tools and ideas that other administrators can turn to again and again in managing their own NT networks. His experience shines through as he shares his secrets for reducing your organization's Total Cost of Ownership.

Planning for Windows 2000

By Eric K. Cone

1st Edition

400 pages, $29.99

ISBN: 0-7357-0048-6

Windows 2000 is poised to be one of the largest and most important software releases of the next decade, and you are charged with planning, testing, and deploying it in your enterprise.

Are you ready? With this book, you will be. *Planning for Windows 2000* lets you know what the upgrade hurdles will be, informs you how to clear them, guides you through effective Active Directory design, and presents you with detailed roll-out procedures. Eric K. Cone gives you the benefit of his extensive experience as a Windows 2000 Rapid Deployment Program member, sharing problems and solutions he's encountered on the job.

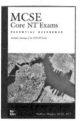

MCSE Core NT Exams Essential Reference

By Matthew Shepker
1st Edition
256 pages, $19.99
ISBN: 0-7357-0006-0

You're sitting in the first session of your Networking Essentials class and the instructor starts talking about RAS and you have no idea what that means. You think about raising your hand to ask about RAS, but you reconsider—you'd feel pretty foolish asking a question in front of all these people. You turn to your handy *MCSE Core NT Exams Essential Reference* and find a quick summary on Remote Access Services. Question answered. It's a couple months later and you're taking your Networking Essentials exam the next day. You're reviewing practice tests and you keep forgetting the maximum lengths for the various commonly used cable types. Once again, you turn to the *MCSE Core NT Exams Essential Reference* and find a table on cables, including all of the characteristics you need to memorize in order to pass the test.

BackOffice Titles

Implementing Exchange Server

By Doug Hauger, Marywynne Leon, and William C. Wade III
1st Edition
400 pages, $29.99
ISBN: 1-56205-931-9

If you're interested in connectivity and maintenance issues for Exchange Server, then this book is for you. Exchange's power lies in its ability to be connected to multiple email subsystems to create a "universal email backbone." It's not unusual to have several different and complex systems all connected via email gateways, including Lotus Notes or cc:Mail, Microsoft Mail, legacy mainframe systems, and Internet mail. This book covers all of the problems and issues associated with getting an integrated system running smoothly and addresses troubleshooting and diagnosis of email problems with an eye toward prevention and best practices.

Exchange Server Administration

By Janice K. Howd
1st Edition
350 pages, $34.99
ISBN: 0-7357-0081-8

OK, you've got your Exchange Server installed and connected, now what? Email administration is one of the most critical networking jobs, and Exchange can be particularly troublesome in large, heterogenous environments. So Janice Howd, a noted consultant and teacher with over a decade of email administration experience, has put together this advanced, concise handbook for daily, periodic, and emergency administration. With in-depth coverage of topics like managing disk resources, replication, and disaster recovery, this is the one reference book every Exchange administrator needs.

SQL Server System Administration

By Sean Baird, Chris Miller, et al.

1st Edition

352 pages, $29.99

ISBN: 1-56205-955-6

How often does your SQL Server go down during the day when everyone wants to access the data? Do you spend most of your time being a "report monkey" for your co-workers and bosses? *SQL Server System Administration* helps you keep data consistently available to your users. This book omits the introductory information. The authors don't spend time explaining queries and how they work. Instead they focus on the information that you can't get anywhere else, like how to choose the correct replication topology and achieve high availability of information.

Internet Information Server Administration

By Kelli Adam, et. al.

1st Edition Fall 1999

300 pages, $29.99

ISBN: 0-7357-0022-2

Are the new Internet technologies in Internet Information Server giving you headaches? Does protecting security on the Web take up all of your time? Then this is the book for you. With hands-on configuration training, advanced study of the new protocols in IIS, and detailed instructions on authenticating users with the new Certificate Server and implementing and managing the new e-commerce features, *Internet Information Server Administration* gives you the real-life solutions you need. This definitive resource also prepares you for the release of Windows 2000 by giving you detailed advice on working with Microsoft Management Console, which was first used by IIS.

SMS Administration

By Wayne Koop and Brian Steck

1st Edition Fall 1999

350 pages, $29.99

ISBN: 0-7357-0082-6

Microsoft's new version of its Systems Management Server (SMS) is starting to turn heads. While complex, it's allowing administrators to lower their total cost of ownership and more efficiently manage clients, applications, and support operations. So if your organization is using or implementing SMS, you'll need some expert advice. Wayne Koop and Brian Steck can help you get the most bang for your buck, with insight, expert tips, and real-world examples. Brian and Wayne are consultants specializing in SMS, having worked with Microsoft on one of the most complex SMS rollouts in the world, involving 32 countries, 15 languages, and thousands of clients.

UNIX/Linux Titles

Solaris Essential Reference

By John P. Mulligan

1st Edition

350 pages, $24.95

ISBN: 0-7357-0023-0

Looking for the fastest, easiest way to find the Solaris command you need? Need a few pointers on shell scripting? How about advanced administration tips and sound, practical expertise on security issues? Are you looking for trustworthy information about available third-party software packages that will enhance your operating system? Author John Mulligan—creator of the popular Unofficial Guide to Solaris Web site (sun.icsnet.com)—delivers all that and more in one attractive, easy-to-use reference book. With clear and concise instructions on how to perform important administration and management tasks and key information on powerful commands and advanced topics, *Solaris Essential Reference* is the reference you need when you know what you want to do and you just need to know how.

Linux System Administration

By M Carling and James T. Dennis
1st Edition
450 pages, $29.99
ISBN: 1-56205-934-3

As an administrator, you probably feel that most of your time and energy is spent in endless firefighting. If your network has become a fragile quilt of temporary patches and workarounds, then this book is for you. For example, have you had trouble sending or receiving your email lately? Are you looking for a way to keep your network running smoothly with enhanced performance? Are your users always hankering for more storage, more services, and more speed? *Linux System Administration* advises you on the many intricacies of maintaining a secure, stable system. In this definitive work, the author addresses all the issues related to system administration, from adding users and managing file permissions to Internet services and Web hosting to recovery planning and security. This book fulfills the need for expert advice that will ensure a trouble-free Linux environment.

Developing Linux Applications

By Eric Harlow
1st Edition
400 pages, $34.99
ISBN: 0-7357-0021-4

We all know that Linux is one of the most powerful and solid operating systems in existence. And as the success of Linux grows, there is an increasing interest in developing applications with graphical user interfaces that really take advantage of the power of Linux. In this book, software developer Eric Harlow gives you an indispensable development handbook focusing on the GTK+ toolkit. More than an overview on the elements of application or GUI design, this is a hands-on book that delves deeply into the technology. With in-depth material on the various GUI programming tools and loads of examples, this book's unique focus will give you the information you need to design and launch professional-quality applications.

Linux Firewalls

By Robert Ziegler
400 pages, $35.00
ISBN: 0-7357-0900-9

New Riders is proud to offer the first book aimed specifically at Linux security issues. While there are a host of general UNIX security books, we think it is time to address the practical needs of the Linux network. Author Robert Ziegler takes a balanced approach to system security, discussing topics like planning a secure environment, firewalls, and utilizing security scripts. With comprehensive information on specific system compromises, and advice on how to prevent and repair them, this is one book that every Linux administrator should have on the shelf.

Development Titles

GTK+/Gnome Development

By Havoc Pennington
400 pages, $29.99
ISBN: 0-7357-0078-8

GTK+ /Gnome Development provides the experienced programmer with the knowledge to develop X Window applications with the powerful GTK+ toolkit. The author provides the reader with a checklist of features every application should have, advanced GUI techniques, and the ability to create custom widgets. The title also contains reference information for more experienced users already familiar with usage, but who require knowledge of function prototypes and detailed descriptions. These tools let the reader write powerful applications in record time.

Python Essential Reference

By David Beazley
300 pages, $34.95
ISBN: 0-7357-0901-7

This book describes the Python programming language and its library of standard modules. Python is an informal language that has become a highly valuable software development tool for many computing professionals. This language reference covers Python's lexical conventions, built-in datatypes, control flow, functions, statements, classes, and execution model. This book also covers the contents of the Python library as bundled in the standard Python distribution.

Lotus Notes and Domino Titles

Domino System Administration

By Rob Kirkland
1st Edition Fall 1999
500 pages, $29.99
ISBN: 1-56205-948-3

Your boss has just announced that you will be upgrading to the newest version of Notes and Domino when it ships. As a Premium Lotus Business Partner, Lotus has offered a substantial price break to keep your company away from Microsoft's Exchange Server. How are you supposed to get this new system installed, configured, and rolled out to all of your end users? You understand how Lotus Notes works—you've been administering it for years. What you need is a concise, practical explanation about the new features, and how to make some of the advanced stuff really work. You need answers and solutions from someone like you, who has worked with the product for years, and understands what it is you need to know. *Domino System Administration* is the answer—the first book on Domino that attacks the technology at the professional level, with practical, hands-on assistance to get Domino running in your organization.

Lotus Notes & Domino Essential Reference

By Dave Hatter & Tim Bankes
1st Edition
700 pages, $45.00
ISBN: 0-7357-0007-9

You're in a bind because you've been asked to design and program a new database in Notes for an important client that will keep track of and itemize a myriad of inventory and shipping data. The client wants a user-friendly interface, without sacrificing speed or functionality. You are experienced (and could develop this app in your sleep), but feel that you need to take your talents to the next level. You need something to facilitate your creative and technical abilities, something to perfect your programming skills. Your answer is waiting for you: *Lotus Notes & Domino Essential Reference*. It's compact and simply designed. It's loaded with information. All of the objects, classes, functions, and methods are listed. It shows you the object hierarchy and the overlaying relationship between them. It's perfect for you. Problem solved.

Networking Titles

Cisco Router Configuration & Troubleshooting

By Mark Tripod
1st Edition
300 pages, $34.99
ISBN: 0-7357-0024-9

Want the real story on making your Cisco routers run like a dream? Why not pick up a copy of *Cisco Router Configuration & Troubleshooting* and see what Mark Tripod has to say? His company is the one responsible for making some of the largest sites on the Net scream, like Amazon.com, Hotmail, USAToday, Geocities, and Sony. In this book, he provides advanced configuration issues, sprinkled with advice and preferred practices. You won't see a general overview on TCP/IP—he talks about more meaty issues like security, monitoring, traffic management, and more. In the troubleshooting section, Mark provides a unique methodology and lots of sample problems to illustrate. By providing real-world insight and examples instead of rehashing Cisco's documentation, Mark gives network administrators information they can start using today.

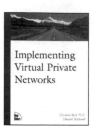

Implementing Virtual Private Networks

By Tina Bird and
Ted Stockwell
1st Edition Fall 1999
300 pages, $32.99
ISBN: 0-7357-0047-8

Tired of looking for decent, practical, up-to-date information on virtual private networks? *Implementing Virtual Private Networks*, by noted authorities Dr. Tina Bird and Ted Stockwell, finally gives you what you need—an authoritative guide on the design, implementation, and maintenance of Internet-based access to private networks. This book focuses on real-world solutions, demonstrating how the choice of VPN architecture should align with an organization's business and technological requirements. Tina and Ted give you the information you need to determine whether a VPN is right for your organization, select the VPN that suits your needs, and design and implement the VPN you have chosen.

Understanding Data Communications, Sixth Edition

By Gilbert Held
6th Edition
550 pages, $34.99
ISBN: 0-7357-0036-2

Updated from the highly successful fifth edition, this book explains how data communications systems and their various hardware and software components work. Not an entry-level book, it approaches the material in a textbook format, addressing the complex issues involved in internetworking today. A great reference book for the experienced networking professional, written by noted networking authority, Gilbert Held.

We Want to Know What You Think

To better serve you, we would like your opinion on the content and quality of this book. Please complete this card and mail it to us or fax it to 317-581-4663.

Name_____

Address _____

City _____ State _____ Zip _____

Phone _____

Email Address _____

Occupation _____

Operating System(s) that you use _____

What influenced your purchase of this book?
- ❑ Recommendation
- ❑ Table of Contents
- ❑ Magazine Review
- ❑ New Riders' Reputation
- ❑ Cover Design
- ❑ Index
- ❑ Advertisement
- ❑ Author Name

How would you rate the contents of this book?
- ❑ Excellent
- ❑ Good
- ❑ Below Average
- ❑ Very Good
- ❑ Fair
- ❑ Poor

How do you plan to use this book?
- ❑ Quick reference
- ❑ Classroom
- ❑ Self-training
- ❑ Other

What do you like most about this book?
Check all that apply.
- ❑ Content
- ❑ Accuracy
- ❑ Listings
- ❑ Index
- ❑ Price
- ❑ Writing Style
- ❑ Examples
- ❑ Design
- ❑ Page Count
- ❑ Illustrations

What do you like least about this book?
Check all that apply.
- ❑ Content
- ❑ Accuracy
- ❑ Listings
- ❑ Index
- ❑ Price
- ❑ Writing Style
- ❑ Examples
- ❑ Design
- ❑ Page Count
- ❑ Illustrations

What would be a useful follow-up book to this one for you? _____

Where did you purchase this book? _____

_____

Can you name a similar book that you like better than this one, or one that is as good? Why?

_____

_____

How many New Riders books do you own? _____

What are your favorite computer books? _____

_____

What other titles would you like to see us develop? _____

_____

Any comments for us? _____

_____

_____

_____

Fold here and tape to mail

New Riders Publishing
201 W. 103rd St.
Indianapolis, IN 46290

New Riders | How to Contact Us

Visit Our Web Site

www.newriders.com

On our Web site, you'll find information about our other books, authors, tables of contents, indexes, and book errata. You can also place orders for books through our Web site.

Email Us

Contact us at this address:
newriders@mcp.com

- If you have comments or questions about this book
- To report errors that you have found in this book
- If you have a book proposal to submit or are interested in writing for New Riders
- If you would like to have an author kit sent to you
- If you are an expert in a computer topic or technology and are interested in being a technical editor who reviews manuscripts for technical accuracy

newriders-sales@mcp.com

- To find a distributor in your area, please contact our international department at the address above.

newriders-pr@mcp.com

- For instructors from educational institutions who wish to preview New Riders books for classroom use. Email should include your name, title, school, department, address, phone number, office days/hours, text in use, and enrollment in the body of your text along with your request for desk/examination copies and/or additional information.

Write to Us

New Riders Publishing
201 W. 103rd St.
Indianapolis, IN 46290-1097

Call Us

Toll-free (800) 571-5840 + 9 + 7494
If outside U.S. (317) 581-3500. Ask for New Riders.

Fax Us

(317) 581-4663